Interpreting Pottery

Anne Anderson

Pica Press New York

Published in the United States of America in 1985 by
PICA PRESS
Distributed by Universe Books
381 Park Avenue South, New York, N.Y. 10016

85 86 87 88 89/10 9 8 7 6 5 4 3 2 1

ISBN 0-87663-743-8

Printed in Great Britain

Contents

6   Contents

Plates

Figures

Glossary

Annona The corn tax which Roman provincials were obliged to pay in kind to maintain the frontier armies

Artefact Any object that has been made, modified or used by man

Assemblage A set of objects found together and therefore assumed to be of the same date of deposition and belonging to one group of people

Auxilia The provinces of the Roman Empire provided troops for the army, to assist the legions. Units were infantry, or part-mounted and approximately 500 men strong

Barrow A mound of earth, circular or elongated in shape, covering a burial or burials

Bronze Age Period when bronze was the principal metal used for the manufacture of tools and weapons. In England it lasted from *c.* 2000–700 BC

Cairn A mound of stones, rather than soil, usually covering a burial

Causewayed camp An enclosure composed of one or more roughly concentric rings of ditches with internal banks. The ditches are broken by frequent causeways of undug material. They date to the Neolithic period, e.g. Windmill Hill, Wiltshire

Chambered tombs A stone built tomb, often used for successive burials over a long period, usually covered by a barrow or cairn. Usually Neolithic in date, e.g. West Kennet, Wiltshire. Sometimes referred to as 'Megalithic tombs', after the large stones of which they are constructed.

Colonia A settlement of Roman legionary veterans, who were usually given land allotments on their retirement, e.g. Colchester, Essex

Fort Headquarters of a Roman auxiliary unit (*see* Auxilia). E.g. Cirencester, Gloustershire; Housesteads, Northumberland

Fortress Headquarters of a Roman legion (*see* Legion). Examples in Britain include Lincoln, Chester and Gloucester

Fosse Way One of the main roads of Roman Britain, from Lincoln to Exeter

Henge A circular or oval embanked enclosure with an internal ditch, sometimes with wooden or stone structures inside. Late Neolithic to early Bronze Age in date. Avebury and Stonehenge, in Wiltshire, are famous examples

Hill Fort A banked and ditched enclosure usually on a hill, following the contours. They date to the Iron Age, e.g. Maiden Castle in Dorset

Iron Age The period when iron was the main metal used for the manufacture of tools and weapons. In England it lasted from *c*. 750 BC until the Roman conquest in AD 43

Legion A military unit composed of Roman citizens, roughly 5,500–6,000 men strong

Limes Name given to a Roman frontier

Oppidum Latin term for any native-defended settlement, but restricted by British archaeologists to an area protected by Gallo-Belgic dykes, as at Camulodunum (Colchester, Essex)

Pre-Flavian Period before the reign of the Flavian Emperors, Vespasian, Titus and Domitian (AD 69–96). Usually refers to the Claudio-Neronian period (AD 41–69)

Radio-carbon dating A method of dating organic materials up to 70,000 years old by measuring the residual radioactive carbon isotopes in a sample and then calculating its age. C 14 enters plants by photosynthesis and is subsequently taken into animals who eat the plants. This process continues until the organism dies and at that point the radioactive isotope of C 14 begins to decay. The half-life of radio-carbon is known and so it is possible to measure the remaining C 14 in a sample and determine its age. However, it has recently been shown, using the dendrochronological sequence for the bristle cone pine (tree-ring dating), that the C 14 concentration in the atmosphere has not remained constant. So radio-carbon dates have to be calibrated in order to arrive at the approximate date in calendar years. Dates quoted in radio-carbon years before calibration are written b.c. or b.p. (before the present) as opposed to calibrated dates written B.C. or B.P.

Skeumorph An artefact that copies in decorative form a feature or the shape of another artefact that was originally functional, e.g. chalk copies of flint and hardstone axes. Skeumorphs are particularly useful when they resemble organic materials like basketry and leather which normally do not survive, e.g. pottery vessels with perforated tops which probably represent the conversion of a leather prototype into clay, with the neck holes originally holding a thong so that the top of the leather bag could be pulled shut

Tria-nomina The three names of a Roman citizen

Preface

This book has been written for the reader who has an interest in archaeology and would like to know more about the way the archaeologist works, particularly how he uses the objects and other information that he gathers from the ground. There are many books on the techniques of excavation but few to inform the reader what happens after the digging has finished. How does the archaeologist arrive at his conclusions, published in the site report, about the chronology and nature of the excavated site? Much is learnt by studying the objects, of which pottery is perhaps the most important due to its durability and abundance. Yet, although it has been a mainstay of archaeology since the subject was developed in the nineteenth century and although the museum visitor is often confronted by cases of pots, there is very little literature available to the non-specialist in this subject. Consequently, many are left wondering why pottery is so important and why the archaeologist spends so much time and energy studying it. The purpose of this book is to explain the significance of pottery and why it has assumed such an important role in archaeology.

Pottery has two main uses, for dating and for the evidence it provides for trade and industry. By illustration, it is shown how the archaeologist establishes the identity, date and origin of the pottery. Having done so, the information can be used to reconstruct the history of a site and to understand something of the social and economic way of life. By drawing examples from British prehistory and the Roman imperial period the many applications of such information are demonstrated, indicating the advantages and also the disadvantages of using pottery as a tool. In addition, recent research on the main pottery types is gathered and presented in a coherent form. By using pottery the archaeologist can come to understand ancient society, from the craftsman who made it and the role he played in society, through possible mechanisms of trade, to its daily use for eating and drinking.

It will be clear from the text that I had a great deal of help and information freely given by museum curators and colleagues. In particular I should like to thank the following people and institutions for their help: Dr A.V. Hubrecht (Riksmuseum, G.M. Kam, Nijmegen), Dr C. Ruger (Bonn Museum), Dr W. Binsfeld (Trier Museum), Mme F. Beck (Saint Germaine-en-Laye), Dr I. Huld-Zetsche (Frankfurt Museum), Dr Decker (Mainz Museum), Dr H. Hellenkemper (Köln Museum), Dr J. Garbsch (Munich), Dr S. Rieckhoff-Pauli (Regensburg), Dr F. Reutti (Rheinzabern), the Trustees of the British Museum, Suzanne Dolby for the cover photograph. I owe especial thanks to my husband, Scott, for improving the quality of the text and to my parents for all their help over the years. I am grateful to S. Vaughan, S. Semmens and M. Taylor for providing the drawings. Finally I would like to express my thanks and gratitude to Graham Webster for all his assistance and encouragement during the preparation of this book.

A.C.A.
Leicester, 1983

1 Why Study Pottery?

An archaeological excavation often appears to be like Pandora's box. Archaeologists are so anxious to rediscover the lost past that they spend their lives digging in the ground hoping to release its hidden secrets. It is the curiosity it inspires that makes archaeology so fascinating. When an excavation is completed, the archaeologist has to piece together all the diverse fragments of information that he has collected, in order to recreate the day-to-day lives and activities of our ancestors. In his attempt to reconstruct past life-styles, he employs two principal types of evidence – the places where people lived, worked and died (structural evidence) and the objects found in close association with them (artefactual evidence). This book concentrates on one particular object – pottery – which in many cases forms the largest body of artefactual evidence recovered from archaeological sites.

Pottery plays an integral part in the interpretation of sites. It is therefore of the greatest importance when it is related to its place of discovery or to other artefacts which have been found with it, rather than divorced from its context or viewed merely as an object of curiosity. On an excavation, as each object is found, its precise location is recorded. In this way the pottery is kept in relation to the chronological development of the site as represented by its 'stratigraphy', (the layers which are formed by the accumulation of rubbish and other debris on any habitation site). Over the years houses will have been pulled down and rebuilt and all manner of disasters (from fire to flood) may have overtaken the site. Year by year more material has been deposited and succeeding generations will have continued the process, leaving behind a record of their ancestors, with only the uppermost layer representing the most recent occupation. The archaeologist has to peel off this debris and in so doing cuts a vertical slice through history (fig. 1). In order to understand the chronological development of individual sites, he must isolate layers, see if they have been disturbed in any way by later human or animal activity and finally ascertain how and in what order those layers accumulated. Each layer

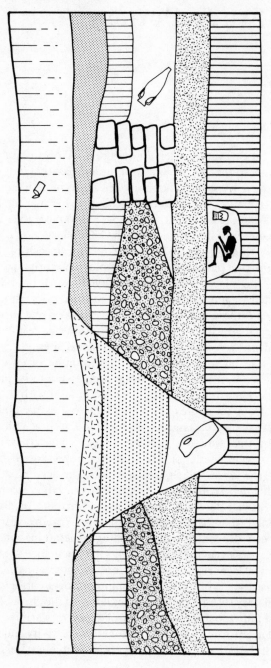

Fig. 1   Stratigraphic section, showing the deposition of layers from *c.* 2000 BC to the present

and its contents must be examined in turn. The importance of the archaeological context in which an object is discovered cannot be over-emphasised. It is a fundamental requirement if the maximum amount of information is to be extracted from both sources.

Numerically pottery is often the most important artefactual evidence from an archaeological site, largely because of its durability. Admittedly complete pots are rare, but in the form of small broken pieces pottery is virtually indestructible. This springs from the very nature of the material, which is simply fired clay. It does not corrode like bronze and iron, or dissolve in acidic soil like bone. Moreover, since clay is widely available and most pots are easy to manufacture, people who live in a fixed abode find them ideal for all manner of day-to-day activities. Pottery vessels have been used since Neolithic times for cooking, eating and storage. Wealthy people could afford vessels of silver, bronze or glass, but the bulk of the population had to rely on cheaper ceramic or wooden counterparts. Not surprisingly, some pottery copied metal and glass originals in shape and decoration so that it was more acceptable to the user (plate 1).

Pottery is particularly plentiful on Roman sites, due to the large-scale production of the wide range of vessels required by current eating habits. In the western Provinces the one aspect of the Roman way of life to be quickly adopted, in the wake of conquest, was the Roman method of cooking and eating, as illustrated by the pottery and metal vessels people started to acquire. The Romans had specialised vessels for specific purposes – the flagon, a type of jug for wine; the *amphora*, a container in which wine or oil was traded and stored; the *mortarium*, a bowl for grinding and mixing food; and glossy red bowls, dishes and cups known as samian ware, which was an expensive tableware. By using such vessels people, either wittingly or unwittingly, emulated Roman practices in the preparation and presentation of food. As metal and glass tableware and cooking pots were much more expensive, most people relied on cheaper and more easily obtainable ceramic ones. Consequently, pottery vessels became a part of everyday life.

Pottery is important therefore to the archaeologist because it survives in greater quantity than any other artefact due to its durability and abundance; 'common things are of more importance than particular things because they are more prevalent.'[1]

A great deal of pottery produced in the home was made and used by the same people. Such pottery may exhibit regional or communal traditions in form and decoration. So pottery can be used as a 'cultural indicator', to identify a specific people or racial group, whereas this is not usually true of metal tools and implements, which were produced by specialists trading over a wide area. The latter were susceptible to outside influences, like the adoption of new ideas deliberately borrowed for commercial reasons. They had to keep up with fashion in a highly competitive market. The comparative scarcity and cost of metal goods often resulted in hoarding or hiding in times of emergency, and their handing down as heirlooms over several generations. By re-use and repair metal objects could stay in circulation far longer than ceramic ones. Metal has a value in its own right, so that once a vessel was broken beyond repair or no longer needed it could be traded as scrap and re-used to make a new vessel. These constraints rarely applied to pottery which was easy and cheap to manufacture and, therefore, to replace.

However, it would be wrong to think that all pottery was produced on a domestic level. Even in prehistoric times it was manufactured by specialists and traded. In these circumstances, rather than reflecting cultural groups, pottery may suggest trading patterns with products from different sources competing with each other for the available market.

Pottery is particularly useful for dating layers and features on archaeological sites, as it has advantages over other artefacts such as stone and metal work, coins and inscriptions. For the prehistoric period, along with other artefacts, pottery is used to create 'cultural assemblages' that are arranged either chronologically or geographically. For the Bronze Age and Iron Age some archaeologists have preferred to use metal work as a means of constructing a chronological framework. Objects of bronze and iron can be classified and typologically analysed more easily than pottery, which can be subject to the vagaries of domestic production. However, the fact remains that pottery is often the only class of artefact found in any quantity which may be used to assess the chronological and cultural affinities of a site. Indeed the strength of pottery lies in the construction of regional chronologies, where the very diversity of the pottery enables greater precision in classification. Pottery is more likely to reflect cultural traditions than a more widely based commercial industry such as bronze working. Many archaeological cultures are therefore basically defined by their ceramics, such as Bronze Age beakers and food vessels. The advent of radio-carbon and other scientific dating techniques has not affected this fundamental role of pottery in prehistory.

For the Roman period pottery is still primarily used for dating, despite the availability of written records, inscriptions and coins.

Inscriptions are comparatively rare and only a few types, such as building records, honorific monuments and milestones, carry a date in the form of imperial titles. Moreover, inscriptions that do not mention a specific date are themselves often difficult to place in time. Coins have special characteristics unlike any other archaeological objects. A coin is a token of exchange with an artificial value determined by the issuing authority and bearing its official stamp. It represents a link in a network of trade. A coin cannot be used for close dating until it has been estimated how long the piece stayed in circulation. The silver coins of Mark Antony, for example, were so debased that they tended to remain in circulation rather than be chosen for savings. Unlike Republican silver, they were not called in by the government for their high silver content, so they are found in hoards long after the reign of Hadrian. Such coins were still current at the end of the second century and even continue into the third.

An indication of the interval between minting and loss may be suggested by the degree of wear, but this is difficult since the coin may have been hoarded and thus not subjected to wear, so that coins issued in the same year may show very different wear patterns. Only a large sample of coins will overcome this problem. While a single coin in mint condition might give a misleading indication of the date because it has been out of circulation, a group of coins of the same date in mint condition will be a reliable indicator. Another hazard, particularly with bronze coinage, is corrosion in certain soil conditions which removes the top surface of bronze and with it any signs of wear. Hence, on sites where there are few or no coins great reliance is placed on pottery for dating.

The use of pottery as a means of dating is itself beset with problems when absolute dates are required. Changes in fashions and marketing patterns are gradual processes, occurring over long periods of time. Absolute dates are derived not from the pottery but from the various associations with epigraphic or historical evidence. For example, a structure dated by coins and inscriptions establishes a date for associated pottery. From this further structures can be dated on the basis of similar pottery finds. Such arguments can be weakened by 'residual' material, i.e. the survival and redepositing of pottery in later contexts. However, this is a problem that effects other artefacts too. Coins in particular can be unreliable for dating due to the residual nature of their provenance. Perhaps as few as ten per cent of all coins are found in the deposit in which they were first lost. Also, in the case of some expensive Roman tableware, a vessel could have been in careful use for many years before it was broken and discarded. In the Roman period the complex mechanisms of supply to the consumer need to be understood, as old stock could cause a serious distortion in a sample of pottery thought to be in current use. Roman military supplies could well have been prone to this type of delay, with consignments lying in the back of a warehouse for many years. These are similar difficulties to those that beset numismatists. Moreover, despite the most extensive studies of pottery, new finds of coins and inscriptions can lead to substantial revisions in the dating of specific types of pottery.

The dating of archaeological deposits by pottery alone is, therefore, unlikely to be precise. Deposits containing vessels dated over a century apart often occur on sites of long, continuous occupation like large towns.[2] However, by examining all the evidence obtained from a layer and comparing it with material from deposits both above and below, a relative sequence of deposition can be constructed. These relative chronologies remain fundamental to our understanding of the social and economic history of individual sites. Indeed archaeology is best suited to studying the broader social and economic aspects of common life not touched upon by historical records.[3]

The economic significance of pottery is its usefulness in studying trade or exchange and the routes by which goods were distributed. Pottery was not the most important commodity to be traded in the ancient world. It is the high survival-rate and abundance that have inflated its significance as an item of trade. The archaeologist is usually limited to studying objects that have not perished in the soil. The geographer Strabo, writing soon after the death of Augustus in AD 14, states that Britain's exports included corn, cattle, hides, slaves and hounds.[4] Obviously this statement would be difficult to substantiate archaeologically. The other exports he mentions are precious metals, gold, silver and iron, while ivory ornaments, amber, glass and other manufactured trinkets were imported in return. The latter exotic and rather costly items were presumably not imported in vast quantities and only reached the highest levels of Iron Age society.

Another continental commodity sought by the Iron Age aristocracy was wine, which was often traded in ceramic containers called *amphorae*. These large, two-handled vessels were used for transporting and storing not only wine but also olive oil and *garum* (fish sauce) throughout the Roman world. A study of Roman *amphorae*, therefore, will reflect the trading of wine, olive oil and *garum*. Few pottery vessels were traded in their own right but travelled as part of a composite cargo. The fine-ware drinking vessels, produced in Baetica, Spain, have a wide but sparse distribution which resulted from river and coastal trading. These vessels were probably transported with *amphorae* full of Baetican olive oil, as there is an epigraphically attested guild of importers of Baetican olive oil at Lyons, France. Pottery may have been traded under similar circumstances in the prehistoric period. The distinctive early Neolithic pottery produced at the Lizard Head in Cornwall was probably traded with Cornish stone axes.[5]

Although pottery may not have been the most important commodity traded in the ancient world it is vital to the archaeologist. It can be used as a general indicator of trade between different regions and may suggest the routes by which goods generally travelled, implying by inference that other items could have been traded in a similar way.

2 Pottery and Research

The potential of pottery as a means of dating and as an indicator of trade was only gradually realised by archaeologists. The 'Three Age' system of Stone, Bronze and Iron, which has been widely used since the beginning of the nineteenth century as a means of ordering objects, is based on technological changes. Thomsen (1788–1865), the first curator of the National Museum of Denmark, devised this classification as a way of arranging the growing collections that came under his care. Thomsen classified the archaeological material into three groups based on the material used to make tools and weapons, which he claimed also represented three chronologically successive ages of Stone, Bronze and Iron. Worsaae, Thomsen's successor at the Museum, went one step further by applying the three age system to field monuments, and proving the stratigraphic sequence of these ages by excavating barrows and peat bogs. Between 1829 and 1843 the three age system was established as a fact and it still forms the basis of prehistory.

It soon became evident that the Stone Age could be further divided into an early and late phase. It was Sir John Lubbock, later to become Lord Avebury, who first used the terms Palaeolithic and Neolithic for these divisions. The Neolithic, or New Stone Age, was the later, a period characterised by weapons and tools of polished flint and other types of stone. The various ages were further subdivided into chronological periods or epochs, characterised by assemblages of specific types of artefact, although these classifications continued to rely on stone and metal. For example the Swedish archaeologist Oscar Montelius (1843–1921) devised a four-fold classification of the Neolithic in Northern Europe. Each phase was distinguished by a specific type of polished stone axe and the method of burial. Montelius believed very firmly in the exact description and classification of prehistoric artefacts. He meticulously arranged artefacts according to their shape and ornament and appreciated the importance of studying the associations between objects. Furthermore, he went on to order them in sequences based on changes in the design, form and decoration. This notion of arranging artefacts in progressive sequences, referred to as typology, was in fact initiated by Worsaae but refined by Montelius, allowing him to establish a relative chronology for Scandinavian artefacts.

Sir Flinders Petrie applied these principles to unpainted pottery from the East, recognising the importance of ceramics as archaeological 'chronometers', following his excavations of a Palestinian tell, Tell el-Hesi, in 1890. The tell was composed of 60 feet (18 m) of occupational debris clearly divided into archaeological levels characterised by different types of pottery (although the pottery types and levels did not always coincide exactly). In his publication *Diospolis Parva* (1901) Petrie arranged the pre-dynastic Egyptian material by means of the technique which he called sequence-dating. His sequence dates were based on the typological evolution of prehistoric pottery. He started his sequence with the figure SD 30, correctly assuming that he had probably not yet discovered the earliest material, and carried it on to dynastic times with SD 80. The pottery was ordered in such a way that the differences were seen to result from a logical series of changes. For example, the handles on one form became progressively smaller, until they were finally reduced to simply a painted line on the side of the vessel. Arranging the pots according to the progressive reduction in the handle size produced a relatively dated series of objects. In this way certain relationships in shape, proportions and decorative style can be ordered to produce a chronological sequence. Petrie wrote: 'This system enables us to deal with material which is entirely undated otherwise. . . . There is no reason now why prehistoric ages, from which there are groups of remains, should not be dealt with as surely and as clearly as the historic ages with recorded dates.'

Petrie was not the only man to be working by these principles. The word 'typology' seems to have been invented and first used in this country by General Pitt-Rivers (1827–1900). He had been concerned professionally with the use and evolutionary history of the musket. Pitt-Rivers studied the development of firearms, arranging collections of individual types in progressive sequences and was influenced in his work by the evolutionary theories of the natural sciences proposed by Darwin. He decided that all material culture could be seen as objects to be arranged in typological sequences developing in an evolutionary way. Pitt-Rivers, like Flinders Petrie, insisted that archaeology was not simply a study of art objects but of all objects. He stressed that his collection was not for the purpose of surprise, through the beauty or value of the objects exhibited, but solely for instruction. For this purpose ordinary and typical specimens rather than rare objects were selected and arranged in sequence.

The work of Pitt-Rivers was paralleled by that of Sir John Evans (1823–1908) who was also busily classifying and arranging sequences of bronze and stone tools. *Ancient Bronze Implements, Weapons and Ornaments of Great Britain and Ireland* was published in 1881. He also laid the foundations of the study of Celtic coins in Britain with the publication of his book *The Coins of Ancient Britain*. In this he recognised, by observing a chronological progression, that the coins did not evolve into more sophisticated types but rather devolved through continuous copying into crude and often illegible forms. All Celtic coinage is in origin imitative, following a chosen classical model. The earliest coins are basically forgeries, substitutes for the originals which were not available in sufficient quantity. Gradually, in the process of copying, local deviations crept in and the traditional patterns were transformed in order to differentiate local coinages. Evans' study demonstrated that not all objects necessarily change for the better.

Between 1880 and 1900, after inheriting the Cranborne estates in Dorset, Pitt-Rivers devoted himself to excavation, investigating camps, villages, cemeteries, barrows and ditches including Wor Barrow, Bokerly Dyke, Wood Yates and Rotherly. He initiated and practised the total excavation of sites, and stressed the importance of stratigraphy and the necessity of recording the position of everything found. He transformed excavation from a pleasant hobby to an arduous scientific pursuit.[1] Like Petrie he recognised the importance of associating objects with the stratigraphic position in which they were found.

However, it was Petrie who refined the technique of cross-dating, whereby objects from different sites are compared in order to establish a date. At Mycenae he recognised Egyptian influences and actual Egyptian objects, all of the eighteenth dynasty, which enabled him to declare that the late Mycenaean civilization flourished between 1500 and 1000 BC. At Tell el-Hesi he was also able to synchronize some of the stratigraphic levels with Egyptian dynasties and so construct an absolute chronology of the occupation on the site.

By the turn of the century the basic archaeological techniques for dating had been formulated: typology (the independent and internal method of arranging artefacts by progressive changes in shape and style) and cross-dating (the comparison of objects with similar types found in historically dated, sealed deposits). On the basis of either or both of these techniques several major pottery classifications were devised, several of which are still in use today.

One of the first major classifications of European prehistoric pottery was J. Abercromby's *Study of the Bronze Age Pottery of Great Britain and Ireland* (1912). In this great work he listed and illustrated all the known beaker pottery from the British Isles and from a study of form and decoration divided it into three chronological groups – A, B and C. Until the 1950s Abercromby's classification, with further refinements of alphabetical subdivisions, remained the basis of beaker identification and dating. In 1963[2] Piggott replaced this alphabetical classification with a descriptive approach based on the form of the vessel itself. He followed Abercromby by retaining a tripartite division, but now British beakers were divided into long-necked, bell and short-necked varieties. These regroupings were still based on the initial corpus and it was only in 1970 with the publication of Clarke's *Beaker Pottery of Great Britain and Ireland* that a new and more comprehensive approach to the pottery was attempted.

As many prehistorians have preferred to use stone or metal work as a means of dating and for constructing site chronologies, some major classifications of Neolithic and Bronze Age pottery did not appear until the 1950s and '60s. Such a classification was the late Neolithic Peterborough tradition named by Piggott in 1954[3] and subsequently divided into three distinctive styles, Ebbsfleet, Mortlake and Fengate (the places where they were first identified).[4] A comprehensive survey of Bronze Age urns was not available until Longworth published *The Origins and Development of the Primary Series of Collared Urns in England and Wales* in 1961.[5]

In contrast, the end of the nineteenth century saw the publication of several major Roman pottery classifications. Many of these dealt with arretine and samian, the red glossy pottery produced in northern Italy and Gaul. Indeed the first attempt at samian typology was published as early as 1859 by Charles Roach Smith, who collected samian from various parts of London.[6] Unfortunately there was nobody else in Britain sufficiently interested to follow this early lead. Instead the foundations of samian studies were laid by Continental scholars, such as Dragendorff who classified the forms of vessels, giving each shape an individual number, in 1895[7] (fig. 27). In 1904 Déchelette distinguished southern from central Gaulish potters by cataloging name-stamps and figure types on decorated bowls.[8] Déchelette relied on stylistic differences between the work of various potters when composing his chronological classification. He grouped the central Gaulish potters who made the early bowl form Drag. 29 between AD 40–75 (fig. 27). Potters who made the later form Drag.37 were dated AD 75–110 if their designs were arranged in panels or had free-standing human figures (fig. 27). His third period included the potters who designed Drag. 37 bowls with coarse scrolls, big medallions or figures, and free-style scenes with animals and arcaded patterns which he dated from AD 110 to about the end of the second century. The main period of production and exportation was, in his opinion, during the period of the Antonine Emperors, and the chief potters of that period were Cinnamus and Paternus. Knorr attempted a similar study of south Gaulish potters,[9] while Ludowici[10] and Folzer[11] distinguished various east Gaulish factories, including Rheinzabern. By the time Oswald and Pryce wrote *Introduction to the Study of Terra Sigillata* in 1920, they were able to state:

> The importance of a careful study of the pottery which occurs in such profusion on all Roman sites is now fully recognised by British and Continental students of the Imperial period, and no investigator can afford to neglect this branch of his subject. Next to datable inscriptions there is, perhaps, no relic of Roman occupation which yields such valuable chronological evidence as *terra sigillata*. . . . The variations and transmutations of its forms, the changing character of its decorative designs in successive periods and the marks of its potters, tell a chronological tale. . . . It is indeed no exaggeration to state that the ceramic results of certain excavations have done much to substantiate modify, or reconstruct views which had hitherto been based upon historical evidence alone.

The scope of their work was confined almost wholly to the study of such details of technique, form, decoration, and design occurring in *terra sigillata* that could be of assistance to dating. No attempt was made to describe all the types which occur but rather to give a full account of those vessels which possess some definite chronological value. The method by which a date for each type was arrived at was based on 'site-values'. Thus the absence or presence of certain types on properly excavated sites which could be dated by external historical evidence was used to determine the period and distribution of specific forms of samian. This method also indicated the activity of the potters concerned in the production of such forms, as well as the period when certain decorative motifs were in fashion. It could easily be applied to south Gaulish samian which was found in large quantities on the historically dated Roman fortresses and forts in Germany. For example, varieties found at Haltern (12 BC–AD 16) were not present at Hofheim (AD 40–51). Hofheim types were rare at Geislingen (AD 74–90), while the later site produced samian forms comparable with only the earliest pieces at Rottenburg and Cannstatt occupied from 90. Oswald went on to amass a great index of potters' name-stamps impressed on samian, published in 1931.[12] This major work on the subject has been superseded by the vast index compiled by Brian Hartley which is yet to be published.

A general study of the decorated bowls of central Gaulish potters was still required and Stanfield began work on this from about 1930. It is clear that before his death in 1945 he had intended it to be a comprehensive survey of the British material, supplemented where necessary by Continental pieces. His research was not only a stylistic study of the work of individual potters but the relationship between potters was also indicated, and the extent to which potters borrowed figure types or decorative details from each other. This work was revised and published by Simpson in 1958[13]. Many other people have contributed, and still are, to the building and revising of these chronological classifications, in which every detail of the decoration or the shape of the vessel is significant.

The first extensive studies of Romano-British coarse pottery were published at the beginning of this century. James Curle realised the importance of pottery, devoting a substantial section of his report on the excavations of the Roman fort at Newstead[14] to the pottery, both samian and coarse wares. The first individual studies of coarse pottery were undertaken by Thomas May, who published the large museum collections at York,[15] Carlisle,[16] Silchester[17] and Colchester.[18] He also researched and published the pottery from the excavations at Hengistbury Head,[19] the Ospringe Cemetery, Kent,[20] Swarling, Kent,[21] Richborough,[22] Warrington[23] and Templeborough.[24] No one before or since has published so much pottery from so many sites in such quantity and variety. Much of his work was on pottery already in museum collections or from his time as a pottery assistant to Bushe-Fox, but at Templeborough he was director of excavations. In May's report on the samian the descriptions are carefully detailed with full references and dates clearly derived from Knorr and Déchelette. The report on the coarse pottery is very different, as illustrated by May's comment on the red, oxidised wares: 'common flowerpot-red or tile-red wares were as offensive for domestic purposes to the Romans, as to ourselves and should generally speaking be regarded as 'wasters – overbaked and distorted specimens which accumulate in heaps beside kilns.'

May obviously considered that all the pottery of the period was intended to be black or grey and he even thought that the black-burnished ware, so common on northern sites, was actually coated with bitumen. Even more surprisingly he appears to have no conception of a dated sequence. Of the 69 coarse ware vessels described in the report only 12 are dated and most of these refer to Wroxeter and Newstead parallels. When discussing the forms that imitate samian vessels May considered them to be all first-century in date like the originals and to have been the products of potters working in the vicinity of the fort. Yet at least three are now known to be fourth-century red colour-coated wares. It appears May had very little conception of the significance of stratified deposits.[25] This is surprising considering his close association with Bushe-Fox, whose ideas and techniques were far in advance. At Wroxeter in 1912[26] Bushe-Fox clearly appreciated the need to arrange the coarse pottery in a dated sequence and he grasped the principal that changes in the form of some vessels was due to a chronological development. Unfortunately this idea eluded May but his work was still of enormous value as it was a great advance to see coarse pottery studied and published in its own right. The excavators at Silchester and Caerwent had found large quantities but regarded it as so commonplace that they hardly bothered to mention it. They ignored the principles laid down by Pitt-Rivers, who attempted to record everything he found.

Although Sir Mortimer Wheeler was not specifically interested in Roman pottery, he nevertheless demonstrated the way it could be used to date the constructional sequences of Roman forts in Wales.[27] Unfortunately he did not develop this line of enquiry in his report on the excavations at Verulamium, St Albans, in which only a small amount of pottery recovered was published.[28] An interesting comparison can be made with Frere's report on his excavations at Verulamium.[29] Although dealing with a much smaller site than Wheeler, 1,293 vessels were published by stratified groups as against 183 vessels from Wheeler's area of the town. Kathleen Kenyon, a student of Wheeler, fortunately took pottery more seriously and her report on the Jewry Wall site, Leicester[30] is one of the first serious attempts to use it on a large scale to date the main sequences of occupation. She also produced a type-series of the pottery from the site, an idea started by Bushe-Fox at Wroxeter (see below). However, it was John Gillam[31] who succeeded in producing a comprehensive survey of the pottery found on northern, principally military, sites.

Gillam's type-series presented a range of dated types of coarse pottery vessels found on these sites. Most of the vessels illustrated were from stratified deposits on or near Hadrian's Wall. Within the region the known history provided a background for dating the pottery. The fact that many of the types used in northern Britain can be found elsewhere provided a range of dated types, of value when dating pottery from other regions. Form and decoration rather than fabric were used as the basis of the general classification. The vessel forms are grouped together by general shape, purpose and other features but may be in different wares.[32] The classes are themselves arranged in order running from tall vessels with narrow mouths to flat vessels with wide mouths. Within each class the order of the vessel form is chronological, from early to late specimens. Site evidence took precedence over typological considerations in assessing the dates of the pottery types.

Erich Gose applied similar dating methods in his formation of a type-series of the Roman pottery from the Rhineland[33] but he paid greater attention to fabric. He proceeds from fine wares, such as samian ware and colour-coated drinking beakers and cups, to coarse wares. The pottery is classified by wares, either relating to decorative techniques, such as mica-dusted ware and marbled ware, to types known to have been manufactured in certain areas or places, such as Gallo-Belgic ware and Speicher ware. Each vessel is meticulously described, including the nature of the fabric, identification of the source where possible and date range.

The 1960s and '70s saw dramatic changes in the archaeologist's approach to pottery. The traditional view, which considered form and decorative differences to be paramount, paid little attention to the fabric of individual vessels. Pottery was used almost solely as a means of dating or for indicating cultural or tribal traditions, with little regard to economic considerations. The origins of some major pottery types, such as Romano-British black-burnished ware, were completely unknown. The situation has been radically changed by the use of scientific aids, in particular petrology and heavy mineral analysis, to ascertain the composition of pottery. For instance, the early Neolithic pottery from the causewayed enclosure at Hembury, Devon had been studied in some detail by Thomas[34] and divided into several groups. The predominant coarse 'A' ware was shown to be local in origin. However, another type, Hembury 'F' ware, was clearly imported from outside the region as it was characterised by fragments of igneous rock. This was also studied by Thomas,[35] who suggested a source on the edge of the Dartmoor granite massif.

Cornwall and Hodges[36] extended this work by indicating that similar pottery had been found at Maiden Castle, Windmill Hill and Robin Hood's Ball, but did not change the assessment of the source. Peacock[37] took the study another step forward by locating the exact source of the raw material. From the mineral assemblage he showed that the only possible origin in south-west England was the Gabbro, an outcrop of rock on the Lizard Head in Cornwall. The clay from this area was mineralogically identical with the pottery. Moreover, it became clear from the homogeneous nature of the pottery, (demonstrated both by the fabric and the restricted range of forms produced) that it was actually manufactured in this area of Cornwall. This has important implications for the whole study of Neolithic pottery, indicating that, while most wares were produced on a local domestic basis, some were manufactured by specialists and traded over considerable distances. Further studies indicated that this clay was an important source in the Iron Age as well.

Similar techniques have been applied to Romano-British coarse wares, locating the source of important types such as Dorset black-burnished ware.[38] These studies underline the need to characterise pottery by the fabric as well as form and decoration. In this way greater refinements can be obtained, with the isolating of specific types of pottery whose origin and distribution can be traced. For the Roman period this has resulted in concentrated work on the manufacture and distribution of pottery, with the realization that this is the only way to understand the development of the coarse ware industry both stylistically and chronologically. This was appreciated by Philip Corder and amply demonstrated by his extensive excavations and reports on kilns in Yorkshire and elsewhere, published in the 1930s and 1940s.[39]

In spite of this, the concept was not advanced until the 1960s with the work on the Colchester industry by M.R. Hull.[40] After another considerable lull, there has been a return to this approach with the work on the New Forest industry by Vivien Swan[41] and Michel Fulford,[42] the Oxfordshire industry by Young[43] and the Lower Nene Valley.[44] Similar studies have resulted in the identification of Continental imports into the Provinces. Dr Kevin Greene's work on Pre-Flavian fine wares has indicated the long distances that pottery, other than samian, could travel.[45] Work continues along these lines with the present study of later fine ware industries, such as Cologne, the Lower Nene Valley and Colchester, concentrating on ways to distinguish and date the products of each industry.[46] Research programmes of this kind aim not only to date the pottery but also to ascertain where the pottery was traded and to trace the development of the industry itself. Thus, the full historical and economic potential of pottery is finally realised.

The present approach to pottery, therefore, is to study the relationship of fabric, form and decorative treatment in order to isolate specific types of pottery. Within each type further divisions can be made by tracing progressive typological changes so that individual forms may be dated. The occurrence of vessels in historically dated contexts will assist in the construction of a series of dated forms. Where possible the origin of the pottery is ascertained and the area in which it was used or traded illustrated by means of distribution maps. In this way pottery can be used not only for dating layers and features on archaeological sites but also used to extend our knowledge of trade routes and marketing patterns in the ancient world.

In order to gain the maximum amount of information the archaeologist must know what to look for and what to ask of the pottery. Three principal factors must be determined: the date, where the pottery was made and by what means it arrived on the site. Only by applying the same criteria to each sherd of pottery found can the archaeologist attempt to assess the complicated social, economic and political history it may represent.

The archaeologist applies strict standards and demands a uniform approach to the study of pottery, so that material from different sites of the same period can be directly compared. A considerable part of an excavation report may be taken up by a detailed pottery report, complete with statistics charting the proportions of each type found and standardised drawings of the pottery. The conventional method of drawing pottery is in full profile with a central vertical dividing line (fig. 2). On the right external decoration is shown and the general appearance reconstructed. On the left a section through the pot is indicated in solid black, illustrating the external and internal profile, and the thickness of the section. Any internal features, such as wheel marks, are also indicated on the left.

In conclusion, pottery is easily mass-produced, yet has a short working life. But, once discarded, it can remain in its archaeological context indefinitely. Due to its great abundance and variety pottery is well suited to the formation of chronological or regional classifications. In addition the distribution of different types of pottery can contribute to our understanding of the ancient economy. Due to its unique qualities pottery has become one of the principle tools of the archaeologist. The following chapters explain and illustrate, by taking examples from the Prehistoric and Roman periods of Britain and the Continent, how the archaeologist exploits this tool to its fullest extent.

3 Pottery and the Archaeologist

Pottery is only of use to the archaeologist when it can be identified and dated. Until classified, both by source and by date, pottery cannot make a positive contribution either to archaeology or history. The wider social and economic implications of the production and use of pottery cannot be appreciated unless the origin and distribution of specific types can be determined. The archaeologist, therefore, requires three basic facts about each sherd of pottery found: identity, date and origin.

Identification

FABRIC

Identification means discovering the fabric, form and decoration of each sherd of pottery. Firstly there is the fabric – the material of which the sherd is made. A description of the fabric should note the nature of the clay – whether it is coarse or smooth. This means looking at the inclusions, grains of sand, particles of iron ore and lumps of rock which may occur naturally in the clay or have been added during manufacture. Vessels made for the table usually have a fine smooth fabric, like Roman samian, and are referred to as fine wares. Cooking pots and storage vessels are normally more coarse, such as Roman Dorset black-burnished ware, and so are known as coarse wares.

The techniques used in the manufacture of the pot are an important element of the fabric description, (e.g. whether the pot was hand-made or wheel-made). Coarse wares are often hand-made and do not have the tell-tale internal spiral finger-marks made as the pot revolved on the wheel. However, in the prehistoric period some hand-made vessels exhibit a remarkably high degree of craftsmanship, such as Iron Age 'saucepan pots' (fig. 2.4). The introduction of the wheel, probably towards the end of the Iron Age, resulted in the mass production of a fairly standard range of forms. As well as internal wheel marks, pots made on a wheel often have spiral marks on the base produced when the potter detached the pot from the wheel with a wire or string. During the Roman period nearly all pottery was produced on the wheel, exceptions being Dorset black-burnished ware and Malvernian salt pots, which were still produced in the Iron Age way. Decorated samian was produced on a wheel, with a mould centered on it by means of a small hole cut in the base. Plain vessels were shaped with templates whilst turning on the wheel, producing the complicated angular profiles so characteristic of some early forms (fig. 28).

Fabric analysis has grown in significance with the development of new scientific techniques for identifying minerals and elements in the clay body of the pot. In the initial stages of identification it is necessary to establish visual differences, using a hand-lens. Later on a full petrological examination may be required to establish, with greater certainty, the origin of the vessel. Features that may be visually discerned include the colour and texture of the clay body and the techniques used in the production of the pot.

The colour of the body, which can be an important criterion, is largely determined by firing conditions. An oxidised fabric is produced when all the carbon in the fuel is burnt. This leaves a surplus of oxygen in the kiln atmosphere, which results in a light brown or red surface colouring. A reduced fabric is produced when the fuel is not fully burnt. Soot and carbon monoxide are carried into the kiln, creating pottery with a grey or black surface. These are the two extremes but in primitive firing the conditions could fluctuate or not be sustained. Consequently, the core of the pot may be of a different colour to that of the surface when the firing is not long enough. In addition the surface may be patchy in colour due to the pots touching during the firing or due to stacking, when the bottom or inside may be of a completely different colour to the top or outside. Vessels in a fine white fabric retain their colour after firing because there is no iron oxide in the clay.

Texture is very important, as the fabric may be coarse or fine. It may contain a great deal of sand 'filler', which is added to make the clay less elastic, to reduce shrinking, to distribute the heat evenly through the pot, so that it does not crack during firing, and to prevent cracking when used for cooking. In prehistoric times flint, shell and fossil shell (oolite) were also used as fillers for the same reasons. Natural inclusions may be noticed, such as the presence of red or black ironstone particles, mica or fragments of igneous rock. These inclusions help to create something akin to a 'thumb print', isolating different fabrics.

The surface finish and treatment may also help in the identification of specific fabrics. Vessels were sometimes covered both inside and out with a 'slip'. Normally the pot was dipped upside down in a clay slip, a liquid mixture of clay and water either with or without the addition of a colouring agent. Adding a colouring agent such as iron compounds, may produce, after firing, a surface colour darker than that of the body, a process which is called a colour-coating (plate 9). This may occasionally have a metallic lustre or sheen. Sometimes the slip was light on a darker body. This practice was frequently employed in the early Roman period on flagons made of red clay to make them look white, in parts of the Empire where white clay was difficult to obtain. A slip or colour-coating is normally considered to be a characteristic of the fabric but the application of a slip with a brush is normally classed as decoration.

Another surface finish is a glaze, when a vitreous or glassy layer is fused onto the surface of the pot (plate 1). This technique was particularly useful for waterproofing a pot and was used on first-century AD St Rémy flagons, vessels used for the serving of wine and other liquids. However, the technique was not extensively used in the Roman period, when only lead glazes were employed. Mica-gilt or dusting was another finish, involving the application of particles of mica suspended in a slip to create a golden sheen. Glazing and mica dusting were ways of imitating the glossy sheen of more expensive bronze vessels (plate 1).

The fabric of a vessel can be linked with the term 'ware', which refers either to the material composition of the pottery, as in 'grey ware', or to the place of manufacture as in 'Lower Nene Valley Ware'. This term should not be confused with the 'class', which designates vessels of the same general form and purpose, irrespective of fabric, date and details of form. Ware can be used in a general sense, as in colour-coated ware or calcite-gritted ware, to indicate a specific technique of production or more precisely to denote vessels of known industries. It must be stressed that the large industries of the later Roman period, such as Oxfordshire, produced several technically different wares, with some forms (e.g. flagons) manufactured in a variety of fabrics including colour-coated, parchment and grey wares.

One notable exception to this rule is Roman samian ware, which despite its name does not derive its nomenclature from its place of manufacture. Instead this term was used generally in the Roman world for a distinctive kind of earthenware.[1] The Romans themselves may have believed that such pottery originally came from the island of Samos, but by c. 200 BC any geographical meaning of the word, when applied to pottery, had been lost. The earliest known references to

samian occur in the musical comedies written by Plautus, long before
the ware now known as samian by archaeologists was first made.
Plautus implies in his humour that samian was well known for being
fragile and easily broken, as well as being in common use.[2] From the
late Republic onwards the word took on a wider meaning, probably
relating to a distinctive characteristic of the original ware which was by
then widely copied. The name continued to be applied to the copies in
the same way that 'china' has come to be used today as a general term for
fine pottery.

The distinguishing feature of samian could have been its glossy
surface as '*samiare*' means to polish.[3] It may have taken its name from
some kind of polishing stone or powder known as *terra samia* which,
according to Galen and Pliny, was originally quarried on Samos but
may also have been extracted from other areas. Employed as it was for
polishing metals as well as having medical uses, this material was
probably Kaolinite. It is used today to create the shine on glossy paper
and furthermore Kaolin deposits are found on Samos. Hence, the term
samian may be derived from some process during the manufacture
which gave the vessel a polished, glossy appearance. As the vessels were
not physically polished this may refer to the preparation of the slip
which coated the surfaces of the vessel, in order to create the glossy
effect. The Romans seemingly believed that the gloss on the pottery
was due to the use of *terra samia* to bring up the shine. The word came
to mean glossy pottery and was probably used to denote fine pottery in
general.

By the time of Pliny's *Natural History*, dedicated to the Emperor
Titus in AD 77, the author was able to comment, 'Samian is still
esteemed for tableware. This reputation is held by Arezzo in Italy and
for cups only by Sorrento, Asti, Pollentia, Sagunto in Spain and
Pergamon in Asia Minor'.[4] Confusion has arisen over Pliny's use of the
term samian, as some archaeologists[5] have made an exception of his
remark, maintaining that in this instance the word was used geographically and that Pliny meant that Samos was still exporting tableware to
Italy. Waage[6] considered the plain red-glazed Roman pottery found
during his excavations of the Agora in Athens to be Pliny's samian. At
this time the native clay of Samos was claimed to be the raw material
from which this red pottery was made. Although the earliest pottery of
Samos was still unknown it was thought that the island was exporting
plain red ware throughout the Mediterranean area during the lifetime
of Pliny. Waage's 'samian from Samos' is now considered to be Eastern
Sigillata B, probably produced at Tralles in Asia Minor.[7] It copies

plain Arretine and production was perhaps started by the migration of a potter from Arezzo in the reign of Augustus. No fine wares are known to have been made on Samos during the whole of the period covered by the references to samian in Roman literature.[8] It seems more likely that Pliny uses samian as a generic term for the pottery produced at Arezzo and a number of other places in the Empire – centres where quality pottery was manufactured. It could be assumed that all these places were producing samian-type pottery in Pliny's day. The existence of a potter called L. Tettius Samia and a number of workshop slaves called Samus at Arezzo support this inference.[9]

So in archaeological circles the term samian has come to be associated specifically with the red-glossy pottery known to have been produced at Arezzo and at other centres in the Empire, even though no ancient writer mentions any colour when referring to samian. This connection with red-glossy pottery was first made at the beginning of the eighteenth century by Samuel Pitiscus.[10] Then Governor Pownall (1779) published some vessels from the Pudding-Pan Rock shipwreck in the Thames Estuary,[11] identifying them as samian by quoting from Pitiscus who had stated that pottery made from samian clay turned to a red colour. Gradually the practice of using the term to describe red-glossy pottery was adopted.[12]

Continental archaeologists, especially those in France and Germany have preferred to use the term *terra sigillata* rather than samian when describing such pottery. This term has enjoyed a vogue amongst Roman archaeologists in Britain but the archaeological use of *terra sigillata* is in reality an abuse of the original meaning of the phrase. *Terra*, referring to earth rather than pottery, and *sigillata*, meaning 'with little figures', should be applied to the practice of stamping tablets of medicinal earth, which was common in the Roman period.[13] Early antiquarians probably mistook sherds of decorated samian ware for these tablets of *terra sigillata* and the term was transferred to the pottery. Today the term should strictly be applied only to decorated ware. This reinforces the case for retaining samian ware as a general term, as it probably derives from a phrase used in the Roman world for red-and-black glossy pottery.

VESSEL FORMS

Once the visual appearance of the fabric has been noted, attention can be turned to identifying the vessel form, i.e. the shape, including the rim, base and handles (where present) and any other distinguishing features. Determining the form will also mean identifying the class to which the vessel belongs, as vessels related by form are likely to share a common function, regardless of date, fabric and minor stylistic differences. A bowl will always imply a round hollow receptacle suitable for containing food, which must be deeper than a dish if it is to perform its designated function. It is generally accepted that it should have a height more than one-third its width.[14] A hemispherical bowl has a round profile, forming one half of a sphere (fig. 2.1). Sometimes bowls are referred to as segmental, when the body forms a segment less than half of a sphere (fig. 2.2). A carinated bowl has a sharp inward change of direction in the wall, often near the centre, but sometimes it is more generally used to refer to any angular change of direction in the wall. The furrowed bowls of the early Iron Age have a sharply carinated profile (fig. 2.3). When more than one change of angle is present the term angular is applied, such as the early Iron Age angular bowls and jars from the Upper Thames region which have distinctly waisted profiles (fig. 19.1,2). This practice can be taken to extreme in the concertina bowls of the primary Iron Age, which have, as their name implies, a multiangular profile. The term champher is sometimes confused with carination but the former refers to an angle in the wall at the junction with the base which should not be confused with a simple sagging base. A campanulate bowl takes the form of an inverted bell (fig. 28.27). The 'saucepan pots' of the middle Iron Age are basically cylindrical bowls and jars of varying height (fig. 2.4), while contemporary bowls common in the Upper Thames Valley have a globular or round profile (fig. 2.6). In the later Roman period a bowl with a flange placed immediately below the rim, providing a stable footing for a lid, was very popular and was produced in a wide range of fabrics (fig. 2.9).

In contrast a dish is a shallow vessel with a height less than one-third but greater than one-seventh of its rim diameter, while a plate or platter, has a height no greater than one-seventh of its diameter.[15] Dishes and platters tend to follow the same pattern as bowls, with straight, curved or carinated walls (fig. 5.6). Sometimes they have elaborately shaped profiles as in the case of Arretine and samian platters (fig. 28.15,17). Platters and plates were common during the late Iron Age-early Roman period (figs. 20.5 and 5.6).

The width of a jar is normally less than its height. It can be constricted at the neck or straight-sided like a bucket. They are usually further distinguished as being either wide-mouthed or narrow-mouthed. The former should have a rim diameter either the same or greater than the width across the shoulder. The latter should have a

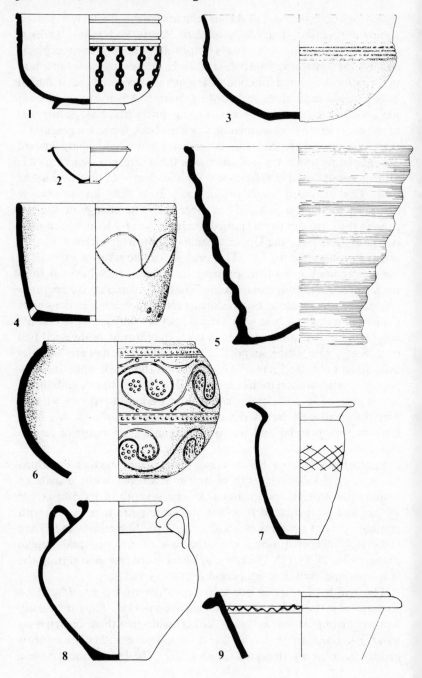

mouth measuring less than the width at the shoulder. A more general approach requires that the mouth of a wide-mouthed jar should be able to accommodate a man's clenched fist. The term cooking-pot is usually applied to jars used for cooking, which may have soot encrusted on their surface. It is often used to describe Dorset black-burnished ware jars, common throughout the Roman period (fig. 11). The Latin terms *olla*, for a pot or clay jar and *dolium*, for a very large jar, are no longer used in archaeological publications as their meaning is imprecise. Also belonging to the Roman period is a special kind of jar referred to as a 'honey pot' which is a double-handled vessel with a narrow mouth (fig. 2.8). It is known that they were actually used for either storing or transporting honey, as examples have been found with the Latin for honey, *mel*, scratched on them. Jars occur in a wide variety of shapes and sizes. Late Neolithic grooved ware jars have wide mouths, straight sides and flat bases (fig. 15.1). Early Iron Age angular jars have carinated profiles (fig. 19.1). In the Roman period a wide range of jars was produced, from cooking pots to storage jars. Narrow-mouthed, high-shouldered jars with ovoid profiles are more common in the first to early second century, while wide-mouth jars proliferate in the later period.

The term vase is used to describe certain very ornate jars. In the early La Tène phase of the Iron Age some distinctive pottery forms were produced, which are commonly known in Britain by their Continental names. The *vase carène* (fig. 4.1) is distinguished by its sharply angular profile normally accompanied by a pedestal base, while the *vase piriforme* (fig. 4.2) has a characteristically high, rounded shoulder with a pear-shaped body and a pedestal base.

The term urn (*urna*) is applied to vessels, often jars or vases, when they are used for funerary purposes, either to contain the cremated remains of the dead or when placed in the grave. In the early Bronze Age the use of such vessels was widespread. The cordoned urn belonging to this period is decorated with large cordons, the areas in between left either plain or decorated (fig. 3.1). The collared urn has a thickened deep area below a bevelled rim, marked out from the body by

---

Fig. 2   Forms: bowls, urns and jars

1 Hemispherical bowl with stamped decoration. *After Webster*
2 Segmental bowl. *After Webster*
3 Furrowed bowl. *After Megaw and Simpson*
4 Saucepan pot. *After Megaw and Simpson*
5 Corrugated urn. *After Birchall*
6 Globular bowl with curvilinear decoration. *After Megaw and Simpson*
7 Wide mouth jar. *After Gillam*
8 Honey jar. *After Webster*
9 Flanged bowl. *After Webster*
Scale 1:4

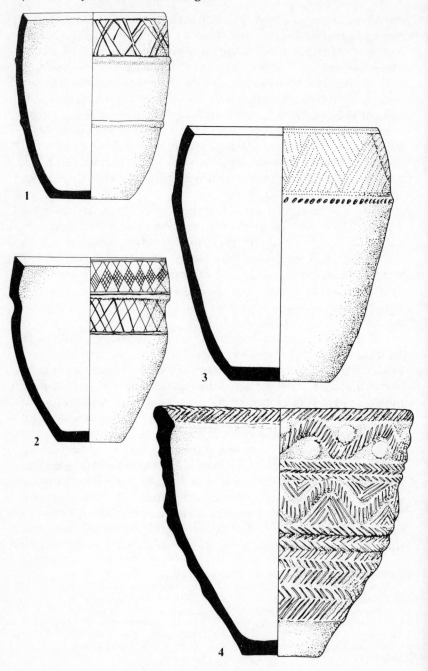

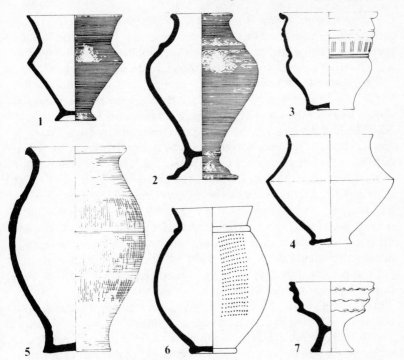

Fig. 4 Forms: vases and beakers
1 Vase Carène
2 Vase Piriforme
After Harding Scale 1:3
3 Girth beaker. *After Swan*
4 Biconical beaker. *After Swan*

5 Butt beaker with rouletted decoration.
After Birchall
6 Poppy-head beaker with panels of
barbotine dots. *After Webster*
7 Tazza. *After Webster*
Scale 1:4

a sharp constriction (fig. 3.2). As its name suggests the bucket urn is very plain, with a flat base and straight-sided walls ending in a bevelled rim. Biconical urns have a carinated profile, with the wall flaring out and then turning sharply in towards the base (fig. 3.3). Encrusted urns are heavily decorated with applied bosses (fig. 3.4).

The later Bronze Age Deverel-Rimbury urns occur in three classic shapes – bucket, barrel and globular. In contrast to earlier practices there is no distinction between the pottery associated with burials and that found on settlements. In the late Iron Age 'Belgic' pedestal urns

Fig. 3 Forms: Bronze Age urns
1 Cordoned urn
2 Collared urn

3 Biconical urn
4 Encrusted urn
Scale 1:6 After Megaw and Simpson

(fig. 20.1,2), conical urns (fig. 20.3 and corrugated urns (fig. 1.5) were commonly connected with the rite of cremation. During the Roman period a jar with a human face applied or modelled on the shoulder of the vessel, called a face urn, often served as an ash container.

There were three main types of drinking vessel, excluding the jar. Firstly the beaker which is typically tall and slender and, like a jar, should be taller than it is wide. Large examples could only be held in both hands and might have been designed for communal use. The term has also been specifically used to describe a complete range of vessels current in the late Neolithic-early Bronze Age. These are associated in this country with the arrival of new settlers, named Beaker folk after their distinctive pottery. Beakers come in many different shapes, sizes and fabrics, the most common are Bell ('S' sided), Barrel, Short-necked and Long-necked (figs 17, 18). The significance of these different forms is discussed below, but by calling them beakers it implies that they were primarily used for drinking. This may be true but it is possible that they were used for other purposes too. The Butt Beaker belongs to both the late Iron Age and the early Roman periods. This is a tall vessel shaped like a butt or barrel and decorated with cordons, rouletting and latticing (fig. 4.5; plate 21). It was produced in a wide range of fabrics. A contemporary vessel was the Girth Beaker which was a straight-sided beaker with horizontal bands of corrugations, cordons and latticing (fig. 4.3). Biconical beakers were also produced during this period. The walls of these vessels flare sharply out from the mouth and turn back in, towards the base, at a point roughly equivalent to half the height, so that they resemble two truncated cones placed base-to-base (fig. 4.4). Poppy-head beakers dating from the late first–late second century have a shape like the seed-head of a poppy and were produced in a grey or black fabric with a polished surface (fig. 4.6). The body is often decorated with panels of barbotine dots.

From the first–early third century colour-coated beakers were used to supplement the range of samian ware beakers and cups. High-shouldered beakers were popular for most of the first century in Britain and the western Provinces. They have a narrow mouth and base, with a high rounded shoulder and globular profile (fig. 5.1). Some vessels are extremely light and delicate, like those made at Lyons in Gaul. Bag-shaped beakers were very popular in the late first and second centuries. They have a wide mouth and straight walls that flare out below the rim, then turn sharply in towards the base at a point roughly equal to one third of the height of the vessel (fig. 5.2). They can have plain, cornice

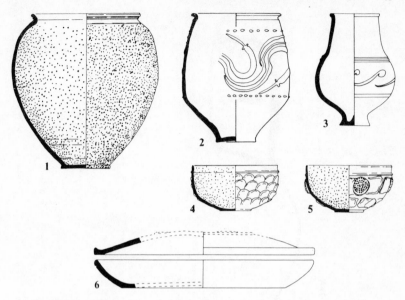

Fig. 5   Forms: beakers, cups and platters
1 Lyons high-shouldered beaker with roughcast decoration. *After Greene*
2 Nene Valley bag-shaped beaker with a cornice rim and barbotine decoration.
After Howe, Perrin and Mackreth
3 Bulbous beaker with barbotine decoration. *After Webster*
4 Lyons hemispherical cup with roughcast interior and applied imbricated scales on
the exterior. *After Greene*
5 Lyons hemispherical cup with applied 'raspberry roundels'. *After Greene*
6 Platter and matching lid. *After Hull*
Scale 1:4

or grooved cornice rims (see below). Bulbous beakers replaced bag-shaped beakers during the late second–early third century. These have a narrow mouth, a long thin neck tapering into a globular or bulbous body often with a small, short foot (fig. 5.3). In Britain the form continued to be produced until the end of the fourth century. All the forms mentioned above – high-shouldered, bag-shaped and bulbous – were often produced with indented sides, the sides of the pot being pushed in to form alternating hollows and bumps (fig. 32.3). Seven or nine indentations are common, numbers which may have been deemed lucky by the owner as small indented beakers were frequently used for shaking dice.

The cup is a wide, shallow vessel, but quite small and likely to have been for personal use. Drinking cups were particularly popular from *c.* AD 40–70, produced in colour-coated fabrics and outnumbering their

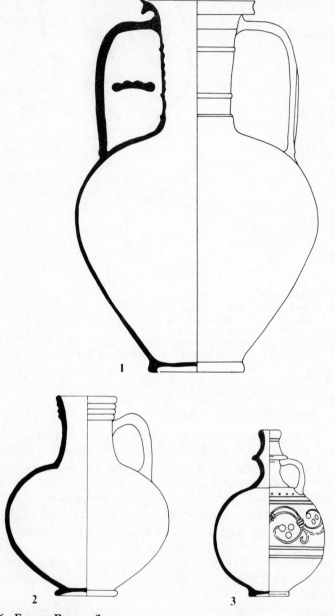

Fig. 6 Forms: Roman flagons
1 Hofheim flagon. *After Swan*
2 Ring neck flagon. *After Webster*

3 Flange-necked flagon. *After Webster*
Scale 1:4

beaker counterparts. They took the form of small hemispherical or carinated vessels (figs 5.4, 5.5). A wide range of cups was produced in samian ware, often with matching small bowls. One form is campanulate in shape (Drag. 27, fig. 28.27), while another has straight sides tapering in towards the base (Drag. 33, fig. 28.33). Small cups could serve other purposes besides drinking. Incense cups have been known since prehistoric times. The 'Grape cups', decorated with numerous round pellets of clay, and 'Aldbourne cups', horizontally perforated through the walls, both belonging to the early Bronze Age Wessex culture, may have been used for incense. They appear to have been made specifically for burial with the dead. Incense cups were widely used in the Roman period. A *tazza*, a cup-like vessel, normally in a light-coloured fabric with a pedestal base and decorated with bands of frilling, was probably used as an incense cup in domestic ritual ceremonies or as a lamp (fig. 4.7).

The third and final main type of drinking vessel is the tankard or mug, normally a straight-sided vessel with a single handle. These were fairly common in prehistoric and Roman times. Beaker tankards have very elaborate decoration, while the simpler Dorset black-burnished ware tankards were made during the late Iron Age and Roman periods (fig. 10.4).

Lids were employed to cover both jars and bowls, in the latter case forming a casserole set. These do not vary greatly in shape, having either a curved, straight or carinated profile. Those with flat tops could equally well have been used as dishes and so are sometimes termed dish/lid (fig. 12.8).

A jug is basically a handled jar with a spout, which is surprisingly rare in the prehistoric and Roman periods. Instead, during Roman times the flagon (from the late Latin *flasca*, flask) was the most common vessel used for holding liquids. It has a tall narrow neck, usually a globular body, a foot ring and one or more handles. Surprisingly few had spouts, except the pinched spout flagon. The form is further characterised by different necks and rims, including ring-necked (a conjoined series of individual rings fig. 6.2), pulley-wheel, screw-necked (a continuous spiral groove), disc-rimmed and flange-necked or collared (fig. 6.3). A type of flagon common in Britain from c. AD 43–70 is named after the well-known military site of Hofheim, Germany, where the form was first clearly defined early this century (fig. 6.1; plate 2). The Latin term *lagena*, meaning a large vessel with a neck and handles, is sometimes used for two-handled flagons at least half a metre high to distinguish them from *amphorae*. The latter are also large two-

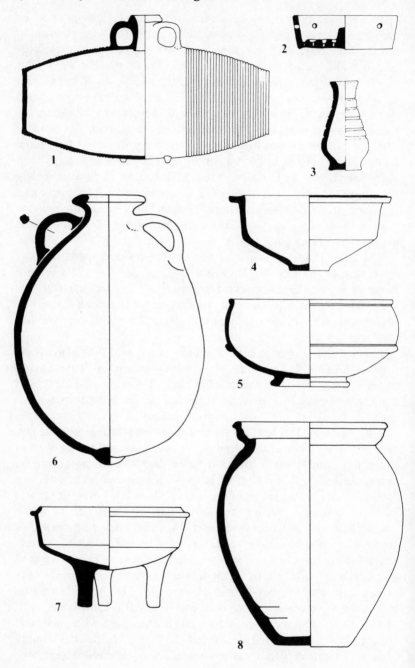

handled containers varying in shape and fabric but with a rounded or pointed base, used for importing oil, wine and *garum* which was a strong fish sauce (fig. 7.6). Often amphorae were stamped, usually on the handles, recording the name of the maker of the vessel, or the producer of the contents, or both (plate 3).

The *mortarium* was a very important vessel in Roman cooking – used perhaps like a mortar and pestle for mixing and grinding food. It is a bowl, with a large overhanging rim adapted for gripping and a spout. Grit is usually embedded in the interior surface, to facilitate the grinding. First- and second-century examples often have the name of the maker stamped on one or both sides of the spout. They are further distinguished by different rims and profiles, for example the wall-sided, bead and flange, and hammer-headed varieties (fig. 37).

The Romans had other very specialized vessels. The cheese-press or wring, is a small, shallow, flat-bottomed dish with holes and concentric ridges in the bottom, probably used for the manufacture of cheese (fig. 7.2). Matching ridged lids without holes are also known. The costrel is a rare form, shaped like a barrel but lying on its side with a small neck and handles on the top and small stud-like feet on the bottom. The body is often rilled to imitate a barrel (fig.7.1). An unguent flask is a small narrow-necked vessel thought to have been a container for ointment or perfume and probably imported into this country (fig. 7.3). The triple vase is another unusual vessel composed of three small jars either attached to the top of a tubular ring-base which is often hollow or simply joined together at the base.[16] These may have been used as lamps or for making offerings at house shrines. Although these are the principal vessels found in prehistoric and Roman times, within each period there may have been many other specialised vessels for specific unknown functions. The Romans had a particularly diverse range of vessels available, covering nearly every conceivable purpose, not matched in Britain until the middle of the nineteenth century.

Further refinements can be made, when identifying the form, by distinguishing rim types. The term 'everted' applies to a rim that turns sharply out and up from the body, like that on a Butt beaker (fig. 4.5). These occur in all shapes and sizes, including square, round, pointed

---

Fig. 7   Roman forms

1 Costrel	*Hartley*
2 Cheese press	6 Amphorae
3 Unguent flask	7 Tripod bowl
4 Reeded rim bowl	8 Lid seated jar. *After Gillam*
5 Cordoned bowl (Drag. 44). *After*	*Scale 1:4 1–4 and 6–7 after Webster*

and triangular. A flat rim means that the rim forms a right-angle to the neck or body, providing a flat surface which is sometimes decorated with rouletting or reeding as on Roman reeded-rim bowls (fig. 7.4). The term simple or plain rim is normally associated with a rim that continues the line of the body of the pot, like that found on early Iron Age angular bowls and jars (fig. 19.1). Sometimes the area around the rim and neck is thickened or turned into a slightly protruding bead (fig. 7.5). The area immediately inside the lip can be bevelled, as is found on early Bronze Age urns (figs 3.1–4). Jars in the Roman period sometimes have lid-seated rims, with a groove for the lid to make it more secure or to seal the contents (fig. 7.8).

There are several very specialized rim forms, belonging to the Roman period. A cornice rim, found on certain beakers, implies a carefully moulded rim which has a stepped or undercut profile (fig. 5.2), as in an architectural cornice. A grooved cornice rim has a central groove cutting the rim into two roughly equal ridges (figs 35.2,3). Flagons sometimes have rims in the form of a disc and are called disc-rimmed or disc-mouthed. The term cavetto rim has been applied especially to Dorset black-burnished ware cooking pots, on which the rim curves out from the shoulder of the vessel to form a concave, quarter-round profile (fig. 11.4).

Bases are also used in the same manner, as a further refinement, coming in a variety of shapes. Nearly all early Neolithic vessels have round or sagging bases, including the pottery styles known as Hembury, Abingdon and Windmill Hill (figs 14, 24). Vessels belonging to the earliest style, of the late Neolithic Peterborough series Ebbsfleet, also have round bases but those of the latest style, Fengate, are flat (fig. 25). This change was perhaps brought about by the influence of contemporary Beaker vessels, which all have flat bases (figs 17, 18). Indigenous grooved-ware vessels apparently developed the use of a flat base independently (fig. 15). The change to flat bases must imply flat surfaces on which to put vessels and may mark the introduction of wooden shelves and tables, as opposed to the sand floors on which round-bottomed vessels would have rested.

In the Iron Age and Roman periods, when pottery styles became increasingly elaborate, bases and feet were designed. A foot-ring is a low ring formed on the base to enable the vessel to stand more securely (fig. 8.1). It also implies a hollow area under the base. Foot-rings were normally applied or made from the surplus clay around the base, after the vessel had been formed on the wheel or in a mould. A more elegant form of this is the pedestal base, which is basically an extended foot-

Fig. 8 Bases
1 Foot-ring   2 Kick base   3 *Omphalos* base
                                          After Webster

ring. It can be found on *vase piriforme* (fig. 4.2) and Belgic pedestal urns (fig. 20.4). The pedestal can be hollow (fig. 4.2) or, as in the case of some late Roman beakers, solid. Vessels with foot-rings or pedestals sometimes have kicked bases, where the base rises towards the centre to form a hollow peak (fig. 8.2). This is a common feature of plain samian forms (fig. 28.18–31), with the potter's name-stamp impressed on the peak (plate 4). Vessels with no foot-ring can also have kicked bases (fig. 2.5). An *omphalos* is similar but with a prominent hollow dome raised in the base (fig. 8.3). When the junction of the wall with the base is bevelled symmetrically it is referred to as champhered and this should not be mistaken for a sagging base (fig. 12.3). Some bowls have feet. The tripod bowl is named after its three solid legs (fig. 7.7); few quadruped bowls are known.

Handles are another distinguishing feature. Short, stumpy, knob-like handles, either solid or perforated, are called lugs and can be found on many types of prehistoric pottery (fig. 14.1–2). Looped handles, which curve sharply and are fixed upright on a pot, are very common (fig. 6.). Handles are entirely missing on some styles of pottery, instead deeply recessed necks and collars were used for gripping (fig. 3.2). Strap handles are looped handles placed lengthways and occur on dishes and platters of late Iron Age and Roman date. The countersunk handle denotes a rounded handle partly sunk into the side of the vessel (fig. 10.3).

DECORATION

Decoration, where present, can play a major part in the identification of pottery styles and types. The main ways of decorating pottery include incised or excised patterns, impressed techniques producing either negative or positive designs, and applied ornament. Incision involves cutting into the pot with a sharp implement, usually at the leather-hard stage. Definite examples of excision, where part of the surface is actually cut away, are comparatively rare as it is difficult to distinguish the final effect from that produced by incision. Excision was used to create the 'cut glass' effect found on some samian vessels of the mid-second century (plate 5). By grooving, fairly broad, shallow lines are drawn on the surface of a pot, again normally at the leather-hard stage. No clay is actually removed, as in excision, nor is the surface itself cut, as in incision. Grooving is not the same as burnishing, which means rubbing the surface prior to firing to produce a smooth, polished effect (see below). Grooves and incised lines can be arranged in all manner of patterns, including horizontal, vertical, chevron, zigzag, lattice or hatched, and wavy designs. Some of these designs were employed in the production of late Neolithic Grooved ware (fig. 9.2).

The introduction of compasses in the Iron Age resulted in compass-scribed patterns in the form of intersecting arcs and curvi-linear designs (fig. 9.3). Channelling is another form of grooving, found on early Bronze Age Aldbourne cups. Slashing, a form of incision, often occurs on the rim and neck of vessels, with short or long narrow gashes arranged in vertical or diagonal patterns (fig. 14.5–6). Rilling consists of fine, parallel, close-set incised lines, arranged either vertically or horizontally, formed with a sharp tool pressed against the side of the pot (fig. 7.1). Furrowing is made by drawing the fingers or a wide tool across the body of a vessel resulting in a series of broad horizontal grooves (fig. 2.3). Scoring is similar to rilling, where fine parallel or random lines are arranged in vertical, horizontal and arc patterns. These are drawn freehand and should not be confused with a similar effect produced by combing. The regular horizontal grooving found on the flange of some types of Roman mortaria and the flat rim of some forms of bowl is often referred to as reeding (fig. 7.4). The most extreme method of incision/excision is perforation, where holes are cut through the wall of the vessel, often around the neck, as found on early Neolithic Windmill Hill style bowls and jars. It has been suggested that these vessels with their sagging bases and perforated tops, represent the conversion of a leather prototype into clay, with the neck holes originally accomodating a thong so that the top could be pulled shut.

Stamping and punching both involve impressing patterns into the plastic surface of the vessel. In its simplest form a sharp implement, like a small piece of bone, a twig or a finger nail, can be stabbed or impressed to form a repeating pattern (fig. 14.3,5). Impressed designs are common on late Neolithic Peterborough pottery, especially arranged in a herringbone pattern (fig. 25.2), probably produced with a small bird's bone. A more elaborate form of decoration was created by impressing lengths of whipped or twisted cord. The earliest Beaker vessels found in Britain are known as 'all-over-corded' beakers as their surface is covered with impressions made with a fine two-strand twisted cord (fig. 17.1). Another type of impressed decoration found on beakers was made with a blunt-toothed comb. Horizontal or vertical lines of such impressions were arranged in a repeating pattern (fig. 17.2) or in horizontal bands of lattice, ladder, zigzag, triangular, lozenge and chevron motifs (fig. 18.3). Comb-stamping and combing were also used in the Iron Age and Roman periods. On large jars combing was used to create sweeping linear, arc, diagonal and wavy patterns. Individually stamped motifs occur on Iron Age vessels, with impressed roundels and dots combined with grooving to produce elaborate patterns (fig. 9.3). Similar stamped decoration was also popular in the Roman period (fig. 2.1). This involved the cutting of individual stamps or dies. A more elaborate form of this is roller-stamping, made with a roller on which patterns have been cut, producing a regular repeated pattern (fig. 9.4). This creates quite a different effect to individually stamped motifs which may have no regular sequence or pattern but a haphazard arrangement, due to the use of one or more independent dies. Rouletting is another form of continuous stamping, produced by impressing a toothed or engraved wheel against the vessel while it turns on the potter's wheel (plate 24). This was particularly popular in the late Iron Age (fig. 4.5) and Roman periods (fig. 31.2).

Whereas stamped decoration creates a negative impressed design, moulded pottery has designs in positive relief, where the motifs stand proud of the original vessel surface. There are two techniques used to produce this effect: vessels are either entirely moulded or the wall of the vessel is pushed into individual dies. Relief-moulded decoration where the entire vessel, was produced in either a one or two piece mould, was a relatively costly process. Most decorated samian bowls were made in this way (fig. 27). The mould itself was a wheel-thrown bowl, its inner profile corresponding to the desired exterior profile of the final vessel (plate 6). A small hole was provided in the base to centre it correctly on the potter's wheel. The patterns were produced with positive relief stamps or *poinçons*, creating negative impressions in the mould, with details added freehand with a stylus. The mould was then fired in the usual way. A vessel was formed in the mould using soft clay, and as it turned on the wheel the rim of the vessel was drawn up above the upper edge of the mould. The ovolo, or tongue and egg pattern, often marks this junction (fig. 27.37). As samian clay is so fine and contains little filler, it shrinks considerably on drying, enabling the easy removal of the vessel from the mould. Decorative details were sometimes blurred by this process. The bowl was then finished by trimming and turning

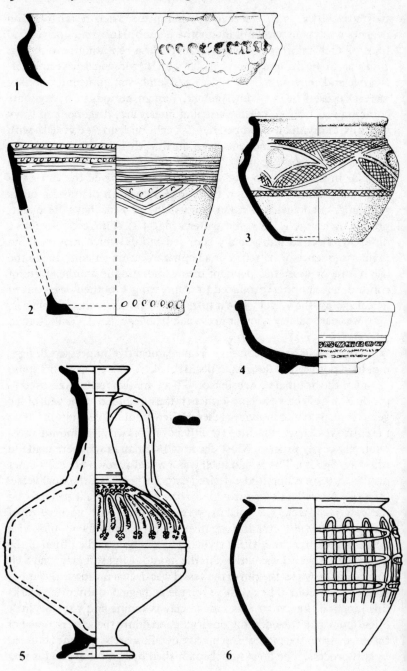

the rim and forming the foot-ring. Apart from samian ware very few vessels were entirely moulded. Some south Gaulish colour-coated drinking cups were moulded thus but they are related to contemporary samian production. Central Gaulish lead-glazed vessels were often moulded and they include flagons (fig. 9.5), handle bowls called *scyphos* (after the comparable Greek vessels) and carinated bowls resembling samian form Drag. 29. Instead of the use of figures, common on samian, scrolls, arcading and gadroons occur with little rosette patterns (fig. 9.5). Again the production of this ware was related to that of samian.

As well as the moulding of entire vessels, or just the top as in the case of some flagons, the wall of a vessel could be pushed into individual negative stamps to produce raised decoration, such as the face-masks found on some late Roman Oxfordshire flagons (plate 7). Other figures produced in this way include representations of Mercury and other Roman and Celtic deities, found on some fourth-century colour-coated bowls made in the Lower Nene Valley.

Indenting is another form of decoration; it may also have been used to provide a better grip. This involved pushing parts of the surface of the vessel inwards to make a series of concavities. In the Roman period many drinking beakers were indented or 'folded' (fig. 35.6). Finger-tipping also produces concavities. This was done simply by pushing a finger-tip into the still damp clay. These indentations are sometimes referred to as pits (fig. 9.1). An opposite effect was produced using the finger-tip to push the wall of the vessel outwards, forming round bosses (fig. 3.4).

Applied decoration – the addition of clay to the surface – takes many forms. Perhaps the most common is the cordon, a projecting strip of clay applied to the surface either vertically (fig. 15.2), horizontally (fig. 3.1) or diagonally. The cordons themselves can be decorated with slashed or notched patterns (fig. 3.4). They were also used with other types of decoration, particularly incised lines or grooves, or with bands

---

Fig. 9 Decoration
1 Late Bronze-early Iron Age jar with fingertip impressions. *After Megaw and Simpson*
2 Grooved ware vessel. *After Piggott*
3 Glastonbury ware jar with incised curvilinear decoration. *After Megaw and Simpson*
4 Argonne ware bowl with roller-stamped geometric decoration. *After Swan*
5 Central Gaulish lead glazed flagon with moulded decoration. *After Greene*
6 Central Gaulish colour-coated beaker with vertical and horizontal 'hairpins'. *After Greene*
1–4 Scale 1:4 5–6 Scale 1:2

of interspersed rouletting (fig. 4.3). In some cases instead of applying a separate strip of clay, a cordon was made by cutting two deep lines side by side, pushing the clay in between up, to form a ridge which is referred to as a 'pseudo-cordon'. These are commonly found on Roman jars. A great variety of applied decoration occurs on prehistoric pottery besides cordons. Blobs of clay, knots and bosses were added to enliven the surface. Some very elaborate raised patterns can be found, like the ladder pattern that occurs on the rim bevel of some Grooved ware jars (fig. 15.1). On early Bronze Age encrusted urns the most characteristic feature is an applied strip of clay, forming a running chevron pattern, with applied blobs or bosses between the chevrons (fig. 3.4).

In the Roman period applied decoration took a variety of forms. The faces on some face-mask urns were produced by applying the individual elements – ears, eyes and nose – to the surface (plate 8). Roughcast decoration involves the application of fired-clay particles or sand, normally to beakers and cups, to create a roughened effect, which may have been to facilitate handling (plate 9). The clay particles or sand could be added to the liquid clay slip, used to produce the colour-coat, into which the vessel was dipped prior to firing. This technique was fashionable in the first and second centuries AD. More elaborate decoration can be found on Lyons ware colour-coated cups and beakers, which was applied free-hand using plastic clay (fig. 29). Designs include imbricated (overlapping) scales (fig. 5.4), vertical gadroons ('hairpins'), arcading (fig. 29.3), lattice and vertical rows of small and large blobs. A very unusual design found on these vessels is the 'raspberry roundel', which consists of a disc of clay applied to the surface and then stamped with a negative relief die. This produces a simple raised design of small knobs arranged either in a spiral or in concentric circles (fig. 5.5).[17]

In the technique known as 'appliqué', negative relief dies were also used to produce 'face-masks', portraying the heads of Bacchus and Silenus and other figural motifs. These were made separately and fixed to the surface and occur, in particular, on certain samian beaker forms (plate 10). These beakers often have a glossy black colour-coat and are sometimes referred to as 'black samian'. Often the vessel was covered with a continuous decorative frieze, with the addition of features, like intertwining leaves, applied en barbotine (see below). They were only made for a short time, during the first half of the second century AD, at the central Gaulish samian factories. Moulded decoration of this kind, actually applied to the surface of the pot, should not be confused with relief moulding using individual stamps, when similar negative dies were pressed against the side of a still damp vessel. The interior surface will display the tell-tale fingerprints where the pot has been pushed out into the stamp.

Barbotine decoration is another applied method for producing a pattern in relief, by trailing semi-liquid clay on the vessel surface. In its simplest form dots are arranged in geometric patterns, particularly lozenge and rectangular shapes (fig. 4.6). A similar type of beaker was made with panels of barbotine dots and circles. 'Thorn beakers', of the Augustan-Tiberian period, take their name from their distinctive decoration, composed of barbotine diagonal spikes arranged in her-ring-bone fashion. More elaborate designs occur on pre-Flavian colour-coated cups and beakers, with the design added before the application of the slip coating. Initially plant motifs were favoured with patterns of interweaving leaves and tendrils (fig. 31.3). The heart-shaped leaves are probably based on the ivy or vine leaf, while in Spain a design reminiscent of a fern leaf was current. Normally the leaves and tendrils formed a running frieze around the pot, often bordered above and below by a series of barbotine dots (plate 11). While in Spain and in the Lower Rhineland the potters preferred foliate designs, those in Central Gaul largely used abstract patterns, mainly 'hairpins' (fig. 9.6), loops and 'tear drops'. 'Raetian' beakers also bear abstract designs, with incised patterns combined with barbotine 'crescents' and 'torcs' (plate 12). Although abstract designs do occur on Cologne beakers, such as simple running scrolls (fig. 32.8) and imbricated scales, (plate 9), from the early second century designs incorporating animals were preferred. These usually depict dogs in pursuit of hares or deer, and for this reason are called 'Hunt cups' (figs 31.7, 32.1; plate 13). Other beakers portray gladiators in combat with each other or wild animals, such as bears or boars, sometimes accompanied by dogs (plate 14). These vessels are known as 'Gladiator beakers'. Vessels of this kind were produced at other places, in particular at Colchester and in the Lower Nene Valley. Both produced some very inventive designs, often with religious significance, like winged phallic symbols and little hooded figures thought to be Celtic *genii cucullati*, symbolising fertility, healing and the unseen world. Appliqué motifs, such as vine leaves, were sometimes combined with barbotine designs to produce hunting and gladiatorial scenes. Lead-glazed wares were sometimes decorated with barbotine designs underneath the glaze, often appear-ing as a light pattern against a dark background. Simple abstract designs are most frequent, dots arranged in a variety of patterns or barbotine 'hairpins' and imbricated scales. Occasionally barbotine hunting or gladiatorial scenes are depicted (plate 16).

Painted decoration is distinguished from barbotine, as it involves the application of a thin white or coloured slip directly onto the surface, over the colour-coat (where present). Concentric orange or brown bands were painted on 'parchment' wares, particularly on flagons and bowls. Colour-coated bulbous beakers were often decorated with white painted patterns. Foliate designs predominate, with vine leaves and tendrils arranged in a continuous frieze running around the main body of the pot. Little triangular groups of white painted dots, hanging from the tendrils, may represent bunches of grapes. Vessels of this kind were manufactured at Trier, in the Moselle Valley (plate 17). They are often referred to as 'motto pots', as Latin words and phrases were sometimes added to the decoration, like BIBE encouraging the user to drink! Some vessels were elaborately decorated with medallions portraying human heads, executed with many different-coloured slip paints (plate 18).

Rustication or finger-pinching is a type of decoration which does not fall into any of the categories mentioned above. The surface of the pot is roughened, with the clay pulled into peaks by the fingers (fig. 29.2). This could be done while the clay was still damp but in the case of Roman examples a fresh layer of thick slip was applied to the surface, which could be roughened without spoiling the pot's profile. During the late first and early second century these vessels were particularly popular and were produced, usually in a grey fabric, at many places (plate 19).

Frilling was also produced by pinching the clay with the fingers, creating an effect similar in appearance to the traditional edging of pie-crusts (fig. 4.7). It is commonly found on Roman tazze, although as a decorative technique it is most closely associated with mediaeval pottery.

During the prehistoric period better-quality pots were often burnished, to create a smooth surface finish. The vessel was allowed to dry to the leather-hard stage and was then polished smooth and shiny with a pebble or piece of bone. Burnishing on Neolithic pots is often uneven, with a characteristic rippled effect which may have been deliberate. Beaker pottery was sometimes burnished, before incised or impressed decoration was added. 'Belgic' pottery often has patterns of burnished lines or areas of burnishing, contrasting with the remaining matt surface. This technique was also used in the Roman period to finish Dorset black-burnished ware (figs 11, 12).

Vessels which have similar characteristics, including form, rim, base and decoration, but which were produced in a variety of fabrics, are often referred to as belonging to a ceramic style. Early Neolithic Hembury style pottery was manufactured in gabbroic, oolitic and other fabrics (fig. 24). Beaker pottery also represents a similar ceramic style, with minor variations in vessel shape and decorative preference perhaps denoting regional sub-styles within the tradition (figs 17, 18). In the case of Iron Age saucepan pottery (fig. 19.3), vessels with comparable variations in style and fabric may instead represent commercial differences, with potters competing with each other for the available market.

When vessels occur in a consistent style and in an identical fabric, not merely similar in general appearance, they are referred to as a ceramic type. Dorset black-burnished ware is a good example of a ceramic type, with a large number of distinctive forms produced in the same fabric for over four hundred years. A type description, therefore, is a statement of a set of consistent traits which can be seen to occur together in most cases. The purpose of creating pottery types is to make possible the arrangement of pottery from a site so that it can be compared with pottery from other sites. By comparing pottery of the same type from different sites it may be possible to observe changes in form or decoration which may be ordered in a sequence. This form of chronological development, represented by progressive changes in the pottery, is usually referred to as a typological sequence.

Dating

TYPOLOGY

Typology involves selecting common and obvious attributes, including shape and decoration, and observing any variations in these attributes which can be arranged in progressive order. The creation of type-series is important for understanding relative chronologies. By comparing diverse ceramic assemblages, and by noticing differences or similarities, the archaeologist can align his site with others in both time and space. Comparison with assemblages which are earlier or later permits sequential dating and the construction of a relative chronology.

Once again Dorset black-burnished ware is a good example of a pottery type exhibiting typological changes, in form and decoration, over a period of several hundred years. It was first produced in the late

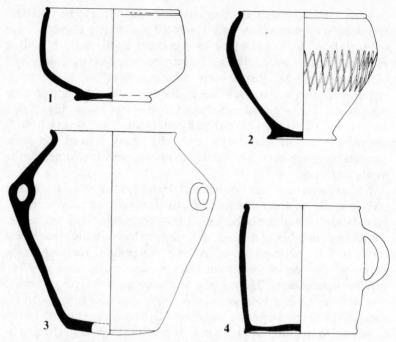

Fig 10   Late Iron Age Durotrigian forms

1 'War cemetery' bowl
2 Wide-mouth jar with a panel of burnished lattice decoration

3 Wide-mouth jar with countersunk handles
4 Tankard or mug
Scale 1:4 After Cunliffe

Iron Age and continued to be made until the end of the fourth century AD. Initially restricted to the area of Dorset, it has been identified as the pottery of a distinctive tribal group living in the region, known as the Durotriges. Throughout production the fabric remained remarkably homogenous. Surprisingly it was always hand-made, even during the Roman period, but this may have contributed to the outstanding success of the ware, as it was undoubtedly cheap to produce. The fabric is characteristically black in colour with a great deal of coarse sand filler. Decoration is confined to burnishing either complete areas, such as the shoulders, necks and rims of jars, or zones of lattice, chevron and intersecting arc patterns. The Iron Age forms include carinated bowls with a foot-ring and sometimes an *omphalos* base, often called 'war-cemetery' bowls after their initial discovery at Maiden Castle (fig. 10.1). Wide-mouth jars with a bead or everted rim were produced with a panel of burnished acute-angle lattice for decoration (fig. 10.2).

Necked jars with countersunk handles were also manufactured (fig.
10.3). Straight-sided mugs with a simple loop-handle, bead rim and
foot-ring (fig. 10.4) and dishes or platters with a bead rim and foot-ring
also occur. These forms continued to be made after the Roman
invasion, with the addition to the repertoire of new Roman vessel forms
like the flagon.

In the Flavian period a diversification of forms occurred, influenced
by wheel-thrown vessels made elsewhere in the Province. The
carinated reeded rim bowl (fig. 7.4) appears to have stimulated the
production of black-burnished ware flat rim bowls and dishes. Early
examples from deposits at Exeter, dated to the late first century, have a
carinated profile with a horizontal rim, the upper surface of which is
corrugated or reeded.[18] In spite of these developments the black-
burnished ware industry remained, for the most part, conservative,
with types that owed anything to the influence of Roman forms making
up only five per cent of the total early assemblage at Exeter.[19]

In c. AD 120 the Dorset black-burnished ware industry suddenly
expanded, with the capture of the whole of the western and northern
military markets. At the same time the ware began to move into civilian
markets in south-central England and the west-central Midlands,
including Staffordshire where the ware is so common that at one time it
was thought to have been made there.[20] The industry supplied only a
limited range of forms to the army in the north, while distributing a
much wider range through south-west England. The standard 'service'
consists of a jar or cooking pot, a bowl and a dish, of which the latter two
could be combined to form a casserole. To these can be added, although
less common, a handled mug and a storage jar, which was in fact no
more than an enlarged version of the normal jar.

Although the makers of Dorset black-burnished ware were remarkably conservative, as the traditions were passed from father to son or
master to apprentice for over 300 years, there were bound to be gradual
changes in shape and decoration. These changes, of which the makers
themselves were probably for the most part totally unaware, led to the
latest vessels having an appearance entirely different to the earlier ones.
Early jars are, in general, wide-mouthed with an upright neck and
everted rim; the profile is globular with a flat base. While the width of
the mouth remained largely constant, in order to admit the hand, the
body became progressively more slender and narrower in proportion to
the mouth (compare fig. 11.1 with 11.6). The whole vessel form
became attenuated, increasingly narrower in relation to the height.
The necks found on the earlier vessels tend to be tall and almost

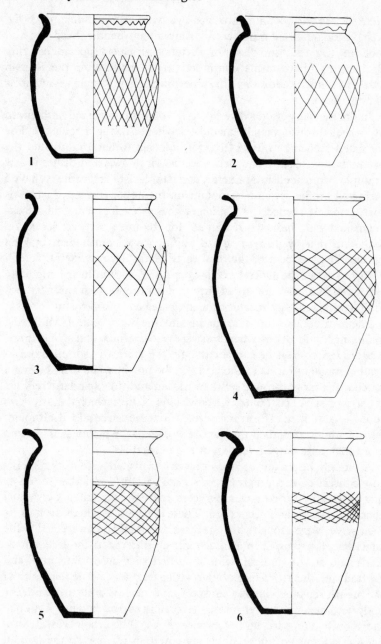

vertical, with the rim thickened, similar to those found on first-century examples (fig. 11.1). The rims on the latest jars, made towards the close of the Roman period, are still thickened but lean so far out that the diameter at the tip of the rim is greater than the width of the body (fig. 11.6). This progression, from near-vertical neck to exaggeratedly splayed neck, appears to have been constant and even – with the result that the relationship of the rim to the shoulder of any jar will provide an approximate but remarkably reliable indication of its date of manufacture.[21]

The panel of lattice decoration around the body of the pot is also a guide to dating, as on the earliest vessels it is at an acute angle (figs 11.1, 11.2) but obtuse on the latest (figs 11.5, 11.6). As a result of this the panel itself became narrower (fig. 11.6). Nearly all the later vessels have a scored line above the lattice zone (fig. 11.5). Generally, from the later part of the third century this scored line is invariably present, while before that date it is extremely rare. A burnished wavy-line is present on the neck of most early second-century jars, though it is not common on any Durotrigian predecessors (figs 11.1, 11.2). After the middle of the second century it became increasingly rare and from the late second century almost disappeared. The production and widespread use of the jar, in developed form, continued to at least the middle of the fourth century.

In deposits dating to the middle of the second century, in Northern Britain, there are about four flat-rimmed bowls to every seven cooking pots of the same type. The earliest flat-rimmed bowls to reach Hadrian's Wall were still markedly carinated, with the angular change of direction of the wall representing one-fifth of the total height of the vessel (fig. 12.1). By the end of the second century they had developed a very small chamfer (fig. 12.3), which on even later bowl and dish forms completely disappears. This process of the 'decline and disappearance of carination'[22] was both even and regular, so that it is possible to place an individual vessel in its chronological position according to the degree of carination. Also the decreasing height of the carination caused the walls above to become increasingly splayed, forming a wider angle with the base (fig. 12.3). Most flat-rimmed bowls and dishes are decorated with acute-angle lattice (fig. 12.1, 12.2). An overlapping

---

Fig. 11   Typological development of BB1 wide-mouth jars

1 Aldborough, early to mid-second century	4 York, mid-third century
2 Milecastle 48, mid-second century	5 Silchester, late third century
3 Manchester, late second century	6 London, early fourth century
	Scale 1:4 After Gillam

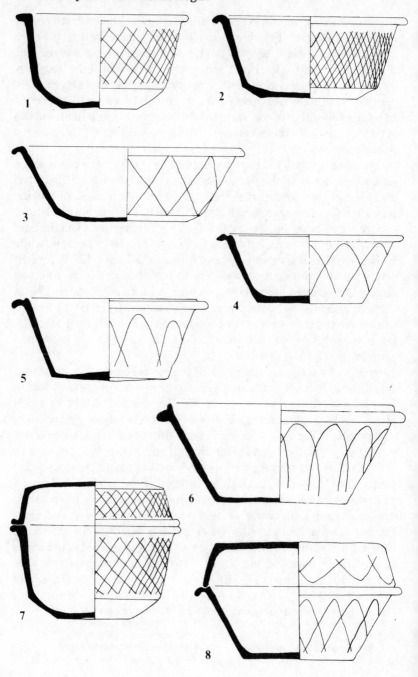

inverted chevron pattern seems to have been introduced around the middle of the second century. Towards the end of the second century and very early in the third, intersecting arcs gradually replaced latticing (fig. 12.4).

Some time towards the end of the second or early third century, the flat-rimmed bowl was converted into the earliest form of flanged bowl (fig. 12.4). These are often referred to as 'incipient' flanged bowls. The flat-rimmed bowl developed into the flanged bowl for practical as well as morphological reasons. The flat-rimmed dish was clearly used as a lid as well as a dish, which when inverted over a comparable bowl formed a casserole (fig. 12.7). Unfortunately this arrangement must have proved unstable, as the flat surfaces of the rims could easily slide apart. So for safety the combination of the flanged bowl with a plain-rimmed dish was developed (fig 12.8). The flange acted as a lid-seating for the dish-lid – precisely the same principle which is used for many modern day casserole sets.[23] The flanged bowl has straight sides, forming a truncated-conical profile. The chamfer present on the earlier bowl form disappears altogether (fig. 12.5). However, its proportions, size and general character are much the same as its flat-rimmed predecessor. It continued in production, although not everywhere in use, until the end of the Roman period. On the earliest examples the flange is formed simply by a groove, cut in the top of the flat rim (fig. 12.4). On later examples the flange has moved down the wall of the vessel, creating a high bead rim (fig. 12.6). This tendency was gradual and even, so it provides a reliable indication of the date of a vessel. Except for one or two early examples with lattice decoration, and a number of late vessels which are not decorated at all, these bowls normally occur with intersecting arcs, exhibiting little change over the course of two centuries.

As well as the typological development of specific types of pottery, as illustrated by the progressive changes of Dorset black-burnished ware, the technique can also be applied to a form manufactured in different fabrics, thus producing a type-series. The Roman ring-neck flagon

---

Fig. 12   Typological development of BB1 flat-rimmed bowls and flanged bowls

1 Shakenoak, early to mid-second century

2 Birdoswald, mid-second century

3 Tiddington, late second century

4 Leicester, late second to early third century

5 Leicester, mid to late third century

6 Downton, late third to early fourth century

7 Flat-rimmed bowl and dish as used to form a casserole

8 Flanged bowl and plain rimmed dish as used to form a casserole

Scale 1:4 After Gillam

exhibits certain morphological changes (fig. 6.2). The neck of this form is composed of several superimposed rings. In the mid-first century the neck was more or less vertical to the body but it soon began to splay outwards. During the second century the top ring-lip became thick-ened and protruded over the lower rings, while they in turn diminished in number or even degenerated into mere grooving. Vessels of the same class but of varying form can also be arranged in chronological order by observing trends of development. In the case of mortaria, vessels with bead rims and thick, broad flanges (fig. 37.4) were superseded by those with either hammer-heads (fig. 37.6) or small flanges. Ring-neck flagons were replaced by flanged necked flagons in the late third and fourth centuries (fig. 6.2, 6.3).

By observing chronological, evolutionary change it does not imply that artefacts necessarily changed for the better. Indeed some types of pottery gradually devolved, from a well-made product exhibiting high standards of craftsmanship to one poorly made, suggesting a lowering of standards perhaps due to mass-production or to the gradual loss of status of the product or the craftsman. The latest samian vessels produced are often crude, the decoration poorly moulded and indis-tinct due to the continual use of the same moulds for too long, thus blurring the original designs. Yet the overheads for producing an inferior moulded bowl were not greatly different from those incurred making a fine-quality one and the distribution costs were the same. It has been suggested that standards declined because samian ware gradually lost its status; increasing prosperity and changing tastes caused a demand for metal and glass tableware. In the case of Lower Nene Valley colour-coated ware, the expansion of the industry, generated by the demand in Britain for a ceramic tableware to replace samian, resulted in the manufacture of a new wider range of forms; but mass-production also brought about a lowering of standards. The large fine-ware industries appear to have relied on the master-apprentice relationship for the teaching and handing down of skills and designs. In some cases the pupils may not have been as competent or as talented as their master – or after his death may have taken up new kinds of work.

The changes that occur in pottery types and styles, allowing the creation of type-series, can be caused by various reasons. Change may be so slow and gradual, as in the case of Dorset black-burnished ware, that it passes unnoticed even by the potters. This is referred to as a 'subliminal morphological trend'.[24] In other cases fashion, new social habits, and economic and political reasons may be contributory factors. The demise of the Lyons fine-ware industry may have been in part due to the devastating civil war fought in Gaul in AD 69. The central Gaulish samian industry was already in decline, due to changing social and economic circumstances, when exportation was finally disrupted by the civil war of AD 196–97 and subsequent large-scale confiscations, by the Emperor Servus, of land and property owned by the supporters of his rival to the throne, Clodius Albinus. The Roman preference for dark colour-coated drinking beakers appears to have been solely due to fashion and tradition. They were manufactured at most samian factories, yet the red-samian repertoire contained mostly cups and few beakers. The chronological, social and economic implications of changing pottery types will be discussed further in later chapters.

The identification of pottery types and the recognition of stylistic changes which have chronological implications are of paramount importance to the archaeologist. Of necessity, descriptions of types or styles must be lucid and sufficiently detailed. Fine divisions can be made within a class of artefacts, depending on how specific the archaeologist is when creating the classification. It must be remembered that such classifications are totally arbitrary and may bear no relationship to cultural groupings. It is in the interpretation of differing pottery types and styles and what they represent in human terms, that archaeologists run into problems. As long as this factor is kept in mind pottery types can serve the archaeologist well in the dating and distributional ordering of his materials. Further interpretation would not be possible until such order is established.

SERIATION

The typological development of ceramic types and styles should not be confused with the related technique of seriation. This is based on the transitory nature of popularity. When a new product is introduced onto the market its popularity tends to grow slowly, rising to a peak and then diminishes gradually as it passes out of fashion. If this sequence is plotted on a bar-graph the slope created, from the introduction until the replacement by another product, will resemble a 'battleship curve'. At the start the curve is narrow but as popularity grows the bars widen, followed by the decline which reduces the bars. This sequence can be applied to most aspects of man's culture – initial small beginnings, growth to maximum popularity and finally a dwindling end. Some sequences last over thousands of years, others persist for centuries, years or only months. It is this distinctive shape of popularity which makes the technique of seriation possible. Seriation, therefore, is a method of relative dating which involves the arrangement of assemblages in such a way that the frequency of various types of artefacts within them form 'battleship curves' through time.[25] By this method of type-frequency it is possible to arrange a series of single-period sites in relative chronological order, in the absence of stratigraphic information. The technique can only be applied to sites belonging to a homogeneous culture but for differing pottery types. These various pottery types are assumed to have chronological implications. By measuring the frequency of each type at every site excavated it is possible to produce a 'battleship curve' graph indicating the relative quantity, correlated with the popularity, of each type through time. This permits the archaeologist to arrange a long series of sites, each of which was briefly occupied, in a relative sequence on the basis of pottery popularity.

However, the application of this technique has certain serious drawbacks. It is dependent on single-period sites. On more complex multi-period sites it would be superseded by stratigraphic evidence. It assumes that the frequency of pottery types can be correlated with their popularity, but in the Roman period it can be demonstrated that a fluctuating quantity of some ceramic types was equally due to their availability. Industrial, economic and political problems could affect the output of kilns regardless of how popular the product was. When samian ceased to be imported into Britain in c. AD 200, it was still so popular that acceptable substitutes had to be found. Oxford red colour-coated ware, of samian type, the production of which may have been started by immigrant potters from the Rhineland, was used to replace imported samian as a tableware out of necessity rather than choice.

More importantly the technique of seriation regards pottery as a local, domestic product rather than one produced on a commercial basis and widely traded. If the latter were true, varying quantities of pottery types might reflect the success or failure of different industries competing for the same market rather than indicate chronological differences. Pottery types and styles can also reflect regional variations within an otherwise basically homogeneous culture. At the borders of each regional grouping there would undoubtedly be some overlap with the styles common in the next region. Therefore, varying quantities of pottery do not necessarily have chronological implication but can be explained in economic and social terms.

THERMOLUMINESCENCE

There is another internal method for dating pottery and other fired-clay artefacts known as thermoluminescence dating which is a chronometric technique. It is based on the principle that ceramic material contains small amounts of radioactive impurities – elements such as potassium, uranium and thorium – which emit alpha and beta particles and gamma rays causing ionizing radiation. This produces electrons and other charge carriers called 'holes' which become trapped in the defects always present in the crystalline structure of the baked clay. Heating the pottery causes the electrons and holes to be released from the traps and they recombine, due to the release of the stored energy, in the form of emissions of light or thermoluminescence (TL). The greater the number of trapped electrons the more intense is the TL. As this is held to increase with time the age can be determined by measuring the TL.[26] The technique is claimed to be accurate to within ± 10 per cent. Although it is a complicated technique it is being used increasingly for authenticity testing of valuable ancient ceramic works of art, such as T'ang tomb figures. Many fraudulent copies have been exposed as nineteenth-century fakes by using this method.

CONTEXT

Typology and seriation are two methods of assigning a relative date to pottery, both internally and independently. Other important factors to be considered are the context in which the pottery was found and the presence of any other associated artefacts. These connections may have some bearing on the date of the pottery. One of the basic principles of archaeology is the relationship between archaeological deposits or layers observed during excavation, particularly through vertical sections, referred to as 'stratigraphy' (fig. 1). If one layer effectively covers another, it can be assumed that the upper one was deposited after the lower and, therefore, is later in date, if only by a short time. The lower layer may be said to be 'sealed' by the upper. In this case any objects recovered from the layer are referred to as a 'group' and it is assumed that they were made, used, discarded or deposited at about the same time. Sometimes artefacts are found *in situ*, i.e. discovered in exactly the same position in which they were discarded or abandoned in antiquity.

In considering any pottery discovered during the excavation of a Neolithic megalithic tomb – a long, low or round barrow covering a stone burial chamber – much will depend on which area of the monument the pottery was recovered from and if it was found in association with any other artefacts. If it was discovered in the chamber alongside a burial, with other personal belongings like flint arrowheads and stone beads, then the pot may be contemporary with the burial. It does not follow that the burial itself will be contemporary with the construction of the tomb, as it appears that old burials were cleaned out to accommodate new ones. It is more likely to represent the last burial to take place before the tomb was sealed for the final time. In these circumstances one cannot rule out the possibility that the pot or the other objects were re-used from a previous interment and belong to different periods of time. The archaeologist must look for the latest artefacts when assessing the final date of deposition (*terminus post quem*).

If the pottery is found in the mound material, it may have already been present in the soil when the material was amassed for the construction. In this case the pottery will predate the building of the monument. On the other hand, it may have been dropped by one of the builders during the course of the work. This emphasizes the importance of inspecting all the material recovered from a layer or feature before deciding upon the significance of individual sherds. Small sherds of pottery may stray from upper layers or surrounding features due to the action of burrowing animals and plant roots. The occurrence of one or two 'rogue' sherds may be due to poor observation or misrecording on excavation and their relevance to the group as a whole is debatable. On sites of continuous occupation where there are several major structural changes, the problem of survival arises, with the disturbance of lower layers by later activity. This occurs when foundation trenches for walls or rubbish pits are dug, involving the displacement of earlier material. The later the date of the layer the more likely it is to contain earlier, or 'residual', pottery and coins. On a Roman town site, fourth-century deposits may contain as much as 75 per cent residual pottery datable to the preceding three centuries. As the excavation progresses and earlier layers are uncovered this contamination decreases, until the primary layers of the very first occupation are reached. These will contain only pottery of that date.

On such sites sealed deposits, not tainted by later material, can occur where all the pottery may be shown to be broadly contemporary by the circumstances of the deposition. When a building and all its contents are suddenly burnt to the ground before anything can be saved, all the pottery will have been in use at the time of the disaster. A similar situation can arise when an area is redeveloped, with the demolition and clearance of old buildings to make way for the construction of new ones. Almost all deposits contain survivals, as some vessels remained in use for a long time, like special vessels treated by their owners with great care and permanently fixed storage jars.

The presence of residual pottery in stratified deposits has for many years confused structural chronology, affecting the dating of the pottery itself. Some outstanding examples have been in the dating of Roman town defences. The movement of large quantities of soil by ditch digging to form the ramparts will include the objects already present in the soil, relating to a completely different period of occupation and not connected with the date of the rampart construcion. At Great Casterton[27] in the first section across the rampart every sherd was collected and recorded, totalling in all some one hundred pieces from the bank, all datable to the first century AD. From this it could have been justifiably concluded that the date of the bank was probably early second century, like that at Verulamium dated by Wheeler to the Hadrianic period, but for the presence of a small hearth immediately below the first layer of rampart soil. This hearth contained seven sherds of pottery, five of which were locally made colour-coated beakers while the other two were typical Lower Nene Valley colour-coated products, including a fragment of a 'hunt cup'. As all these vessels were in use from the middle to the end of the second century it meant that the defences could not have been erected before c. AD 160,[28] This in turn led to the theory that the ramparts were the work of Clodius Albinus, as part of a defensive policy for the Province while he took most of the troops to Gaul in his unsuccessful attempt to gain the imperial throne. A review of the excavation reports of similar town ramparts demonstrated that in many cases the defences had been dated far too early on the basis of residual coins and pottery.

There was also a tendency among excavators of earlier generations, when assessing pottery assemblages, to aim at an average date for the whole group. If a few sherds appeared out of keeping with the main body of the assemblage they were ignored as 'intrusions'. Consequently, Wheeler dated the defences at Verulamium to the reign of Hadrian, although Antonine pottery was found in the rampart. These pieces were dismissed with the statement 'the overwhelming pre-Antonine character of the mass of associated pottery suggests the earlier rather than the later of Dr Oswald's limiting dates (c. AD 130–150) for the exceptional sherd'.[29]

As well as the stratigraphic position of the pottery on a site, other artefacts found with it must be taken into consideration. This is particularly true of Roman sites where coins and epigraphic evidence may provide an absolute or calendrical date for the deposition of a layer. On sites which have produced both, such as large military installations and civilian settlements, they have been used to provide exact dating for associated pottery and other finds. In this way when these ceramic types or forms occur on smaller sites, where no other dating is available, they can be used to establish a date for a layer by the cross-referencing of finds. By this method of cross-dating a chronology can be established and sites historically linked. The danger inherent in this pattern of dating is the creation of a circular argument in which all the evidence for one region may rest on one dated type-site or deposit. If that assumption proves to be incorrect the whole sequence for the area will be invalidated.

Hadrian's Wall and the Antonine Wall in Scotland have provided many sites and deposits dated not only by coins and epigraphic evidence but also by literary information and Imperial records. The date and purpose of Hadrian's Wall is recorded by Hadrian's biographer, in the *Scriptores Historiae Augustae*, who states that a wall was constructed for 80 miles from sea to sea to divide the barbarians from the Romans. It is also known that Hadrian came to Britain in 122 from Germany, where he was responsible for the construction of another artificial frontier. The discussion of the frontiers in the biography is so closely related to the accounts of the visits that there is little doubt that the frontiers were initiated by Hadrian while in the respective Provinces.[30] The construction of Hadrian's Wall, therefore, began in or soon after AD 122. Hadrian died in 138 and by the following year Britain had a new governor, Quintus Lollius Urbicus. The building projects started by this new governor demonstrate that a new policy for the northern frontier had been devised. An inscription for Corbridge recording the construction of a granary in 139 is the first manifestation of this new policy, which is mentioned in the Life of Antoninus Pius, Hadrian's successor to the throne, 'for he conquered Britain through the governor Lollius Urbicus and after driving back the barbarians built a turf wall'. The abandonment of Hadrian's Wall marks the end of Wall Period I, the primary occupation.

When and why the Antonine Wall in turn was abandoned has become one of the most difficult problems of the northern frontier (see below). Over the last 100 years the suggested dates have ranged from the 160s through the 180s to 197 and 207 then finally back to the 160s. There is no guarantee that the date of c. 163, which is at present accepted by most scholars, is correct as it is based on the archaeological evidence available at this time.[31]

Hadrian's Wall, with its outpost and hinterland forts, was repaired marking the beginning of Wall Period II. The last decades of the second century were particularly turbulent and the wall suffered serious destruction on at least one occasion. Large destruction deposits have been found at several milecastles, turrets and wall forts. These deposits contain much of the latest central Gaulish samian exported to Britain. At Corbridge one such deposit consisted of some 4,300 sherds, representing at least 500 separate vessels, of different types of pottery.[32] One-fifth of this pottery was samian, largely from central Gaul. It is also known that the governorship of Virius Lupus saw the beginning of a long building programme, indicated by over 30 inscriptions surviving from the period c. 197–250 and relating to forts on Hadrian's Wall and its hinterland. Several of the stones record the buildings either erected or repaired: the gates and walls, granaries, headquarters building, bath house and aqueduct. This building programme, taken with the slightly earlier destruction deposits, has been used to suggest that the repairs were carried out following an attack on the northern frontier while the army was away in Gaul with Clodius Albinus. However, the destruction (mainly in the eastern sector of the Wall in the vicinity of Halton-Chesters and Corbridge) is now considered to relate to an earlier attack mentioned by the Roman historian Dio Cassius, dating to the early 180s and not the late 190s. The repair work at other sites, including the forts in the western sector and the hinterland, may be interpreted as part of a policy of refurbishing and improvements necessitated by the ravages of time rather than the ravages of an enemy.[33] This case serves to illustrate the problems of relating literary and epigraphic evidence with archaeological deposits and materials. Such correlations are not infallible. In the course of time they may have to be revised in the light of new archaeological evidence.

Pottery dated by associated epigraphic evidence or related to an historical event may in the course of time prove to have been incorrectly assigned. In spite of this limitation, the pottery from Hadrian's Wall and the Antonine Wall is still used extensively when seeking parallels for pottery found on sites less securely dated. It is also often assumed that types of pottery current in the north will also have been available in the south and that if these types are not present on a site it is due to chronological rather than geographic or economic reasons. Great reliance is placed on the presence or absence of pottery types as a chronological indicator with little regard to alternative explanations. These attitudes can lead to inflexibility in the construction of site chronologies (see below).

The context in which the pottery is found affects not only the dating but also has social and economic implications. Pottery used in burial rites will sometimes differ greatly from that in domestic use. If the pottery from various sites is to be compared, then ideally there should be no economic or social differences in the function of the sites. It would be unwise to compare directly the pottery from a Roman town or military installation with that from a villa or farmstead. The latter tend to be ceramically impoverished compared to large towns, forts and fortresses which, due to their larger populations and many social divisions, have diverse pottery types, often in large quantities. Exotic imports are often relatively common in these circumstances, but rare on villas to which they would have been taken by individuals. The history of many towns spans the whole period of Roman domination, whereas the heyday of the villa was during the late third and fourth centuries. Some pottery was made exclusively for burial, either accompanying the body, such as specially made miniature vessels, or for containing the ashes after cremation, like face-mask pots (plate 8). The context of a vessel or sherd may have some bearing on its original use as tableware, a cooking pot, or container or its re-use with a completely different function, such as the conversion of Roman amphorae tops and bases to urinals, buried upright in the ground.

Origin

A full appreciation of the social and economic significance of pottery cannot be fully realised unless the origin can be determined. In some cases the kiln sites known to have produced certain wares have been recognised for many years. The large Roman pottery industry in the Lower Nene Valley, situated near Water Newton, has been well known since the publication of *The Durobrivae of Antoninus* in 1828, by Edmund Tyrell Artis. Work on the New Forest kiln sites began in the 1850s with the research of the Rev. J. Pemberton,[34] whose main interest was the finer and decorated New Forest wares. It was not until 1917 that Heywood Sumner began his study of the kiln structures themselves.[35] Many kilns of the Roman period have been excavated. They are often large, substantial affairs, composed of a flue and a chamber with a raised floor, and are usually constructed of clay. In the prehistoric period most pottery appears to have been fired in bonfires or clamps, which were just as effective as the more elaborate structures but leave little trace. Where kiln sites are not known the distribution of specific pottery types has been used to indicate either likely sources of production[36] or to define the area of use. However, distribution patterns can sometimes be misleading when used to trace the origin of a type of pottery. The large quantities of what is now known to be Dorset black-burnished ware, found in Staffordshire initially, suggested that this ware was actually made in that county. Indeed the origin of this important pottery type remained a mystery to archaeologists until very recently, when the problem was solved by a very careful and detailed fabric analysis. The use of scientific aids, like petrology, heavy mineral and chemical analysis, has revolutionised the study of the origins and distribution of pottery types. Attitudes and concepts have changed with the realisation that pottery, even in so-called primitive societies, was not always a locally made domestic item but could have been commercially manufactured and traded over a wide area.

PETROLOGY
The petrological analysis of pottery involves the identification of the various mineral inclusions in the body of the pot. By studying the shape, size, relationship and proportions of each different mineral present further inferences can be made about the material. This includes not only the minerals which occur naturally in the clay but also the alterations made to its composition by man during the different processes of pot making. Washing, mixing with fillers and firing may radically alter the nature of the clay and it is often the information obtained about the various techniques employed by the potter that provide the most profitable lines of inquiry.

The petrologist will either study a clean fracture under a normal binocular microscope or make a 'thin section', an almost transparent slice of pot only twenty-thousandths of a millimetre thick, which can be examined under the microscope. The petrological microscope has a polarizer and an analyser which transmits light in one direction only. The identification of minerals seen in thin section depends not only on the characteristic shape and cleavage of the crystals that form them but also on the fact that many of them interfere with the passage of light through them, each mineral differing in the nature and degree of this interference.[37] Much depends on measuring the effects that various minerals have upon light – their so-called refractory qualities.

Fillers, or tempering, added to the clay to reduce the plasticity of the material, can range from chaff or other chopped vegetable matter to sand or crushed rock fragments. The first concern of the petrologist is to distinguish the basic clay used from the added filler. Many clays contain a fair amount of naturally occurring mineral inclusions and it may prove difficult to tell these from deliberately added mineral fillers. However, there is often a difference in size between the smaller natural inclusions in the clay and the larger added material. Particle shape may help to distinguish between the two, as a clay may naturally contain small, angular quartz particles, while the filler may take the form of water-worn quartz sand, with its more rounded particles. The quantities of filler may vary from one sample to the next, due to the vagaries of early potting techniques, while the natural inclusions will remain at a fairly constant level. Once the constituents of the natural clay and the fillers have been isolated, the next step is to identify them. The natural clay may not be particularly distinctive, as sedimentary deposits can be fairly uniform and widely spread. The mineral fillers can be of two types, natural sands or artificially crushed rock. Natural sands may vary from a composition of almost pure quartz to that of a mass of different minerals depending on the parent rock. Particle shape varies from angular, representing recently weathered material, to almost completely rounded, as in the case of wind-blown sand. By contrast, artificially prepared fillers are invariably angular and each particle may contain more than one mineral. One other type of filler, which may present problems, is crushed pottery or grog. This may or may not be of the same composition as the main body of the pot. Finally in the case of shell it is important to recognise if it was added as fresh or fossilized material.

This kind of analysis obviously leads to speculation about the source of the material and whether the pot was produced locally or imported into the area where it was found. Sometimes a filler is detected which could not have been obtained near the find-spot of the pottery, although it may not be possible to point to the precise source of the filler. However, in some cases broad regions or exact sources from which the clay or its filler may have come have been defined. The petrological examination of early Neolithic pottery found in Wiltshire revealed that some contained a type of igneous rock which can only be found at the Gabbro, an outcrop which covers about seven square miles of the Lizard Head in Cornwall.[38] This clay was an important raw material used throughout the prehistoric period (see below).

HEAVY MINERAL ANALYSIS

This technique is used to determine the geological source of the sand inclusions in the clay body, in order to identify the probable area of manufacture. It involves crushing 10–30 grammes of pottery and then floating the resulting powder on a heavy liquid, such as bromoform. The heavy minerals, like zircon, garnet and tourmaline, sink while the quartz and clay float. These heavy minerals are separated, identified and counted under a microscope, to ascertain the parent rock from which the sand was formed. Distinctive combinations of heavy minerals can often be assigned to a specific geological formation, thereby suggesting a likely source. Since Peacock drew attention to its potential for ceramic petrology, this technique has been used increasingly to provide an objective means for classifying sand used as a filler in pottery.[39] In the case of black-burnished ware it has been used to confirm the division of the pottery into two categories: black-burnished ware 1, which was largely made in Dorset in the Wareham-Poole Harbour area and black-burnished ware 2, much of which appears to have been manufactured around the Thames Estuary.[40] The technique has also been successfully applied to Roman amphorae, indicating a variety of sources from which these vessels originated and suggesting patterns of trade in the late Iron Age.[41]

CHEMICAL ANALYSIS

Atomic absorption spectrophotometry, a physical method of analysis used to determine the chemical composition of the material, has been applied to pottery.[42] Several research programmes have been undertaken at the Research Laboratory for Archaeology and History of Art at Oxford University. Basically this technique requires taking a powder sample from a sherd of pottery. A small area on the edge of each sherd is cleaned before sampling so that the powder obtained is not contaminated by a slip-coating or weathered material. It is important to get a representative sample of the composition of the body fabric. The spectrometer requires liquid samples, so 25 milligrammes of the powder are dissolved in acids. This method identifies and measures the concentration of certain elements in the material, usually sodium, magnesium, aluminium, calcium, titanium, iron, manganese, chromium and nickel.

This technique has been used particularly for analysing fine wares, which have few inclusions visible under the microscope. The method relies on elements rather than minerals, which means that very small samples will suffice rather than the much larger ones required for heavy mineral analysis. This is a great advantage as many fine-ware vessels are too precious to be destroyed for analysis. Instead a small sample can be discreetly obtained from the interior or the base. The technique is also extremely precise, as the relative amount of each element is measured over a range as wide as four orders of magnitude, i.e. from 0.0001 to 10 per cent. However, there are drawbacks. Each element has to be measured separately, so that analysis for a large number of elements is time consuming. Contamination may result from the high dilutions necessary for elements present in high concentrations, so that the method is used for the analysis of minor and trace elements rather than the major ones. The technique has been successfully used to ascertain the origins of certain colour-coated drinking vessels of the late first and second centuries AD, which from a visual comparison of their fabrics were virtually indistinguishable.[43]

From this discussion it can be seen that the application of scientific methods of analysis can be of great use when seeking the origins of a type of pottery when the relevant kiln sites are lacking or for separating the products from different industrial centres which are visually indistinguishable.

DISTRIBUTION

If distribution maps can be somewhat unreliable as a means of indicating likely places of manufacture, they are still vital for tracing the movement of pottery from its source. Distribution means defining the spread and limits of artefacts, structures or settlement types within an area. The distribution of objects is represented by plotting the 'find-spots', the places at which the pottery was found, on a map. This may be done on a simple presence or absence basis, but a more informative result may be obtained by quantifying the pottery recovered from each site. For instance, within a 10-mile radius of its source the pottery may form 80 per cent of the assemblage recovered from a site, up to 20 miles away only 40 per cent and over 30 miles away less than 20 per cent. In this way the amount of pottery is seen to diminish as it moves away from its source, perhaps indicating the difficulties or cost of transportation or competition from rival firms. This concept, called distance-decay function, can be expressed mathematically to ascertain the rate at which quantity declines as the distance from the source increases.[44] Distance-decay tends to vary according to the value of the object traded, with costly items travelling further afield than cheap or easily produced ones.

This statistical procedure is a specific example of linear regression analysis, which is used to determine the relationship between two variables. One variable, in this case distance, is regarded as independent, while the second, quantity, is dependent upon it. By observation it is possible to estimate the relationship between the two, in this instance that quantity diminishes with distance. This is demonstrated by the distribution of a certain type of early Neolithic pottery made of gabbroic clay from the Lizard Head in Cornwall.[45] These pots were evidently transported, from Cornwall through south-west England into Wessex, largely by coastal traffic (fig. 13). As it moves away from its source the proportion of the ware falls in relation to other types of pottery present on sites. At Gwithian and Carn Brea nearly all the pottery found was from the Lizard, further east at Haldon only a quarter of the pottery found was gabbroic in origin and still further east at Windmill Hill, Wessex, it was represented by only two sherds. The limitations of the theory are that it assumes a linear relationship between the variables and uses only one variable to explain all the variations in the other. It does not consider the method of transportation.

The Antonine mortaria produced at Colchester, Essex, provide an instructive example of how transportation can effect distribution patterns, since their market consisted of a south-eastern 'home' area with another predominantly concentrated on the Antonine Wall and the Corbridge area with few vessels occurring in the intervening areas.[46] The clustering on the Antonine Wall and around Corbridge lend support to the inference, from the distribution pattern, that coastal shipping to the Tyne and Forth was involved. Water transport must have played a very large part in the movement of pottery, which is heavy and prone to breakage. Even if the material being studied is not quantified the relationship of the plotted find-spots to the natural terrain may reveal something about communication or trading networks. Concentrations along river valleys or coastal plains may indicate water-borne transportation.

As not all pottery was produced and marketed on a commercial basis but rather made for local, domestic use, the identification of the source may be of secondary importance to finding out who used the pottery. The clustering of find-spots may suggest a cultural or tribal entity, while a wide scattering may indicate the diffusion of a new technology spread by the arrival of a new people. The occurrence of one trait alongside another within a given area can prove contemporaneity or association, as in the case of late Neolithic grooved ware and Henge monuments. Conversely a chronological sequence may be demonstrated, like the replacement of Iron Age Durotrigian pottery by its successor Dorset black-burnished ware in the Roman period. Mutually exclusive distributions can not only imply contemporaneity but also trade or tribal restrictions. The main drawback to this visual representation of distribution is the tendency to accept the information, suggested by the pattern of find-spots, at face value without inquiring about the processes of deposition, like casual loss or

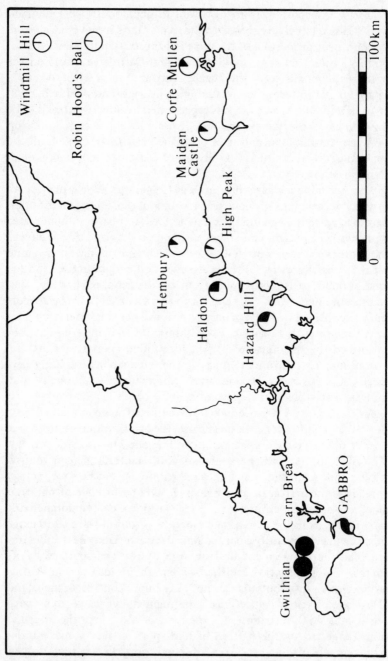

Fig. 13 Distribution of Neolithic pottery made from the gabbroic clay of the Lizard Head, Cornwall. The black sectors in the circles represent the proportion of vessels from the Lizard. *After Peacock 1969*

deliberate burial for instance, which might affect the results. Gaps in distribution patterns may reflect the limits of archaeological knowledge rather than actual gaps.

Pottery distribution can also be used to study exchange or trading patterns between different communities. In a 'market' economy large settlements, such as towns and villages, act as distribution points for goods. The town supplies goods and services to the surrounding area but in return draws its resources, food and raw materials from the same territory. In this way each major settlement has its area of influence. Concentrations of population in turn encourage the local production of goods, which has obvious advantages over goods traded over long distances. Transport costs will be lower, making the product cheaper. However, it may be of inferior quality, being the work of local craftsmen rather than that of highly skilled professionals. The distribution of local pottery, with manufacture geared to a nearby town, will illustrate these points. The bulk of the pottery will be consumed by the inhabitants of the town, with less travelling to the outlying settlements and farms. Moving away from the town the quantity of pottery will be seen to diminish but the area of consumption may be extended along the main roads. The pottery may occur at the next town in even greater profusion than on the outlying settlements due to the ease of access provided by an efficient road system. The pottery may then have to compete with this town's own local types. Any settlement lying between the two towns may have a variety of types present, as their inhabitants could choose from the goods available at both centres. In this way pottery is seen to gravitate towards the larger centres of population, where it is redistributed, being bought by the residents or traded over short distances to nearby settlements and farms.

This type of trading pattern involves an understanding of 'central place theory', concerning the spatial organisation of sites offering goods or services to the surrounding area, developed by the geographer Walter Christaller.[47] Central places are those towns or larger sites within a settlement pattern that act as centres for regional communities by providing certain amenities, such as economic, religious or administrative services. Despite various drawbacks, central place theory may suggest factors which have affected the redistribution of goods and it has been applied to the location and functioning of Roman towns (see below). The idea need not be restricted to the Roman period. During the Iron Age hill forts and *oppida* may have fulfilled a similar purpose within the community, while in the Neolithic period causewayed enclosures and henges may have acted as religious, social and economic centres.

Another mathematical theory that has been applied to distributional problems is Thiessen polygons, which are constructed on a map around a series of centres by drawing perpendicular lines at the mid-points between each centre and all its neighbours. The polygons created enclose the area nearer to one centre than to any other. This theory is useful for defining theoretical territories related to each other. They could be areas served by an industrial or market centre or the regions from which communities drew their resources. These theoretical territories can be tested by comparison with the available archaeological data, like artefact distributions. However, the theory assumes that all the chosen centres are contemporary and of the same social status, assumptions that are difficult to prove archaeologically. The polygons give equal weight to all centres regardless of size, even though a larger centre may have a bigger catchment area. It is possible to weight the polygons by drawing lines at a point between one centre and its neighbour in proportion to their relative sizes, thereby creating a larger territory for the larger centre.[48]

Conclusion

It can be seen, from the above discussion, that the research and writing of pottery reports requires a careful study of all aspects of the subject. Statistical evaluation of the material is being increasingly utilised, to assess the relative quantities of pottery types found on a site, to gauge the impact of a new pottery type, and to appraise the range and number of forms present within each type. By exploiting statistical and analytical techniques the potential of pottery as a socio-economic indicator can be fully realised. Once the archaeologist has at his disposal all the information he can extract from the pottery – including identity, date and where possible origin – the next task is to interpret the results. This is invariably the most difficult and controversial side of archaeology. The misuse of techniques or the suppression of evidence at variance with the bulk of the other available information can lead to distortions. It is important to remember, when assessing the historical and economic implications of pottery, that several theories may be postulated to explain the occurrence of one phenomenon.

4 Pottery and History

The production and use of pottery has often been taken to reflect a 'civilized' way of life, denoting certain social and craft specializations and a stable population. The nomadic hunter-gatherers of the Paleolithic and Mesolithic periods had little use for cumbersome and fragile pots. Portable equipment was constructed of leather or basketry, both of which are light and durable – ideal for a transient way of life. As the use of pottery is normally linked with a settled existence, archaeologists have traditionally dated its inception to the Neolithic or early farming period. In this way pottery became a prerequisite for defining cultures belonging to this period. Before the advent of radio-carbon dating, the established framework of prehistory – from the Paleolithic to the Iron Age – was seen primarily as a chronological development, implying a gradual progression from a simple to a more complicated way of life. It was assumed that one stage had to be completed before another could start.

This rather simplistic approach to the development of man's existence proved to be inadequate when faced with the complexities exposed by new methods of dating. Radio-carbon dating has demonstrated that different societies, of both hunter-gatherer and early farming types, existed side by side, and furthermore could draw upon the experience of each other. The people of the late Mesolithic Errtebølle culture of Scandinavia were dependent on sea fishing for their existence. Two features, traditional 'hallmarks' of the adoption of a Neolithic way of life – pottery and axes with a cutting edge sharpened by grinding – made their appearance in the coastal settlements of this culture without otherwise disrupting the strong Mesolithic background. They were able to do so, because, although these people were hunter-gatherers, their efficient exploitation of the sea enabled them to lead a settled way of life rather than a nomadic one. The thriving Mesolithic cultures in this part of Europe were able to retain a strong influence, absorbing the new techniques of pottery production, agriculture and the domestication of animals from the neighbouring

Neolithic Danubian culture without suffering any immediate profound change of their own culture and way of life. From this it can be seen that the terms Mesolithic and Neolithic largely denote different economic systems, which are reflected archaeologically in the different cultural equipment adopted. In the case of pottery usage the main prerequisite is a settled existence, whether in a Mesolithic or Neolithic context.

Having established that pottery can be a characteristic of the Neolithic age the archaeologist can go on to use different types of ceramics to define individual cultures. In the Prehistoric period this is the principal use of pottery, to define in time and space the life of particular groups of people or so-called cultures. A culture represents human activity which is transmitted from individual to individual by following an established pattern, not by genetic inheritance. The archaeologist of necessity equates human activity with artefacts (material culture), as he can only guess at cultural traits, like religious beliefs and practices, by implication. The equation of culture with society is very imperfect, though it is the best the archaeologist can achieve, unaided by literary evidence. Problems of definition often occur when separating adjacent or successive cultures. Hence, it would be unwise to distinguish a culture by its pottery alone. The ideal situation is to isolate a group of distinctive objects – a cultural assemblage – of which pottery is only one component. For instance, the late Neolithic-early Bronze Age Beaker culture of north-western Europe takes its name from the distinctive pots with elaborate decoration which are often found associated with archers' equipment, gold jewellery and copper and bronze tools. This culture is also characterised by a distinctive burial rite – single inhumations under a round barrow, usually surrounded by a ditch. The arrival of the Beaker culture in Britain has even been related to the appearance of a new skeletal type (Brachycephalic) indicating that these people were of a different race to the indigenous population. Although the Beaker culture has been subdivided into both chronological or regional groupings, largely on the grounds of stylistic differences of the pottery, the material culture, on the whole, remains a cohesive group. Pottery in this instance is only one aspect of a cultural group.

The same cannot be said for other types of Prehistoric pottery. Late Neolithic 'Peterborough ware' does not represent a culture in its own right. It does not occur consistently with any other characteristically late Neolithic objects, such as transverse arrow heads or convex scrapers, but it has been found with other types of pottery and on a variety of occupation sites. In other words Peterborough ware shares no closed association with any objects or monuments of the late Neolithic. There was no Peterborough culture as such, rather it may represent a regional style or fashion that developed in south-eastern England and was used by a variety of different cultures.

Once a culture has been defined, there still remains the problem of explaining how it came into existence, by the movement of people, objects or ideas ('diffusion'), or by local development without external stimulation ('independent invention'). Diffusion has been credited with a major role in human development by spreading ideas and techniques rapidly over wide areas. However, on occasions it has been credited with too much. Multiple origins, even within Europe, for megaliths and metal working are now accepted. The days of Eliot Smith and his school of Diffusionists, when nearly everything was deemed to have spread outwards from Egypt, like the ripples formed by throwing a pebble into a pool, have long since passed. Now the onus of proof is on the Diffusionist to prove conclusively that the trait in question was the same in both areas, that communication was possible and that there was no difference in the relative dates. The difficulties of meeting all these criteria have led to some of the great debates of archaeology, such as the much speculated relationship between Bronze Age Mycenae and the British Wessex culture. As will be demonstrated, in many cases an easy explanation cannot be found. This is particularly true of Britain where its insular character compounds the problem. Where the arrival of a new culture has been ascribed to the movement of people, as in the case of the Beaker culture, there often follows a period when the culture evolves independently from any development on the Continent.

Neolithic and early Bronze Age

In early Neolithic Britain nearly all the pottery was produced and used locally, creating many regional types. Within the territory of the Windmill Hill culture of southern Britain several different pottery styles have been identified. These styles are characterised by their forms (including handles, rims and decoration), but may occur in a variety of fabrics. Although each style has a regional concentration, there is considerable geographic overlapping. The pottery found at the promontory enclosure at Hembury, Devon, has after analysis been shown to be largely of local origin. Petrological examination has indicated that the predominant coarse 'A' ware contains flint, chert and

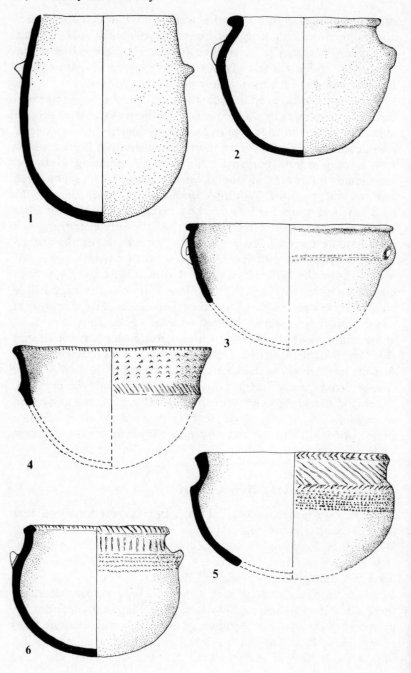

quartz – all of which could have been obtained in the vicinity of the site.[1] Work on the Neolithic pottery from Windmill Hill, Wilts, points to a local clay source for roughly 69 per cent of the vessels found.[2] The dominant forms are deep bag-shaped vessels with simple rims (figs 14.1, 14.2). Their rather leathery texture may indicate the original organic prototypes of the form. The shell-gritted ware found in the Upper Thames Valley, referred to as the Abingdon style after the causewayed enclosure in Berkshire, would also appear to be of local origin. The dominant form is a wide-mouth bowl, with an elaborately thickened, and rolled over rim, ornamented with incised or stamped impressions (fig. 14.3). Such bowls often have lugs developed into elaborate strap handles. In south-eastern Britain the typical form is a wide-mouthed carinated bowl, decorated on the rim, neck and shoulder (fig. 14.4). North of the Thames, in East Anglia, a further series of vessels, named after the site of Mildenhall, Suffolk, is also characterised by a carinated bowl with thickened rim and incised ornament (fig. 14.5).

Not all early Neolithic pottery was produced locally. In south and south-western Britain the materials for several types of pottery were obtained some distance from their ultimate find-spots. One distinctive group known as Hembury ware, characterised by fragments of igneous rock, was clearly imported onto the find-site. Petrological analysis has established that this pottery was made in Cornwall and yet it occurs on sites in Devon and Wiltshire.[3] Distinctive forms were made (fig. 24), which were widely copied. Another group is oolitic ware, vessels made from clay containing fossil shell and oolites derived from a Jurassic outcrop, probably in the Bath-Frome region. These constitute about 30 per cent of the pottery so far found at Windmill Hill,[4] and are known from other sites in Wiltshire including the West Kennet Long Barrow. At Windmill Hill the oolitic ware appeared as Hembury style forms, imitating the Cornish prototypes, and also as ornamented bowls closely comparable with the Abingdon and other decorated styles. The pottery

Fig. 14(a) **Plain early-middle Neolithic pottery**
1 Hembury, Devon
2 Chelms Comb, Sussex
Scale 1:4
(b) **Decorated early-middle Neoltihic pottery**
3 Abingdon, Berkshire
4 White Hawk, Sussex
5 Ipswich, Suffolk
6 Haylands House, Isle of Wight
Scale 1:5 After Piggott

from the deeper silts of the ditches can be identified as follows:
1. Hembury Style: (A) Cornish prototypes (2 sherds) (B) Imitations in oolitic ware (C) Local imitations.
2. Abingdon and other decorated styles: (A) Oolitic ware (B) Local wares.
3. Ebbsfleet style: (A) Oolitic ware (B) Local wares.
4. Various other stylistic groups in local wares.[5]

From this it can be seen that pottery was imported into Wiltshire from several sources, as far afield as Cornwall.

The situation in early Neolithic Britain was, therefore, already complicated due to the co-existence of several regional pottery styles in southern England. Much of the pottery was made locally but often copied styles imported from other areas and was used by people who shared an otherwise similar cultural background. The conventional approach to pottery, which assumes that pot-making must have been domestic, communal work and that pottery styles must express communal traditions, is not necessarily applicable here. The identity and origins of Neolithic communities cannot always be sought in a study of their pottery. The new model for pottery production, as suggested by Peacock, offers a new approach. The apparent anomaly of the co-existence of different ceramic traditions within a comparatively restricted area may now be attributed to the vagaries of trade or fashion. Mutually exclusive or partially overlapping distributions and minor stylistic variations might be the result of competition. Innovations may have been introduced by a few inventive or itinerant potters.[6] Seasonal movements would also help to spread ceramic styles. Evidence from causewayed enclosures suggests that groups or tribes came together from far afield. Consequently, although the Hembury style is largely found in the extreme south-west, examples have been found as far away as Whitehawk, Sussex.

However, it is always difficult to distinguish the diffusion of styles by the movement of people from the spread of objects by trade. In Yorkshire, Wales and Scotland plain vessels with lugs have often been interpreted as representing a colonization from southern England. These vessels are basically a simplified version of Hembury style pots, which might indicate their ultimate origin. Was the Hembury style carried beyond its area of invention by migrating communities or was the idea spread by trade?

GROOVED WARE

This clearly demonstrates that a culture cannot be defined by its

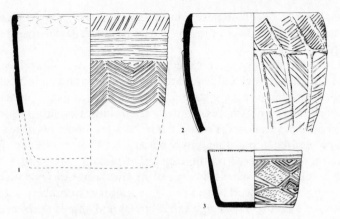

Fig. 15   Grooved ware
1 Clacton style: internal rim bevel with applied relief decoration. Example from Clacton. *After Piggott*
2 Woodhenge-Durrington Walls style: vertical panels formed by incised lines or cordons, often infilled with grooved chevron designs. Example from Durrington Walls, Wiltshire. *After Megaw and Simpson*
3 Clacton style: particularly common are dot-filled triangles, lozenges or rectangles and multiple chevrons. Example from Creeting St Mary. *After Megaw and Simpson*
Scale 1:4

---

pottery alone. Pottery can only be used as an indicator when it is but one element of a distinctive material culture. In the late Neolithic period a major pottery tradition, known as Rinyo-Clacton or grooved ware, represents a remarkably homogeneous group in both form and decoration, found from the extreme north to the extreme south of Britain, yet almost totally absent from Ireland. In the case of grooved ware it has been demonstrated that the pottery is only one aspect of a range of equipment and monuments which characterises a distinctive archaeological culture.[7] The basic vessel form is bucket-shaped with a flat base and thick walls. Generally the vessels are poorly fired. Four sub-styles have been recognised, all apparently contemporary – Clacton (figs 15.1, 15.3), Woodlands, Woodhenge-Durrington Walls (fig. 15.2) and Rinyo[8] – taking their names from the sites at which they were first discovered. These sub-styles have largely been defined by their different decorative motifs, but all use grooved and applied ornamentation rather than the corded techniques so characteristic of contemporary beakers. All the styles are present at Skara Brea, on Orkney, indicating that, despite their regional concentrations, there is no strict territorial separation. The division of the material into northern and southern provinces is, therefore, inappropriate. The excavations at Glenluce have emphasized that the grooved ware of southern Scotland owes more to the southern sub-styles than to the north.

Grooved ware appears to have been a product of insular development, which, although influenced by other contemporary late Neolithic styles, maintained a distinctive character. The occasional appearance of cord and comb-impressed decoration indicates absorption of Peterborough and Beaker skills, but no formative influences have so far been recognised in any other type of pottery. Rather the style appears to be an innovation based on the copying of basketry techniques. The cordons and filled panels so typical of this ware are essentially a rendering of wickerwork. Ideas from other sources were also incorporated, such as the grooved concentric circles and spirals derived from the art of the Boyne passage graves of Ireland. How such decorative motifs were transmitted from west to east remains uncertain. It may have been through the movement of small objects, like the carved chalk cylinders from Folkton, Yorks or even of some form of personal decoration, either on garments or on the skin in the form of tattoo marks.[9] Connections with Ireland, direct or indirect, are certainly implied and this evidence has even been taken to suggest that the passage graves of the Maes Howe group in Orkney, which are closely linked to the Boyne group, were constructed by the communities that used grooved ware.[10]

Other monuments associated with grooved ware, or its makers, include the class of archaeological sites referred to as henges. It has occurred at six henge monuments, and three other ceremonial sites, including those at Avebury, Stonehenge (I), Durrington Walls, Marden and Woodhenge, all in Wiltshire. That some henges were constructed by grooved ware users is indicated by the overwhelming preponderance of such pottery at the last three sites. Although the pottery was sometimes used at ceremonies connected with the henges, it is rarely found in funerary contexts. Only two direct associations have been recorded, but it has been found in secondary contexts at five chambered tombs. Grooved ware also occurs on domestic sites, the most notable being the groups of stone built houses found at Rinyo and Skara Brae on Orkney. Sherds have been found in storage pits of one form or another, although their interpretation as grain storage pits is unlikely as no pit or sherd of grooved ware has produced either carbonised grain or grain impressions.

Grooved ware has also been found with other objects such as flintwork, in the form of transverse or cutting arrowheads and the so-

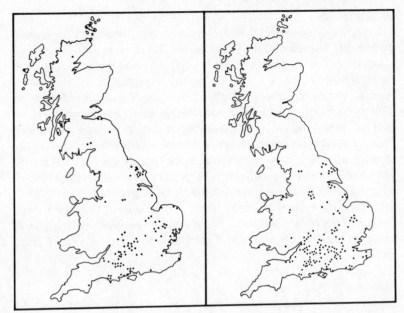

Fig. 16 **Distribution of grooved ware and Peterborough ware.** *After Smith*

called plano-convex knives. Igneous rock axes also figure prominently, from the Cornish axe factories and from Graig Llwyd and Great Langdale. This is not a surprising connection as, like grooved ware, the axes seem to be linked in some way with the ceremonies performed at henges. Carved chalk objects, skeumorphs of rock axes, and decorated plaques, are also associated with grooved ware and in the case of the former with henges too.

The picture established above is one of an insular British culture, characterised not only by its pottery but also by other equipment, including distinctive flint and stone tools, occupation and ceremonial sites. Cremation cemeteries, found at Dorchester-on-Thames, which have produced similar flint, stone and bone artefacts but no distinctive pottery, may also be included in this cultural grouping. In addition a series of cremation burials beneath very large round barrows, particularly in Yorkshire and the Pennines, may be connected with the group. It is possible that the largest of all the round mounds in Britain, Silbury Hill, was built by grooved ware users. As grooved ware clearly reflects a distinctive material culture composed of other types of artefacts and archaeological sites, it has been suggested that the name Rinyo-Clacton should be retained, denoting the homogeneous character of the culture from north to south.

Several pottery styles besides grooved ware flourished in Britain during the late Neolithic. Whereas the latter represents a ceramic innovation, contemporary Peterborough ware was the continuation of early Neolithic traditions. This ware developed from the earlier regional forms of pottery associated with the Windmill Hill culture. The name Peterborough ware has been given to a sequence of styles that are chronological, rather than regional as in the case of grooved ware. This series of styles forms a ceramic tradition with continuity through a typological sequence, which does not appear to represent one aspect of a distinctive culture. The pottery has a wide distribution, which disregards the territorial boundaries of grooved ware (fig. 16). The dynamic expansion of the ware, as seen against the rather static nature of other late Neolithic decorated styles, taken with a loss of cultural status, suggests that Peterborough ware may have been traded.[11]

BEAKER POTTERY

Against this background of native development, exemplified by grooved and Peterborough wares, the appearance of a new intrusive pottery tradition and other equipment, including the earliest metal objects found in Britain, serves to illustrate the way pottery can be used to recognise the movement of people. The complexities of the Beaker culture have also resulted in many conflicting views and opinions. The last decade has seen several studies on the subject by both British and European scholars. The principal writers include D.L. Clarke,[12] Lanting and van der Waals[13] and H. Case.[14] These classifications are all primarily based on the distinctive Beaker pottery, combined with metal and flint artefacts and field monuments. The traditional and easily comprehensible threefold division of British beakers – (A) Long-necked, (B) Bell and (C) Short-necked – based on the original classification by Abercromby in 1912,[15] has been totally rejected. In its place Clarke proposed that the development of British beakers was the result of seven major incursions of people reaching the island in two main waves, with small dispersed groups of settlers arriving over considerable periods of time. These successive arrivals shaped the development of two distinctive insular beaker traditions, a northern and a southern, each capable of further typological and chronological subdivision and forming, in Clarke's opinion two individual social groups.

Clarke based his seven intrusive groups on a typological consider-

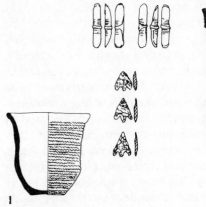
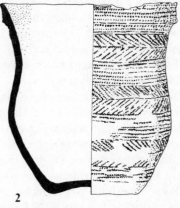

Fig. 17 Beaker grave groups
1 'All-over-corded' beaker from
Cassington, Oxfordshire

2 Bell beaker from Radley, Oxfordshire:
barrow 4A
Scale 1:4 After Case

ation of Beaker pottery, with specific regard to decorative motifs and
designs. Beaker pottery is characterised by the use of cord and comb
impressed ornamentation (figs 17, 18). The earliest wave of settlers is
marked by the arrival of all-over-corded (AOC) beakers (fig. 17.1).
Clarke's second group, the European bell beaker, is also characterised
by vessels with a bell-shaped profile. The third group, Wessex-middle
Rhine beakers (fig. 18.1), which is found in the area previously
occupied by the makers of European bell beakers, played an important
part in the emergence of the early Bronze Age Wessex culture. Group
4, north British-middle Rhine beakers, is contemporary with the
Wessex-middle Rhine group and has a complementary distribution.
The north British-north Rhine group 5 is concentrated in eastern
Yorkshire and Northumberland. Vessels of group 6, or 'barbed wire'
beakers, take their name from their distinctive decoration, which was
made with a thread-wound stamp with three prongs. The seventh and
final group, primary north British-Dutch beakers, is considered to
have provided the foundation for the insular development of the late
and final phases of the north British beaker series. In the south primary
southern beakers developed from the Wessex-middle Rhine group.
The southern and northern native traditions were geographically
separated by the East Anglian group, another insular development,
representing the mixing of beaker groups with the indigenous Neolithic population who used Mildenhall ware.

Clarke's methods have been criticised. There are objections to the formation of groupings, the use of the archaeological evidence, the comparison of pottery forms in Britain with those on the Continent, and the dating and distribution of the pottery. From the technical point of view Clarke based his classification on decorative motifs and style, referring to the way motifs are used to create different patterns, arguing that these are non-functional and more likely to reflect a tradition. Body-shape is dismissed on the grounds that it is largely dictated by function. Greater weight is given in his analysis to motifs and style than vessel shape. Conversely, it can also be argued that variation in shape, within certain limits, is just as likely to be the result of fashion, taste or convention as the decoration. Another element to be considered in Clarke's methodology is his use of the technique of matrix analysis. As his results were not sufficiently precise certain traits had to be emphasised or weighted at the expense of others. Archaeological evidence, associated objects, and stratigraphic position were also used to supplement the result. However, the exact means by which the classification was finally formulated is not fully explained by Clarke, leaving some doubt as to the validity of the results.[16] Further problems are raised by the distribution maps, devised by Clarke, of certain beaker types. A surprising number of beakers, representing supposedly different intrusive traditions, can all be found within one area, while vessels thought to indicate one intrusive group can be found scattered across the country. The reason for this is that, when preparing the distribution maps, Clarke relied on motifs rather than entire vessels. A beaker is not a Northern beaker because it was found in the north; rather that is the area where the motifs on it are most commonly found. Thus considerable numbers of Northern beakers occur in Wessex and both Northern and Southern beakers are found in the same grave.

Lanting and van der Waals approach the problem from a different viewpoint. Their scheme sees only a single initial migration of people bringing 'all-over-corded' beakers to Britain. These vessels can be paralleled exactly on the Continent, whereas the Dutch have been able to demonstrate that Clark's north British-middle Rhine and north British-north Rhine groups cannot be sufficiently paralleled on the Continent to support the idea that they were themselves of European origin. This is a major factor in assessing the likelihood of later migrations, though continued contact with foreign Beaker groups is implied by subsequent British developments. The basis of Lanting and van der Waals' study relies on the distribution patterns of Beaker vessels, which appear to indicate concentrations of settlements in certain areas, particularly Wessex, East Anglia, Yorkshire and north-east England/south-east Scotland. They suggest that a more realistic appraisal of the development of the Beaker culture in Britain would be achieved by studying the pottery and its associations in these four focal areas. This approach emphasizes local development, making it un-necessary to envisage repeated movements of individual Beaker groups across the North sea. Development in these focal areas would be the product of continuing contact with other regions of the British Isles and Europe.

The Dutch propose an evolutionary sequence for British beakers. In Wessex the sequence is represented by seven successive steps and in the other areas studied a similar sequence was revealed. The scheme is based on the typological development of the pottery, supported by a number of important associations. In Wessex, step 1 is marked by the arrival of all-over-corded beakers, which are considered to be typologi-cally early but have no significant associations. Step 2 sees the start of regional development, with beakers that still owe much to the first step (fig. 17.2). AOC beakers also continue. These are associated with gold basket-shaped earrings, copper daggers and archers' bracers (fig. 17.2), which continue into the next stage. In step 3 the vessels are more slender in their proportions and the decorative motifs considerably more varied, and by step 4 they have accentuated necks. Steps 3 and 4 are associated with broad-tanged copper daggers. Vessels belonging to step 5 continue to emphasise the neck, in both size and decoration (fig. 18.2). Decorative designs are more complex with the disappearance of repetitive patterns. By step 6 the distinction between the neck and body begins to fade and the decoration is arranged in two or three broad bands. Jet buttons and pulley rings are restricted to steps 5 and 6. In the final, seventh, stage, the distinction between the neck and body of the beaker is lost altogether and the decoration reverts to all-over designs. In the last two stages riveted daggers occur for the first time.

The Dutch, therefore, envisage one major influx of people, repre-sented by AOC beakers, followed by regional developments with sustained contacts both between regions and the Continent. The latter are most clearly demonstratable in Wessex, as the whole sequence for the area (as outlined above) can be closely paralled in the Rhineland. Eventually other areas of Britain caught up with Wessex and with European developments.[17]

In his appraisal, Case divides the Beaker culture into three consecutive phases. The early phase, represented by AOC beakers, is considered to be the result of trade or exchange between peoples on both sides of the Channel, rather than direct migration. The middle phase saw the arrival of people from the Continent, represented by a new distinctive physical type and the introduction of metal working. The late phase, entirely insular, persisted after the Beaker culture had disappeared on the Continent and is an uninterrupted continuation of the middle phase with some new metal and stone implements. Case concludes, like Clarke and Lanting and van der Waals, that the earliest vessels are the AOC beakers but it does not necessarily follow that they belong exclusively to an early phase. He points out that radio-carbon dates and other associations suggest that this style persisted throughout the duration of the Beaker culture in the British Isles. This apparent lack of specific associations seems to favour a fashion, with the movement of the pottery through the exchange of gifts or by trade. Seasonal movements of small groups of people might also spread the idea of making cord-impressed pottery.

There followed a middle phase in which, unlike the former, there is a major complex of associations, including Clarke's European Bell Beaker, Wessex-middle Rhine and north British-middle Rhine groups. The Wessex-middle Rhine group has particularly rich associations which may suggest an aristocratic class. Finds include copper tanged daggers, awls and tubular beads, decorated gold discs and archers' equipment, including flint barbed and tanged arrow-heads and stone bracers or wrist guards (fig. 18.1). This group may have been responsible for the erection of the bluestone structure (Phase III) at Stonehenge. Also included in this middle phase are Barrel beakers (Clarke's north British-north Rhine group and 'barbed-wire' group) and Short-necked beakers (Clarke's primary north British-Dutch, north British 2 and the East Anglian groups). In Lanting and van der Waals' scheme these beaker groups belong to steps 2, 3 and 4. The middle phase marks the arrival of settlers, bringing their own economy, technology and ritual. They mark an intrusive element against the late Neolithic indigenous background. The evidence includes the apparent arrival of a new racial type (Robust Brachycephalic) which is different to the native (Gracile Dolichocephalic) human skeletal type. Users of middle-period beakers seem to have been exceptionally energetic mixed farmers, who may have introduced a new breed of cattle (bos longifrons) to Britain and the horse to Ireland. Barley appears to have been the principal crop grown, following a Continental trend. Indeed beakers may have been used for drinking beer, and formed part of a

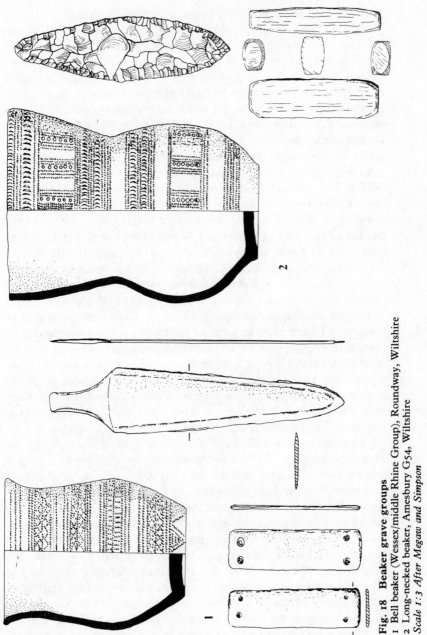

Fig. 18 Beaker grave groups
1 Bell beaker (Wessex/middle Rhine Group), Roundway, Wiltshire
2 Long-necked beaker, Amesbury G54, Wiltshire
Scale 1:3 After Megaw and Simpson

religious 'cult package' that was spread across Europe by migrating peoples.[18] The earliest metallurgy also belongs to this phase but the view of the Beaker folk as wandering prospectors or specialist metallurgists has been challenged. Due to the recalibration of radio-carbon dates the middle phase is now considered to have lasted for roughly half a millennium in Britain and Ireland (2500–2000 BC). This creates a picture of more or less static mixed farmers, similar to many other late Neolithic populations in Europe and Britain. Once the Beaker culture became established in this country, changing pottery styles were probably part of the emergence of regional traditions.

Case's late phase is characterised by the long-necked beaker (Clarke's northern and southern traditions; Lanting and van der Waals steps 5, 6 and 7). The material culture shows a massive continuation from the middle phase, representing an insular continuation of the Beaker culture after it had ended on the European mainland. In the south, Beaker groups survived long enough to overlap with the Wessex culture but by c. 1500 BC, the last Beaker elements had been absorbed.

The work on Beaker pottery illustrates two points about ceramics in general. Firstly, it is unwise to use pottery, or any other artefact, alone to suggest the migration of people from the Continent. New pottery types could have been brought to Britain by settlers or might have arrived through the course of trade and exchange. The argument for migration should be backed up by corroborative evidence: other equipment, new burial rites or distinctive house types. Secondly, pottery classifications can be too complicated, compiled without any regard to what the divisions mean in human terms. At first sight Case's sequence for the Beaker culture might seem oversimplified, with a return to the approach of Abercromby and Piggott. However, a broad, overall classification, which encompasses several different elements, can provide a general cultural background, with the potential for further regional and chronological subdivision. Complicated classifi-cations like Clarke's and Lanting and van der Waals', based primarily on minor stylistic variations of the pottery, come into their own when studying regional divergences and relationships. The profusion of ceramic styles can inflate the significance of pottery in a culture and obscure any basic underlying similarities. Ceramic development should be seen in proper perspective, reflecting folk traditions, technological advances or the economic background. In the past too much emphasis has been placed on pottery signifying cultural differences rather than regional variations of the same culture.

Iron Age

The pottery of the Iron Age presents many problems for the archaeologist, many of whom have preferred to use metal work for constructing a chronological framework. Objects of bronze and iron lend themselves more readily to typological analysis and classification than pottery, which is often subject to the vagaries of local domestic production. For this reason some archaeologists have rejected its use as a 'type fossil' for the British Iron Age:

> Fine pottery styles are so numerous in Britain and western Europe during the Iron Age that any cultural division based primarily upon these would immediately provide too much fragmentation, too many cultures. Coarse pottery on the other hand is so unspecialised and difficult to treat as types that a classification based on this would be far too generalized and subjective.[19]

Hodson goes on to recommend that in formulating a general classification for the Iron Age the archaeologist should 'avoid pottery as far as possible . . . or if pottery is used, select really distinctive pottery types'.[20]

This argument for the total rejection of pottery is unfounded. The fact remains that it is frequently the only artefact recorded, certainly in any quantity, which may be used to assess the chronology and cultural affinities of a site. As demonstrated, the strength of pottery lies in the construction of regional chronologies, where the very diversity of pottery enables a greater degree of precision in local classification. As the product of domestic or local craftsmen, it is more likely to reflect the cultural traits of a given region than a more widely-based commercial industry such as bronze working. Pottery cannot be ignored or relegated to a minor role in classification; 'it is the bread and butter of Iron Age archaeology and forms the closest contact we have with the domestic culture of actual population groups'.[21]

South-eastern Britain maintained a vigorous ceramic tradition throughout the Iron Age. Regional innovations and distinctive local styles soon emerged. The effect of this has been to focus attention in this area, to the detriment of the north and western areas. Recent petrological analysis has revolutionised ceramic studies of the period, highlighting economic factors. This, coupled with stylistic considerations, has enabled the formulation of a series of 'style zones', overlapping both geographically and chronologically,[22] of the type already seen constructed for grooved ware and beakers. The pottery of south-eastern Britain has been grouped in this way, with the distribution of each style well established. The resulting 'style zones' represent the area within which the style was predominant. Each style can also be relatively dated, by reference to local stratigraphic sequences. The interpretation of each zone – whether cultural, economic or technological – is another matter.

Some style zones can be related to social or tribal identity. This is true of a pottery tradition which occurs within a fairly restricted territory in Dorset. This area retained a ceramic identity over a substantial period of time represented by several succeeding styles. The cultural isolation of the area is also reflected in its coinage, in its retension of hill forts for defence as opposed to adopting the *oppida* of south-east England, and finally by its reaction to the advance of the Roman army. In this case a style zone can be equated with a tribal confederacy known as the Durotiges.

In other instances an economic interpretation seems more likely. It is clear that the bulk of Iron Age coarse wares were manufactured domestically but even in the early Iron Age some wares, which have a wider distribution, display techniques beyond those of the locally produced wares. During the third and second centuries BC the pottery over a wide area of southern Britain developed a remarkable degree of uniformity, characterised by vertical-sided 'saucepan pots' (fig. 19.3). This style covered Sussex, Hampshire, Wiltshire, Surrey, Berkshire, Somerset, Gloucestershire and parts of south Wales. Only minor stylistic variations occur – largely regional preferences in decoration and fabric. Petrological analyses have demonstrated that such variations may be due to several potters competing within the area, and bear little relationship to cultural boundaries.

If a technological explanation is preferred it may raise further problems of identifying the source of new ideas. For instance, the fine-ware angular pottery (figs 19.1, 19.2) from Long Wittenham, Berks, stands out from the coarse native pottery made in imitation of it and found on the same site. These finer vessels may have been the work of technically advanced invaders, who wished to maintain the habits of their old homeland. Alternatively, it may be argued that this was the work of a group of skilled potters, the inception of a professional industry, who by sustained contacts with the continent kept abreast of ceramic innovations. Preference for either argument will ultimately depend on the nature of the British distribution and the relationship to Continental antecedents. In this case, while the pottery in Britain does

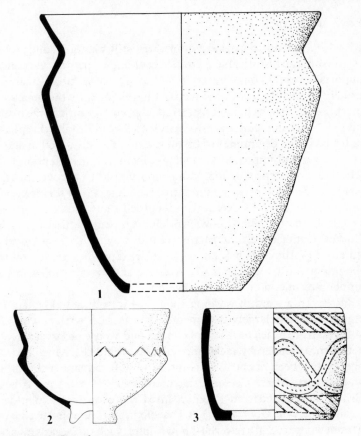

Fig. 19   Early Iron Age pottery
1 Fine ware angular jar from the Upper Thames region. Example from Long Wittenham, Berkshire. *Scale 1:5*
2 Fine ware angular bowl from the Upper Thames region. Example from Chinnor, Oxfordshire
3 Saucepan pottery. Example from Blewburton Hill, Berkshire
Scale 1:4 After Harding

display obvious similarities to Continental material, it nevertheless exhibits individual characteristics which mark it out as distinctly British, and few definite imports have been recognised here. This suggests the influx of a limited number of people, who were responsible for such innovations but who thereafter lost contact with their homeland, developing their crafts along individual, insular lines. Commercial connections would almost certainly have resulted in the appearance of more exotic articles of foreign manufacture.

Late Iron Age

In a 'proto-historic' period pottery can still play a leading role in establishing an historical sequence, even though it may be of secondary importance to coins and literary evidence. The term 'proto-historic' is usually applied to a phase of cultural development which marks the inception of certain characteristic traits that emerge fully in the historic period. In the immediate pre-Roman Iron Age in Britain, this phase is reflected in the beginnings of urbanised life, the introduction and use of coinage, and improved technology, including the adoption of the wheel for pottery production. More important still is the evidence from written records, kept not by the native Iron Age people themselves but by the Romans and Greeks, who recorded their contacts with such people. Perhaps the best known work for this period is Caesar's *de bello Gallico*. Contact with the Mediterranean way of life resulted in the imitation of Roman habits among some Celtic peoples, as illustrated by the import of luxury goods like Arretine and samian tablewares and amphorae containing wine or olive oil.

However, a word of warning should be introduced. The late Iron Age period was largely documented by classical writers who often suffered from a lack of personal contact and whose observations were sometimes clouded by racial and cultural prejudices. Much time and energy has been spent in attempting to substantiate such authors' words, particularly Caesar's statement that the maritime tribes of Britain had crossed from 'Belgium' into Britain in search of plunder by invasion (*de bello Gallico* 5.12). Archaeologists are tempted to construct a framework around a few well-known dates, such as Caesar's invasions of *c.* 55 and 54 BC, directly relating archaeology to history in an arbitrary fashion.

The introduction into Britain in the late Iron Age of wheel-thrown pottery has been taken to correspond to the actual migration of people from Gaul, as recorded by Caesar. In addition, several major waves of imported Gallo-Belgic coinage, in particular coins of types A and B[23] dating to the end of the second century BC, may also point to these incursions. There remains the problem of demonstrating that these two phenomena were contemporary or geographically linked before they can be used to substantiate Caesar's comments.

The pottery from the Belgic cemetery sites at Aylesford[24] and Swarling,[25] both in Kent, immediately presents problems. This pottery is different to any previous pottery group found in Britain, not least because it is all wheel-thrown. It also denotes a more highly organised pottery industry. The concept of a ceramic typology again comes to the fore, with the production of vessels of standardized shape such as pedestal urns, cups or tazze, platters, and girth beakers (fig. 20). However, hardly any grave goods from these sites can be dated any earlier than the middle of the first century BC. Despite this some 'early' types have been identified by Birchall. The principal vessel of the 'early' group is the pedestal urn which is characterized by a series of horizontal grooves (fig. 20.1).[26] A related form of pedestal urn also has girth grooving (Birchall Type IX fig. 20.3). Vessels of crude manufacture, with vertical and random scored ornament (Birchall Va), may also belong to this group. The principal early forms do occur elsewhere, though not frequently, as for example at Shoebury (Ia) and Heybridge (Va), both in Essex. By comparison with all the wheel-thrown pottery from burial sites of the Aylesford-Swarling series, the examples for which a pre-Caesarian date can be tentatively advanced are extremely few. They will certainly not fill the ceramic vacuum created at present for, even if they were more numerous, it is doubtful if the sequence of these pottery-types could be extended back to before c. 100 BC, to coincide with the coinage. The apparent absence of 'Belgic' pottery, and for that matter cemeteries, of the late second and early first centuries BC may reflect that the presence of invaders does not necessarily make an immediate impact on the archaeological record. Some time may elapse before new characteristics emerge. Existing indigenous forms of pottery may have been adopted, albeit temporarily, by the immigrant 'Belgic' population in lieu of better wares during the initial stages of settlement. For instance, there exists in south-eastern Britain a series of dumpy pedestal vases and *omphalos*-based bowls whose distribution could be regarded as complementary to that of the coins.[27] The general distribution of this 'Wealden culture' pottery[28] in the Lower Thames Valley and along the south-eastern coast, corresponding to the primary areas of 'Belgic' settlement, is certainly thought-provoking.[29] The archaeologist would do well to reflect upon the number of invasions or large military raids which would pass unnoticed if recognition were solely dependent upon material evidence. Indeed could Caesar's invasions be archaeologically detected, or even suspected, without the written record of the event?

The bulk of the material from the Aylesford-Swarling cemeteries, dated largely by associated metal work, belongs to the period from c. 60 BC onwards. Supplemented by Roman imports, this pottery, therefore, provides a more reliable guide to the dating of contexts belonging to the century following Caesar's raids than to the previous century.

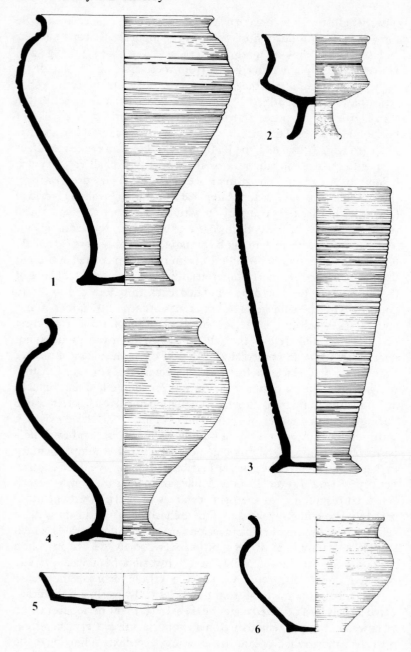

Roman

It has been illustrated that in the Prehistoric period pottery and other artefacts are used to create cultural assemblages that are arranged either sequentially or geographically. In the historic period pottery is still used to construct site and regional chronologies, even where coins or inscriptions may be present. The reason for this is that in Britain inscriptions are not only rare but many, on tombstones and altars, are themselves difficult to date precisely. Normally only building inscriptions, dedications and milestones carry exact dates. Coins often do not occur in sufficient quantities to determine a valid chronology. More importantly the very nature of coins can create fresh problems, with some staying in circulation for great lengths of time.

The life of a coin is determined by its type. Gold and silver coins tended to be used as bullion and their metal value sometimes outweighs their face value in a time of inflation. Base metal coins, on the other hand, could have a very long life. The coins from the theatre at Verulamium,[30] the orchestra of which was used as a rubbish dump at the end of the fourth century, demonstrate this point, giving a clear indication of the coinage in circulation at that time. Out of a total of 2,192 coins only 31 belonged to the House of Theodosius, the rest were all older, including the House of Valentinian (189), House of Constantine (1,445) and the third century and earlier (52). Therefore, only 1.4 per cent of the coins can be used to establish the final date of deposition but in this case it could be even later as there are no more Roman coins found in Britain after the House of Theodosius.

Many important deposits have been erroneously dated by residual coins. For example, a well at Margidunum (an auxiliary fort on the Fosse Way in Nottinghamshire) was published in 1926 by Felix Oswald.[31] The pottery group from this well was dated by Oswald to c. AD 300 on the presence of only two coins, of Tetricus I and Carausius. Following this Philip Corder dated a pottery group at Brough-on-Humber[32] to the Constantian revival, on the basis of two coins of Carausius and one of Tetricus II, in parallel with the material from the

---

Fig. 20 Principal forms of 'Belgic' pottery
1 Pedestal urn with horizontal grooving, Swarling, Kent. (Birchall type 1A)
2 Carinated cup (tazza) with tall pedestal, Welwyn, Hertfordshire
3 Conical urn with horizontal grooving, Swarling, Kent (Birchall type 1X)
4 Plain pedestal urn, Swarling, Kent (Birchall type 1B)
5 Platter with low foot-ring, Watlington, Oxfordshire
6 Necked bowl with low foot-ring, North Leigh, Oxfordshire
Scale 1:4 After Harding

Margidunum well. This date was arrived at even though there were later pottery types in the deposit, which should have belonged to the end of the fourth century. This also demonstrates a tendency among excavators to cling to coin evidence, so that a few sherds of pottery, apparently out of line with the date, can be dismissed as 'intrusions'. The two coins in the well filling had a serious effect on the dating of fourth-century pottery for two or three decades, before it was realized that the coins were either residual or still in circulation and could not provide a *terminus post quem* for the deposit.

Another reason why the earlier date had been favoured was its apparent substantiation of a then widely held historical view of the period. Wheeler had proposed that the decline of urban life in Britain in the third century was so catastrophic that it was followed by only a partial and short-lived revival under Constantius Chlorus before a steady decline into the Dark Ages. A later fourth-century revival seemed out of the question. Even now there are doubts about the great burst of wealth, manifested in large country villas such as Chedworth, Gloucestershire, and Bignor, Sussex, now assigned to the first half of the fourth century.

Although the archaeologist has at his disposal literary evidence, it can often compound the problem of constructing a viable chronology. The literature mentions events, places and people and it can provide a few important dates but often vital details are omitted or long periods glossed over because they are of little interest to the writer from an historical or political point of view (e.g. Tacitus, *Agricola*). Inherent in this is the danger of using archaeological evidence to flesh out bare historical facts. Problems arise when the evidence will not drop into a neat historical framework or when uncomfortable facts are minimised in order to make an hypothesis more acceptable. Some archaeologists have become obsessed with attempts to prove history and provide evidence for the deeds and acts of the Roman Emperors. Unfortunately most archaeological evidence is open to various interpretations and often raises as many questions as it answers. Therefore, when Wheeler dated the rampart at Verulamium to the reign of Hadrian he did so by regarding historical grounds as sounder evidence than the pottery, even though it included Antonine pieces.[33]

THE BOUDICAN REBELLION

One of the main preoccupations of the Roman archaeologist has been to produce the material evidence for great historical events such as the Boudican rebellion of c. AD 60, which happened during the reign of the

Emperor Nero. Neither the event itself nor the basic chronology as laid down by Tacitus can really be disputed, but can archaeology add to the picture? Is there confirmation of the destruction of three Roman cities – London, Colchester and Verulamium (St Albans) – which he describes?

Perhaps the most important ceramic collection so far published is that from Colchester (Camulodunum), in particular the material from the pottery shop which is believed to have been destroyed in the rebellion.[34] This lay in insula 19 of the Roman *colonia*, which had only been founded some twelve years before in *c.* AD 49. Below a layer of burnt daub and wattle, representing the fallen walls of the building, the excavators found masses of broken pottery and glass. The bulk of it consisted of samian imported from southern Gaul (fig. 21.1). The range of forms present was small and so too the list of potters' names found stamped on the vessels. Several names occurred many times, particularly the workshop of *Primus*. Other exotic tablewares were also present, including drinking cups in Lyons ware (fig. 21.2) and *terra rubra* platters which were produced in Gallia-Belgica. The pottery was accompanied by vast quantities of fine glass, much of which had been burnt and distorted by the fire. The site also produced fragments of an extremely rare type of drinking cup in the form of a grotesque head with an open mouth, called a ryton (fig. 21.4). Only six vessels of this form have been recorded from the whole of the Roman Empire. The homogeneous nature of the pottery, the exotic forms present, and the large number of vessels recorded are sufficient evidence to suggest that this had been a pottery shop.

The significance of this group lies in its dating and the fact that it does not represent an isolated phenomenon in Colchester, as similar deposits have been found elsewhere inside the *colonia*, including another pottery shop. The pottery can be dated quite closely, the decorated samian to the pre-Flavian period (i.e. before AD 70, though it is more Neronian than Claudian in character), while the stamped plain vessels cover the period *c.* AD 45–65. A shop can be destroyed by fire at any time due to an accident or deliberate destruction, but in this case, when the other sites are taken into consideration, especially the desecration of a nearby cemetery, it would appear that a large part of the city was destroyed sometime in the Neronian period.

According to Tacitus, after Colchester, the rebels then turned their attention to London, newly founded but already 'an important centre for businessmen and merchandise' (Tacitus, *Annals* XIV). Many inhabitants fled from the city and those who stayed behind were

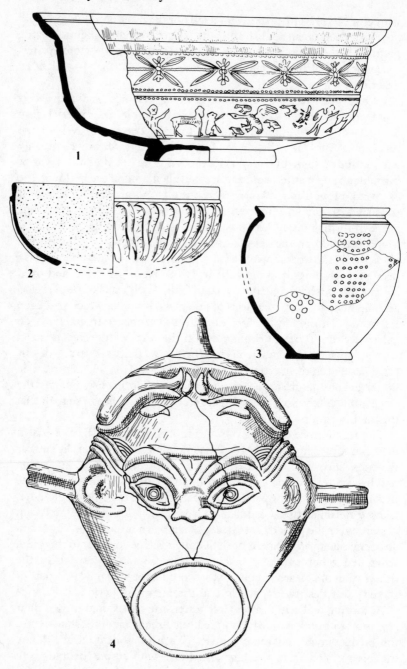

slaughtered. The main evidence for this destruction comes from deposits containing imported pottery – principally the samian, which had been blackened by the fire. A careful study of the pottery[35] revealed that it fell into well-defined chronological groups, relating not just to one but to several large-scale fires which had swept across large areas of the city. One of these, the earliest, may correlate with the destruction by the rebels. As at Colchester buildings consumed by fire, containing Neronian pottery and coins, have been revealed at various sites including Aldgate[36] and St Swithin's House.[37] A similar pattern has emerged at Verulamium on Watling Street, the road taken by the rebels in their pursuit of the Roman army. A large area of the town was destroyed at this time, indicated by a layer, at least a foot thick, of burnt daub and ash. The flames swept along the main street in front of the forum, destroying the shops fronting onto it,[38] but there were no striking discoveries like those made at Colchester. This suggests that most of the inhabitants had time to evacuate and take their portable belongings with them.

The evidence for the sacking of Colchester, London and Verulamium, therefore, rests principally on extensive destruction deposits which can be found at all three sites and dated by associated artefacts, specifically the pottery, to the Neronian period. This evidence can be justifiably related to the rebellion of the Iceni led by Queen Boudica, substantiating the written account of the event as told by Tacitus. Despite this it is unusual to find deposits that can be directly related to historical events. Often buildings are accidentally destroyed by fire (e.g. one building at the Great Casterton villa[39]) and have no relevance to any historical event. The destruction of the forum at Wroxeter in *c.* AD 165 was a much larger and more dramatic event. The so-called 'gutter find' – the remains of the contents of a pottery retailer's shop found buried in the gutter of the street in front of the shop[40] – illustrates the extent of the damage. It is tempting to see serious conflagrations as evidence for rebellion by restless natives with, in this case, an uprising of the tribes of Wales destroying Wroxeter.[41] The archaeological support for this from other sites is, however, rather

---

Fig. 21 **Pottery from the first pottery shop at Colchester, Essex**
1 Samian ware, Drag. 29 bowl
2 Lyons ware cup with applied decoration
3 San Remy lead-glazed ware beaker with barbotine dots below the glaze
4 Ryton or drinking cup in the form of a grotesque human head with a large mouth from which to drink
1–3 scale 1:2; 4 scale 2:3 After Hull

slim. Large fires have been recorded at other towns; Verulamium suffered this fate in c. AD 155[42] and London sometime earlier in the second century.[43] These three fires all occurred at different times, well dated by samian burnt *in situ*, and can all be attributed to accidents like the Great Fire of London in 1666. The Romantic theories of Victorian antiquaries, who readily saw any trace of burning as belonging to some great catastrophe, are no longer credible. Their favourite cause was the great Barbarian Conspiracy of c.AD 367 and the many villas that suffered destruction were considered to be its victims. This idea has since been disproved.[44]

SAMIAN PRODUCTION

For the Roman period pottery is still used to formulate site and regional chronologies on the presence or absence of certain ceramic types. These differing types are rarely taken to indicate cultural or racial differences, but rather chronological, economic or social patterns. In the past too much emphasis has been placed on chronological reasons, particularly relying on the evidence of samian, to indicate when a site was or was not occupied. It has been assumed that some of the Roman forts in Wales were evacuated in the Hadrianic period,[45] mainly depending on the presence or absence of Hadrianic samian in each fort, rather than the structural remains. At the fort of Gelligaer 'the occupation was not prolonged beyond AD 130 or thereabouts'[46] – on the basis of two coins, one of Nerva and one of Hadrian and the evidence of the samian.[47] Implicit in this and similar hypotheses is the assumption that the supply of samian remained at a constant level without any violent fluctuations in quantity, from the Claudian period to the end of the second century, when samian ceased to be imported into Britain. On this assumption the ratio of samian recovered from different periods on a site would be an approximate indicator of the relative densities of occupation.[48]

It is now becoming clear that, far from being a well-organized industry with constant production, development was comparatively haphazard. Production seems to have been a sequence of expansion and collapse, first in Italy with the manufacture of Arretine and then in southern, central and eastern Gaul. These industries did not decline because of rival factories conquering their markets. The industry at Arezzo was apparently falling into decline before La Graufesenque, the main factory in southern Gaul, began to take over its markets. It would appear that the 'home market' was fundamental to survival. In the case of Arezzo, Goudineau[49] has suggested that the crucial sales areas were not the long-distance consumers in the Rhineland but the local market in Italy. The decline in the popularity of the product may have been due to increasing prosperity in Italy, with changing taste demanding metal and glass dinner services rather than pottery ones. The industry contracted to supply a new social level, changing its output to suit new demands. The moulded wares were abandoned but the plain wares, often decorated with appliqué, continued to be produced until the end of the first century. The 'quality' of samian may be more a reflection of hard-headed business decisions than incompetence on the part of the potters.[50]

The same pattern of decline may also apply to La Graufesenque. The use of this samian started to decline in the Mediterranean area during the early Flavian period, while it was reaching its peak in the northern market (fig. 22). Perhaps the collapse of the Mediterranean market eventually led to the total collapse of the industry. The consumers in the north, including the army, may have had little or no control over suppliers, having to chase after a dwindling quantity of samian like everybody else.[51] This may in turn have led to alternative fine-ware production in the Rhineland and Britain. The start of large-scale samian production in central Gaul and at scattered sites in east Gaul does not represent a 'movement' of the industry as such, rather the adaptation of existing pottery manufacture to a different situation. Central Gaul had been producing samian and other fine wares on a limited scale from the Augustan-Tiberian period. The industry was stimulated by some potters migrating from the south.[52] Despite this, central Gaul never matched the output of La Graufesenque and could only recover part of the latter's market-area, while Spain, Italy, North Africa and the south of France were left to local manufacturers or in the case of Aquitaine, nothing at all (fig. 23). Time saw an increase in the quantity produced rather than the area supplied. Lezoux took roughly 30 years to reach its maximum capacity in c. AD 150–65, corresponding with the massive output of the Cinnamus factory, which supplied Britain with approximately one third of all its decorated wares. During the period c. AD 100–120, when La Graufesenque was in decline and central Gaul had only just started mass-producing samian, there was undoubtedly a shortfall in the amount of samian available for purchase. The consumer, whether civilian or military, seems to have had little control over supplies and all were exposed to shortages. From this it follows that the amount of samian appearing on a site of continuous occupation will not reflect the level of consumption but will rather vary according to the output of the kilns supplying the site.

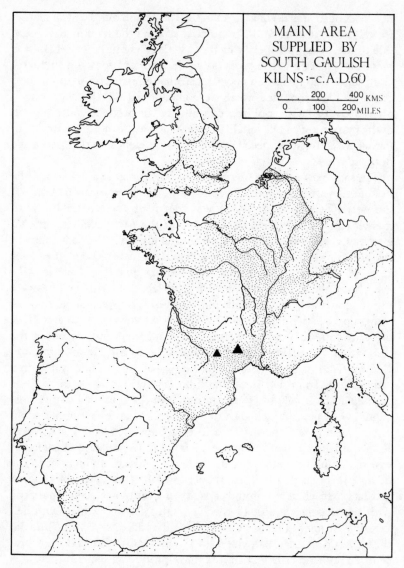

MAIN AREA
SUPPLIED BY
SOUTH GAULISH
KILNS:–c.A.D.60

| 0 | 200 | 400 KMS |
| 0 | 100 | 200 MILES |

Fig. 22 **Main area supplied by the south Gaulish kilns c. AD 60.** *After Marsh*

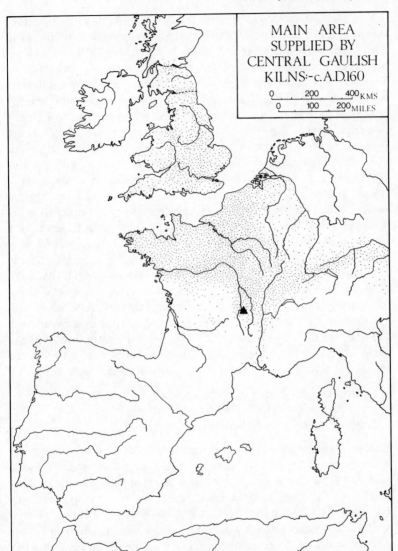

Fig. 23 Main area supplied by the central Gaulish kilns c. AD 160. *After Marsh*

The period c. AD 90–140 presents many problems, when a shortage of samian coincided in Britain with the retreat from the Scottish forts and with the military movements in Wales and northern Britain associated with the establishment of the Hadrianic and Antonine frontiers. At Watercrook, Cumbria, it might be argued from the samian that the fort was abandoned in the Trajanic-Hadrianic period and subsequently reoccupied at a later date. Unfortunately the coins and particularly the coarse pottery indicate the opposite – continuous occupation.[53] There is now no need to argue from the samian evidence for abandonment, given the fluctuating samian supply at this time, if it conflicts with other information. A similar pattern can be illustrated by the material from the fort at Littlechester, Derbyshire, founded in the Flavian period, which has also produced few Hadrianic-early Antonine pieces. This prompted Hartley (1961) to write, 'So there would seem to be a strong probability of a break in occupation or alternatively of a drastically diminished use of the excavated part of the site'.[54] Given the new outlook, continuous occupation might now be argued. Again the danger is revealed of relying too heavily on one class of artefact without integrating the evidence of coins and coarse pottery. At Chesterfield, Derbyshire, the fort was apparently occupied in two successive phases, the first fort dating to c. AD 55/60–80/85 with the second to c. AD 85– early second century. The evidence from the samian would support a Hadrianic abandonment, to provide troops for Hadrian's Wall:

South Gaul, to c. AD 110 – 400 sherds
Les Martres de Veyre, c. AD 100–125 – 4 sherds
Lezoux, c. AD 125 – 1 sherd.

However, there were also large quantities of coarse pottery, especially black-burnished ware I which was not current in the north until after c. AD 125. The site must have occupied after that date, probably at least until c. AD 140 suggesting an evacuation associated not with Hadrian but with the advance into Scotland under Antoninus Pius.

One way to overcome this problem, so that samian can be used as a reliable indicator of site occupation, is to establish a 'supply norm' like that established for coins. The results for individual sites could then be compared against this norm and weighed to give a balanced picture. For example, a sherd of Les Martres de Veyre samian of Trajanic date is likely to be at least three times more significant than an early Flavian sherd. Thus, the samian statistics for sites continually occupied could be calibrated in order to measure the significance of the sherds found.[55]

THE ANTONINE WALL

Unfortunately there are times when the archaeological data clashes with the historical record or epigraphic evidence. Far from substantiating an historical event, doubt can be thrown on its real significance or even its actual occurrence. Much controversy still surrounds the date of the abandonment of the Antonine Wall in Scotland. The evidence from the pottery, particularly the samian, would suggest that the Wall itself and the other forts in Scotland (except Newstead and probably Cappuck) were abandoned shortly after c. AD 160. This conclusion is based on the lack of stamped and decorated samian manufactured by potters thought to have been working in the period 160–200.[56] It is considered that the work of these potters is represented in two very important groups of pottery, the Wroxeter 'gutter' find, mentioned above and the Pudding Pan Rock shipwreck. The latter is from a ship wrecked off the coast of Kent, which was probably destined for the port at London. Material from the wreck has been collected over the years, being gathered off the beach or in more recent times dredged from the river. Neither group can be dated exactly but they both fall within the period c. AD 160–200. The total absence of Pudding Pan Rock stamps and the very low proportion of Wroxeter 'gutter' examples at forts along its course have been taken to indicate that the Antonine Wall was abandoned soon after c. AD 160. Also the most typical late-Antonine forms of plain samian are largely absent from Scotland. This is supported by the lack of stamped mortaria of the period c. AD 160—200 on the Wall, while Gillam has concluded that the course pottery confirms a date of abandonment at this time. The evidence of the samian mortaria and coarse pottery is all in agreement. Despite this, none of the evidence is self-dated but instead relies on a relatively small number of deposits dated and interpreted by highly specialised scholars. A second aspect to emerge from a study of the samien is the likelihood that the Antonine Wall and Hadrian's Wall, plus the hinterland forts, were never held simultaneously, except for the minimum period necessary for the repair of one before the evacuation of the other. This must have been short for there is only a 5 per cent overlap in the distribution of stamps, considering that the same potters would have supplied both walls.

The archaeological evidence is not, however, in complete agreement with the literary and epigraphic record of the later second century. The proposed evacuation of the Antonine Wall in or soon after AD 163, perhaps under the orders of the Governor Calpurnius Agricola, who wished to consolidate the Roman position in northern England, leaves unresolved the question as to which frontier was crossed by the barbarians during the reign of Commodus in c. AD 180. Dio Cassius, in his *History of Rome*, records that the tribes in the island crossed the Wall that separated them from the Roman forts, doing much damage and killing a general and the troops he had with him. Commodus in alarm sent against them Ulpius Marcellus, who ruthlessly put down the barbarians. It would obviously be difficult equating the Wall mentioned by Dio with the Antonine Wall if Scotland was totally unoccupied by Rome.

It may be that it was Hadrian's Wall that was crossed but it seems that only a limited sector, in the vicinity of Halton-Chesters and Corbridge, could have been affected. The destruction at Corbridge might be assigned to this event, thereby relieving the problems posed by the samian in the deposit,[57] and providing corroborative data. This deposit has also been related to a later incident involving a breach of Hadrian's Wall in c. AD 197 but this is now disputed.[58] The evidence from Newstead, in particular the late samian found there, would indicate that the fort was held until the 180s. It may be that Dere Street, with Newstead and Cappuck and perhaps Risingham and High Rochester, formed part of a patrol system on the fringes of Selgovian and Votadinian territory, separating these two tribes and maintaining law and order in the area. This may have been held from the time of Calpurnius Agricola (162–166) down to that of Ulpius Marcellus, Governor of the Province in c. AD 180–184/5. There is further evidence to suggest that Rome did not abandon all her interests in Scotland. Late Antonine samian, with one stamp paralleled in the Wroxeter 'gutter' find, has been found at Castlecary on the Antonine Wall, which is further supported by the inscription on an altar also discovered at the site. The altar, dedicated to Mercury, records the erection of a shrine and statue by soldiers of the *VI Victrix*, who were citizens of Italy and Noricum (Austria). It is this later aspect that is most intriguing, as the most obvious way that these men could have entered the legion was by transfer from the *II Italica*, the one legion of Noricum raised in Italy in c. 165. Only new legions recruited Italians as most entered other military units such as the Praetorian guard or the Urban cohorts. As the inscription mentions both Italians and Noricans the legion must have been stationed in Noricum long enough to recruit local men. Finally, it is unlikely that soldiers could have been spared from the Danube before c. 180. This altar, if correctly dated to after c. 180, does confirm a continuing Roman presence as far north as the Forth-Clyde isthmus

1 Roman pottery vessels that copy metal originals (Cologne, W. Germany): bronze flagon (*rear left*), its pottery counterpart (*rear right*), silver cup (*front left*), a copy in lead-glazed ware (*front right*) (Cologne, W. Germany)

2 Hofheim flagon, mid-first century AD (Leiden, Netherlands)

3 Roman amphorae handle with name-stamp

4 Samian dish, Drag. 18 with name-stamp on the base. The actual stamp used can be seen to the left (Rheinzabern, W. Germany)

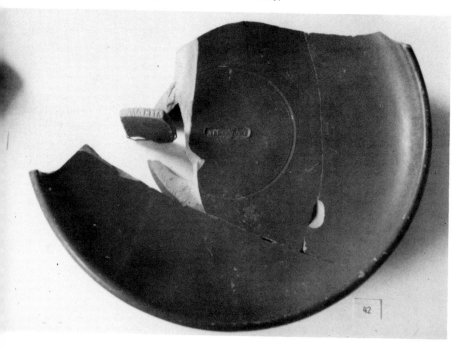

5 Samian beaker with 'cut glass' decoration, mid-second century AD

6 Moulds for producing samian bowls, Drag. 37 (Trier, W. Germany)

7 Face-mask forming the
spout of a late Roman
Oxfordshire flagon
(Wanborough, Wiltshire)

8 Large Roman face-mask
urn (Vienna, Austria)

9 Cologne bag-shaped beakers with roughcast decoration (*left*) and barbotine imbricated scales (*right*), late first-early second century (Nijmegen, Netherlands)

10 A central Gaulish vessel with an appliqué figure, mid-second century (Wanborough, Wiltshire)

11 LEFT A Cologne high-shouldered beaker with barbotine decoration, of foliate design, in a continuous frieze around the pot, mid-late first century AD (Nijmegen, Netherlands)

12 LEFT, BELOW 'Raetian ware' beakers decorated with barbotine 'torcs' (*left*), rouletting (*centre*) and barbotine 'torcs' and incised lines, mid–late second century (Straubing, W. Germany)

13 Cologne 'hunt cup', depicting dogs in pursuit of hares, *c.* AD 160–190 (Copyright: British Museum)

14 LEFT Cologne 'gladiator beaker' depicting a bestiarius (animal fighter) stabbing a bear with a spear, mid-second century (Cologne, W. Germany)

15 LEFT, BELOW 'Gladiator beaker' showing a chariot race. The potter may never have actually witnessed such an event, since he has depicted the charioteer dressed in gladiatorial armour. Mid-second century. From Colchester, Essex (Copyright: British Museum)

16 RIGHT A Cologne lead-glazed ware beaker with barbotine decoration, a hunting scene, under the glaze. Second century AD (Cologne, W. Germany)

17 Two Trier 'Rhenish ware' motto beakers, with messages applied in white paint over the colour-coat, late second-early third century AD (Cologne, W. Germany)

18 Trier 'Rhenish ware' motto beaker, decorated with four medallions which contain human heads, late second-early third century AD (Trier, W. Germany)

19 RIGHT, ABOVE Roman 'rusticated' coarse ware jar (Mainz, W. Germany)

20 RIGHT Two samian bowls, Drag. 37, dating to the second century AD

21 LEFT A Terra Nigra platter copying a samian form, with an imitation name-stamp in the centre. Mid-first century

22 LEFT, BELOW Base of a samian bowl, Drag. 37, with the name of the mould-maker in cursive script, late first-second century AD

23 BELOW A reconstrucion of a Roman potter's wheel at Trier Museum, W. Germany. The base-stone does not appear to have been kicked round, as there are no signs of wear. Instead the two holes cut into the upper surface may have held the tip of a pole used to turn the apparatus

24 Bronze wheel, with a design cut into it, originally mounted on a wooden handle (reconstructed) used to make rouletted decoration (Frankfurt, W. Germany)

25 Whitehill Farm, kiln 6, before the removal of the contents, in this case broken pottery dumped from nearby kilns, late second century AD

26 Whitehill Farm, kiln 6, showing the elongated barrel-shaped oven cut into a deliberately built mound of clay, late second century

27 Whitehill Farm, kiln 2: a section through the interior, revealing a sequence of five different floor levels, seen as bands of burnt clay

28 Reconstruction of a Roman up-draught kiln, showing the raised and pierced floor, under which the fire was set and the covering dome with vent-hole to allow the gases and smoke to escape (Heerlen, Netherlands)

29 BELOW Kiln equipment used in the production of samian: (*rear*) hollow pipes, probably imbedded in the walls of the kiln to circulate the heat and at the same time to prevent the pottery from coming into direct contact with the gases and smoke; (*front*) spacers used for separating the pots during firing (Munich, W. Germany)

during the later part of the second century.

There is further literary evidence to suggest that the Antonine Wall was held after c. 163, in some shape or form. Referring to the northern campaigns of the Emperor Septimius Severus in 209–11, Dio Cassius mentions that 'the Maeatae live close to the wall which divides the island in two and the Caledonians beyond them'. It is known that the Maeatae lived just north of the Forth and so the Wall which they lived beside must have been the Antonine Wall. This, together with the inscription from Castlecary, is the best evidence for the continuing occupation of the Antonine Wall but it is not unequivocal proof for a late date of abandonment. It directly contradicts the evidence provided by pottery, which is unanimous in suggesting a date soon after c. 160 and the lack of epigraphic and numismistic information later than the 180s. The evidence provided by the samian has been challenged by insinuating 'that the supply of samian ware to the whole of northern Britain was drying up'.[59] This, according to Hartley, is 'an hypothesis constructed as special pleading to account for the absence of late Antonine samian ware in Scotland'.[60] After all there is late Antonine samian in Scotland at certain sites. There is samian from Crammond and Carpow (the latter, only occupied in the Severan period, has a legionary supply base for the campaigns of AD 209–11) including central Gaulish ware, even though the factories undoubtedly ceased exporting by the time of the civil war in c. 196–7.

East Gaulish samian, from the factories at Rheinzabern and Trier, was reaching Britain in increasing quantities during the period 160–200, being present at Birrens, Newstead, Cramond and Carpow.[61] If the Antonine Wall was occupied after c. 163, why has it not produced such samian, when sites close to it have? If samian was not available to the Scottish garrisons in sufficiently large quantities, would not a substitute tableware have been found, like Lower Nene Valley colour-coated ware for instance? If so, it is not found in anything like the quantity to be expected. The same is true for the later forms of Cologne colour-coated ware, which are totally absent from the Antonine Wall even though they are common on the Upper German Limes, occupied from c. 160–230. Unfortunately this problem may never be fully resolved but it serves to illustrate the difficulties of matching archaeological data with historical events.

5 Pottery and Trade

For the archaeologist 'trade' has become a general term used to cover the complex process by which certain objects, with specific characteristics, travel considerable distances. The previous chapter has already highlighted the problem of distinguishing the movement of people, including their personal belongings, either peaceably or by force, from the movement of goods by exchange or trade. Part of the problem lies in the fact that it is difficult to show the processes of exchange in archaeological terms. Objects can be moved hundreds of miles from their place of origin or manufacture but it is often impossible to discern why or by what means these objects travelled. Goods may simply have passed from one group of people to another as outright gifts, like a wedding dowry or on the basis of an equal exchange of resources, by swapping goods of comparable value to both parties. A more sophisticated level of exchange is barter or haggling where the parties hope not only to acquire the goods but also to make a profit. Even more complicated is the movement of goods indirectly through a medium of exchange, by using an established currency. A currency has to be acceptable to both sides but can take many forms, from bone-discs and bronze ingots to officially minted coins. All manner of things can serve the purpose but the archaeologist will not necessarily be able to recognise all of them, even if they survive.

The structure of exchange-trade mechanisms is, therefore, complex. In some cases, people obtain goods for their own immediate purposes, in which case the goods have a value in their own right and are not intended to be converted into capital profit or to be used for further trading exploits. This 'subsistence orientated' trade is an extension of domestic production and consumption and there is no reason to assume that it will generate a range of new activities in terms of specialised production. This trade may be carried out seasonally, on trading expeditions with no specialist traders. A more sophisticated pattern of trade is one in which goods are acquired for their 'exchange value', allowing profits to be made either directly or after a series of conversions. This system relies on differences in the evaluation of goods, which can occur with the operation of different rates of exchange or when physical barriers, either geographic or political, separate the parties involved. This situation can promote the activities of the specialist trader – an intermediary operating between different communities. Unlike subsistence orientated trade, such commerce aims to buy and sell goods under the best conditions, enabling the trader to make a profit. The activities demanded – the collecting, transporting and trading of goods – create a specialist role, although it can still be seasonal in practice.

A development in the pattern of trade can stimulate changes in the methods of production. In order to satisfy external trade, craft specialisation increases. The development of the 'market economy' results from the need to redistribute goods on a large scale. The growth of industry and the emergence of towns and cities as centres of industry and trade are the outward signs of a 'civilised' way of life, along with literacy. With craft specialisation, the industrial worker needs to trade for his daily needs, food and other necessities that he no longer has time to produce himself. Trade then reaches all levels of society, with the commercial network supplying products at one end of the scale and at the other the industrial worker reliant on trade for his very existence.

This picture is true of Roman society. Landowners and farmers, by trading their surplus produce, could acquire the manufactured goods and other commodities necessary to sustain the Roman way of life. Only by producing and selling a surplus could they pay either their taxes or their rents. A considerable proportion of the Empire's population lived in towns and the bulk of these people must have been dependent on trade and the manufacturing industries for a living. Trade was vital to the economy as a whole, as a means by which the surplus of the largest wealth-producing activity of the Empire, agriculture, could be transformed into goods, taxes and the other material needs of the Empire. Without an adequate trading system the complex administrative and social structures of the Empire could not have existed.[1] However, despite its obvious importance, trade is rarely mentioned in Roman literature. There are a few records that describe the nature of commerce in perishable commodities or manufactured goods. Some historians have argued that the almost total neglect of commercial affairs by Roman writers is a reflection of the role of trade in the Roman economy. Such a view, in the light of archaeological evidence, cannot really be sustained. Rather the situation reflects the low esteem in which trading was held in Roman society. Traditionally the Roman senatorial class did not directly involve itself in sordid business matters. So it is likely that prevailing social attitudes discouraged literary references to trade. It is only through archaeological evidence that trade, as an important area of the Roman economy, can be demonstrated.

Archaeologically it is virtually impossible to detect all the levels of human behaviour connected with the exchanging and trading of goods. All that remains in the archaeological record is the object itself, whether it arrived there as part of a dowry, in exchange for something else, or purchased with money. In archaeological terms trade between different societies is postulated when objects identified with one cultural assemblage are found associated with artefacts characteristic of another contemporary culture. To use trade as the explanation for the movement of objects, as opposed to other possible reasons, depends on the quantity and quality of the objects and the consistency of their distribution. A small concentrated distribution may indicate the arrival of settlers, while a widespread, uneven distribution may reflect the vagaries of trade. Distribution patterns are also helpful in establishing trade routes (figs 13, 30).

For the archaeologist it is necessary to demonstrate that trade occurred, before it can be understood how and why it took place. For this reason the arguments for trade have relied principally on the movement of artefacts, based on similarities or dissimilarities in their form – whether style, technology or function: are the cultures sufficiently contemporary with each other to allow trade, and which sources of raw material could have been exploited? Objects made from a material not found naturally within the cultural area in which they are distributed may indicate trade. Likely sources of the material may be sought and confirmed either through compositional studies or from supporting evidence of wider exchanges. The compositional approach is being increasingly applied to pottery, as in the case of gabbro ware and Cologne ware discussed below.

The recognition of trade in the archaeological record is, therefore, dependent on the objects traded. As pottery often forms a major part of the surviving evidence for past cultures it can be used to increase our knowledge of the organisation of trade and the economy in general. This is particularly true of societies which have left no written records. Pottery is well suited to the demonstration of trade and marketing patterns, due to its indestructibility and abundance. Various wares can be recognised and characterised with comparative ease, and sources can be identified either scientifically or by comparison with kiln assemblages. Despite this, the archaeologist must remember that an artefact is not necessarily important in the society that produced it merely because it survives in the archaeological record. Pottery was clearly widely traded and had some intrinsic value, but it was a commonplace, mundane object. In many instances it was the contents of the pot, as in the case of Roman amphorae, that were important. Even though some pottery was traded in its own right, it was often accompanied by other, perhaps more important, perishable goods. Despite its lowly position in ancient society, by studying pottery the archaeologist can reveal the existence of a widespread network of trade through which many other types of goods were distributed.

Neolithic

GABBROIC WARE

There is evidence to indicate that Neolithic man exchanged goods and that certain crafts became specialised, including the manufacture of pottery. It has already been shown that in south and south-western England the materials for several types of early Neolithic pottery were obtained some distance from their find-spots. A group clearly imported into Wiltshire is gabbroic ware, characterised by fragments of igneous rock in the clay body which have been traced by petrological examination to the Gabbro, an outcrop which covers about seven square miles of the Lizard Head in Cornwall. This rock weathers in places to form a yellow clay with abundant mineral inclusions and is mineralogically identical with the pottery found in Wiltshire.[2] In the early Neolithic period the vessels produced in this fabric are a stylistically homogeneous group. The principal forms are a simple open bowl with a plain rim (fig. 24.1) and a carinated bowl (fig. 24.2). Both have thin walls and are usually finished with burnishing. A carefully made 'trumpet lug', a tubular handle with expanded trumpet shaped ends, is characteristic of the open bowls (fig. 24.1), while vertically perforated lugs are occasionally found on the carinated bowls.

Although the antecedents of the style are difficult to pin down it represents a tradition which reached south-west England from the Brittany region. The restricted range of forms is important since it precludes distribution of the raw material instead of the finished pots. If the vessels had been made at their find-spots such homogeneity is unlikely to have been maintained, due to the influence of more predominant local styles. This situation is confirmed by the petrology,

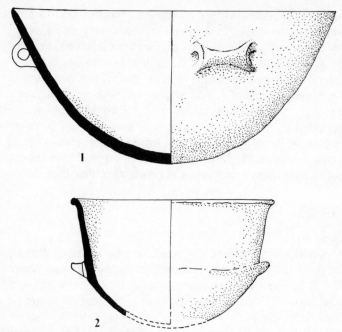

Fig. 24 Early-middle Neolithic gabbroic ware
1 Hembury, Devon
2 Carn Brea, Cornwall
Scale 1:4 After Megaw and Simpson

as the clay never contains intrusive material such as flint which may have been incorporated accidentally had the vessels been made in Wiltshire from imported gabbro clay. It is reasonable to postulate instead that these vessels reached Wessex by trade, as the number of finds negates the suggestion that they were personal items introduced by occasional visitors. The pots themselves support the idea that they were produced by specialists, as in technique they are superior to most other early Neolithic wares. Gabbroic ware influenced the manufacture and development of ceramics further to the east but the local copies of the Cornish imports were less carefully made and sometimes the diagnostic trumpet lugs were reproduced solid rather than hollow as on the original vessels.

Both imported and local vessels occur side by side on sites such as Hembury, Maiden Castle and Windmill Hill. It was at Hembury, Devon, that the style of pottery was first recognised (Hembury F ware) and this name is still used to design the general style. In the Hembury-style assemblage found at Windmill Hill the finer gabbroic ware vessels constitute only a small percentage, the bulk being made up of imitations in oolitic ware, probably from the Bath-Frome region and imitations apparently made locally. So it appears that the style of pottery used in south-west England and over much of Wessex originated in workshops situated in a remote corner of the region, produced by specialist potters, if only on a seasonal basis, and dispersed eastwards along channels of trade where it was repeatedly copied. This proposed system was not, apparently, short-lived but persisted for several centuries. Hembury-style gabbro ware has been recorded in contexts dating approximately to the period 3330–2580 bc.

The distribution of gabbroic ware also indicates that its dispersal may have been linked with that of Cornish stone axes. The flint and hardstone industries were also specialised occupations, again probably on a seasonal basis. Axes, and other stone implements, were apparently regarded as a form of wealth by the people to whom they were a technological necessity. Numerous small hoards of used and unpolished flint axes are common, which may be interpreted as personal possessions buried for safe keeping or as votive offerings. It is possible they were even used as a convenient medium of exchange. The dispersal of axes over extensive areas may have been the result of barter, as it is unlikely that such wide distributions could have been achieved solely by visits to the workshops. In this respect the causewayed enclosures, like those at Hembury, Maiden Castle and Windmill Hill, may have acted as tribal or communal 'foci', meeting places where people could exchange goods as well as perform social and religious ceremonies. This would explain the great variety of pottery and axes found at such sites.

PETERBOROUGH WARE

The social and economic pattern in the late Neolithic period becomes increasingly complex as native ceramic traditions flourished alongside the completely new Beaker pottery, brought by people migrating from the Continent. The development of this pottery, and of indigenous grooved ware, has already been mentioned as representing in both cases one aspect of a distinctive late Neolithic culture. But contemporary Peterborough pottery is quite different in character. This name has been given to a sequence of styles that are chronological rather than regional. They appear to represent a ceramic tradition with continuity through a typological sequence, rather than one which is associated with any specific culture. Three main styles have been defined, called

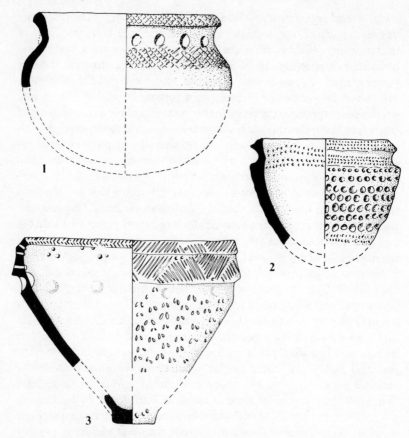

Fig. 25 The Peterborough tradition
1 Ebbsfleet style. Example from Ebbsfleet. *After Piggott*
2 Mortlake style. Example from West Kennet, Wiltshire. *After Megaw and Simpson*
3 Fengate style. Example from West Kennet. *After Megaw and Simpson*
Scale 1:4

Ebbsfleet, Mortlake and Fengate (fig. 25). Initially the three styles follow one after another, but latterly all were contemporary. This stylistic classification, supported by radio-carbon dates and stratigraphic evidence, only applies to southern Britain as far north as Yorkshire and even within this area there are regional variations of the style. Its antecedents can also be sought in this area, as the style seems to have developed from the earlier regional types of pottery associated with the Windmill Hill Culture of southern Britain.

The earliest style, Ebbsfleet, emerged in and around the Lower

Thames Valley, apparently deriving from the earlier local wares. The typical form is a necked bowl with a rounded base, sometimes with an 'S'-shaped profile or otherwise with a sharp carination (fig. 25.1). The subsequent Mortlake style continued the tradition of the round-based bowl but the vessels were clumsily made and poorly fired compared to earlier examples. Rim forms become increasingly elaborate, with the development of an internal bevel or ledge which was lavishly decorated (fig. 25.2). In the final stage, the Fengate style, the vessels continue to be poorly fired and thick walled but the profile changes. The developed rim forms, first seen on Mortlake style pots, become even more exaggerated. The rim evolves into a collar, or overhanging rim, invariably with an internal rim bevel. The body becomes conical in shape with a flat narrow base, often disproportionately small in relation to the width, so the vessels look top heavy (fig. 25.3).

The Peterborough series is not associated solely with any specific types of monuments or artefacts. The majority of the associations are related to the Windmill Hill cultural grouping. The pottery has been found, though usually in a secondary context, at causewayed enclosures. At Combe Hill and White Hawk, Ebbsfleet ware was associated with the primary silting of the ditches and at the latter site it was in fact the only pottery represented in a primary context.[3] Seven earthen long barrows have produced Peterborough ware, with again only the Ebbsfleet style connected with a primary deposit, and in no case related to the actual burial beneath the mound. It occurs in secondary contexts in nine chambered tombs but there is no indication that the makers of the later styles of Peterborough ware were responsible for the construction of these monuments, even though continued interest is implied. The flint and stone associations with the Peterborough series reinforce the concept that this pottery forms a tradition rather than a distinctive archaeological culture. The distribution of the pottery reflects the dynamic expansion and development of this ceramic tradition, which contrasts with the apparently static nature of other late Neolithic decorated wares.[4] A comparison with the distribution of grooved ware (fig. 16) indicates that Peterborough ware does not observe its territorial limits but extends right across them except in the extreme north, thus demonstrating that the pottery could cross cultural divisions and that it cannot be related to any particular group of people.

The widespread distribution, taken with the gradual loss of cultural status of the later styles of Peterborough ware, may indicate a change in the organisation of pottery production at this time.[5] Perhaps the development of a new fashion for decorated bowls, which arose in the area of the Lower Thames Valley and subsequently spread, reflects an organised industry. Peterborough ware may be likened to the gabbroic ware of the early Neolithic period – a specialist product, traded over long distances and even imitated by other potters producing regional sub-styles. However, the emergence of Peterborough ware could also be interpreted as reflecting a socio-economic change. A great deal of this pottery has been found in rivers or in pits dug in their banks. The frequent use of bird bones to decorate the vessels suggests the importance of wildfowl as a source of food to the potters. The predominance of cattle amongst the bones of domestic species from sites, and the varied conditions under which Peterborough ware is found, may imply a nomadic pastoral society whose way of life discouraged the construction of large ceremonial or funerary sites or even substantial domestic sites. However, this does not account for the lack of other diagnostic artefacts associated with the later styles of Peterborough ware. All that can be definitely stated at the moment is that Ebbsfleet represents one element of earlier Neolithic society, Mortlake and Fengate represent elements of later Neolithic society, but there was no Peterborough culture as such.

There is plenty of evidence for the trading of goods in the late Neolithic and Bronze Age but this largely relates to the stone axe factories and metal working. It is not until the Iron Age that specialization in pottery production and the trading of pottery is again clearly seen. The manufacture of fine pottery was a specialist craft by the first century BC and in some regions specialization probably dates back to the fourth century or even earlier. Some degree of commercial manufacturing does not preclude domestic production and it is likely that a large percentage of the local early Iron Age coarse wares were home-made. By the second and first centuries BC even the plainer and simpler vessels take on a mass-produced appearance, suggesting that 'commercial enterprise was now dominant'.[6]

Iron Age

GLASTONBURY WARE

In the late Iron Age the communities of south-western Britain used a range of ceramics, including very distinctive, highly decorated bowls and jars, which are referred to as Glastonbury ware. A petrological study of the fabrics in which this pottery occurs has distinguished six regional groups, each group characterised by a different parent rock ranging from the gabbro of the Lizard Head to the carboniferous limestone of the Mendips.[7] Once again it is clear that Glastonbury ware is in reality a ceramic style rather than a homogeneous type. It is also clear that a number of different production centres must have been in operation but these were not necessarily contemporary. The origins and development of this style are extremely difficult to trace, largely due to the lack of well stratified deposits. It is probable that Glastonbury style pottery began to be produced locally in Cornwall, perhaps as early as the third century BC, influenced by styles current at this time in Brittany.[8] The bowl form, with its internally grooved rim and elements of the curvilinear decoration (fig. 9.3) are techniques which suggest an origin somewhere in the Amorican peninsula, but there is no evidence for the actual importation of pottery.[9]

Skilled potters may have settled in the Lizard area and manufactured vessels in the local gabbro clay for the neighbouring communities which had previously been virtually aceramic. Unfortunately few sites have produced any reliable evidence for the subsequent development of the style. At Castle Dore, Cornwall, a plausible sequence can be constructed starting with early decorated ware from the Lizard and continuing into the first century BC, when it was superseded by cordoned ware. The latter is characterised by wheel-made necked jars, tazza-like bowls and large jars, all ornamented with horizontal cordons, sometimes combined with grooves, which also appear to have derived from Amorican ceramics. At Castle Dore, cordoned ware could be shown to be chronologically later than Glastonbury style pottery. Throughout Cornwall cordoned ware traditions generally flourished into the Roman period.

The development of Glastonbury ware in Somerset need not have followed the same course as in Cornwall. Early Cornish wares were imported into Somerset but it is possible that local production of the style began somewhat later. At the other end of the spectrum, it would appear that in Devon and Somerset the Glastonbury style continued in use for several decades longer than in Cornwall and may even have flourished until the time of the Roman occupation. Peacock's study of the Glastonbury wares implies that within a restricted area specialist potters were at work at several different centres, supplying pottery to the communities in the region. Only in the case of Group I, the gabbroic ware, is there any evidence of widespread trade, with some vessels in this category reaching Devon, Somerset, Hampshire and

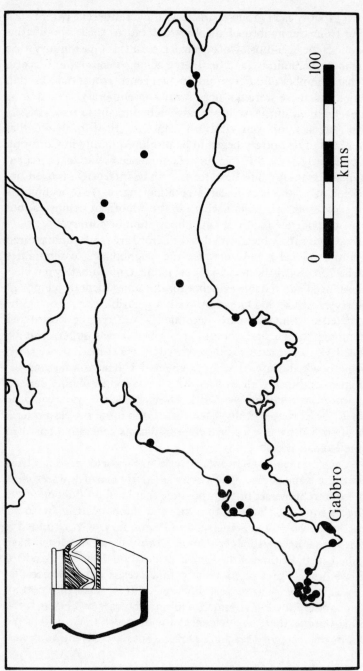

Gabbro

Fig. 26 Distribution of Group 1 Glastonbury ware. *After Cunliffe*

Northamptonshire (fig. 26). It may be that the Cornish ware was the prototype subsequently imitated on a local basis in many different fabrics.

Since Peacock's examination the distribution of Glastonbury ware has been explained in terms of commercial, rather than tribal or cultural, factors. This view has been disputed by Blackmore, Braithwaite and Hodder.[10] The aim of this study was to examine in great detail the distributions of specific motifs found on Glastonbury pottery and to see what light these could shed on the production and dispersal of the pottery. Thirty-four decorative design elements and their regional distributions were selected. Spatial analysis was used to provide information about patterning and associations between the distributions of different motifs. The results indicated that there were no discrete distributions, i.e. no traits found in completely separate areas without overlapping. However, two distinct distribution structures did emerge. The first consisted of localised distributions in the 'core' area of south Somerset, the second was more widespread, but with the same centre, spreading from south Wales to Maiden Castle and Hengistbury Head in Dorset. The more widespread distributions were mainly of simple geometric rectilinear designs, while the more localised group included many curvilinear designs, the traditional hallmark of the Glastonbury style. This distributional hierarchy could have been due to commercial factors, with local low-value wares highly decorated with curvilinear designs, and the more widespread trade of high-value wares with simpler geometric designs. The authors ruled out commercial value as no correspondence could be found between the decorative motifs and Peacock's petrological groups. Instead, complete cross-cutting between style and petrology was found. This evidence, they conclude, did not lend support to the idea that a few separate production centres were making their own types of pottery and distributing them to different marketing areas. Also Peacock's distribution maps of the petrological groups did not indicate the 'core and wider' distribution pattern. Very localised and distinctive motifs occurred at one site only or at two or three neighbouring sites. It would be difficult to equate this type of localised use with centralised production and dispersal.

On this evidence the authors returned to the cultural approach, that the distribution was controlled by ethnic rather than commercial factors. However, they do not specify whether they favour a return to the household production model or if they envisage that marketing was controlled by tribal groupings. They conclude that the core area of the distribution pattern, centred on south Somerset, represents a group of people who were conscious of their identity, in other words a cultural or tribal grouping. The classic Glastonbury designs are found in the 'home area', while the less distinctive motifs were used peripherally, perhaps diluted by contact with other tribal groupings. They use the pottery to indicate territorial boundaries, implying that in this case material culture is an expression of tribal identity.

This study of Glastonbury ware is based on the misconception that typological analysis is an alternative to fabric study.[11] In fact the two are complementary, each providing information with a different bias, with fabric indicating the source of raw materials and the techniques of potting, while form and decoration relate to function and the influence of tradition and new fashions. The fabric is also an essential indication of tradition since 'it is less susceptible to ephemeral influences as basic technological recipes will not be changed lightly'.[12] From this it follows, when interpreting ceramic data, that greater weight should be given to the fabric. It is more profitable to study the petrological groupings and then the typology within the fabric framework. Blackmore, Braithwaite and Hodder failed to do this, conducting their spatial analysis across the petrological groups. It is true that many decorative motifs are common to several groups but the study of individual elements of the ornament in isolation is liable to blur rather than clarify the subtle distinctions that certainly exist.[13] For example there are distinct differences in the frequency with which decorative traits occur and also in the techniques used in their execution. Thus hatched triangles are common to several groups but there are clear differences in the way they were produced.

Blackmore, Braithwaite and Hodder concentrate on Glastonbury ware in the Somerset region. The distribution of Peacock's Group 2, characterised petrologically by Old Red Sandstone, Group 3 by Mendip Limestone and Group 4 by Jurassic Limestone, all centre on Somerset. The 'core and wider' distribution pattern may apply to these groups but it is hard to see how Group 1 (Gabbro) and Groups 5–6 (Fermian with Sanidine and Permian) with their Cornish-Devon distribution, relate to it (fig. 26). If Somerset Glastonbury ware is thought to represent an expression of tribal identity its relationship with neighbouring Cornish Glastonbury ware must be established. There is no need to attribute the 'core and wider' distribution pattern entirely to ethnic differences, as commerce could easily be influenced by cultural groupings. Durotrigan black-burnished ware, a contemporary type of pottery, has been shown to relate to a distinctive tribal grouping centred on Dorset. After the Roman conquest of Britain, the same forms continued to be made and used locally by the indigenous natives. The ware was exported beyond Dorset, particularly to the south-west, perhaps distributed by coastal trading and occurs on Roman military installations at Exeter, Devon and Nanstallon, Cornwall. A restricted range of forms is present at these sites, suggesting that the more traditional forms manufactured to meet local demand did not find favour with the military market. The 'core and wider' distribution pattern need not be equated with lower (home) and higher (export) value wares but rather indicates that the more culturally distinctive wares found favour with the 'home' market, while less characteristic wares could be more widely traded. Both types of pottery could even have been manufactured by the same potters, who may have simply aimed their products at different sections of the market. In this way tribal traditions could determine how goods were traded. Moreover, Peacock never implied that one petrological group represents a single workshop, as a good source of clay could have been exploited by a number of neighbouring workshops. This in itself may account for the 'core and wider' distribution pattern, as potters working in proximity to each other could sell their products in very different places.

In conclusion it is possible for pottery to be made along traditional lines and still be produced and traded commercially. Somerset Glastonbury ware may be equated with the tribe of the Dobunni, whose coins place their territory in Gloucestershire extending into Somerset down to the Mendips, north and west Wiltshire, and west Oxfordshire. Within this area a twofold division can be traced in the native pottery of the first century BC.

North of the Bristol Avon the principal types include jars and saucepan pots which recent petrological examination[14] has demonstrated were manufactured in the Malvern area and exported widely – east to the Cotswolds and west to the Welsh borderlands. Four different groups were defined by Peacock's study, each group characterised by a different filler present in the clay (A- Malvernian, B I & II-Limestone, C-Landovery sandstone). The forms belonging to all four groups, while generally similar, were shown to have distinctive features and some degree of differential distribution was also observed. The implication seems to be that within one culturally related area potters were at work in at least four places, supplying the ceramic needs of the communities living within a 50–80 mile radius of the production centres.[15] In the north Somerset region, on the other hand, the inhabitants preferred Glastonbury ware. At first sight this appears to negate the suggestion that Glastonbury ware was an expression of tribal identity but in the last two decades before the Roman invasion of AD 43 the tribal territory of the Dobunni appears to have been split between two ruling houses. Comux, followed by Bodvoc, controlled Gloucestershire and west Oxfordshire, while Corio remained dominant in northern Somerset. The numismatic evidence, taken with the similar internal division in pottery styles, would indicate that both areas retained a separate identity throughout the late Iron Age. So, even within a politically defined tribal area, cultural or social divisions could still be present.

It is still necessary to establish the relationship between the Glastonbury ware used by the Dobunni in Somerset and that by the Dumnonii, the tribe occupying Cornwall and Devon. What this represents in cultural terms is difficult to say but at the very least it must reflect social or commercial contact between the two areas.

Late Iron Age

Trading contacts between Britain and the adjacent continent seem to have intensified after *c.* 100 BC. Strabo and Caesar expressly refer to cross-Channel trade controlled by the Amorican tribe called the Veneti, with whom some of the British communities maintained close diplomatic relations. The Dumnonii in Cornwall and Devon were linked both commercially and politically with the area, if Caesar's statement that the Amoricans summoned reinforcements from the adjacent coast of Britain at the time of the Roman conquest in 56 BC is accepted. The archaeological evidence reinforces this connection with the demonstrated links between the local Cornish ceramics, Glastonbury ware and Cordoned ware, with those in Brittany.

These contacts are further emphasised by the appearance in and around Hengistbury Head, Hampshire (in the tribal area of the Durotriges), one of the principal ports in the south-west, of typical Amorican and Norman pottery, in particular the characteristic graphite coated vessels and elegant wheel-made cordoned vessels referred to in this country as Hengistbury class B ware.[16] In Britain the distribution of these exotic types clusters around Hengistbury Head. Trade through the port is also demonstrated by the appearance of a rare type of wine amphorae, Dressel Type 1A, which was used for transporting Italian wine. Several have been recorded at Hengistbury Head and isolated examples from Green Island (Poole harbour), Dorset and from Ventnor on the Isle of Wight. Otherwise the type is unknown in Britain and furthermore has not been recorded in Brittany. This suggests that shiploads of Italian wine were brought direct to southern Britain, via the Atlantic sea route, bypassing the Venetic middlemen. One load at least foundered and sank off Belle-Ile, Morbihan, where the wreck complete with cargo still lies.[17] The Roman conquest of Gaul in the mid-first century BC, particularly the savage reprisals against the Veneti and other maritime tribes, seems to have curtailed this cross-channel trade. At Hengistbury Head and neighbouring sites in Dorset, a few examples of the latter Dressel 1B amphorae have been found but as these were coming into use in the years immediately prior to Caesar's campaigns they do not in themselves necessarily imply that trade continued after the mid-fifties. Present evidence suggests that after Caesar destroyed the Venetic fleet the south-west was denied direct commercial outlets to the Roman world.

In contrast, the last hundred years before the Claudian conquest in AD 43 saw the development of a lively trade between south-eastern Britain and Roman Gaul. During the second half of the first century BC, Italian wine was imported in large quantities, as the widespread occurrence of Dressel Type 1B amphorae demonstrates. Along with wine came the tablewares appropriate to its consumption, notably the bronze jugs and cups found in the burials at Aylesford and Welwyn, Herts, which were imported from the Ornavasso region of northern Italy between 80 and 10 BC. In return a wide range of British goods were exported, 'corn, cattle, gold, silver, hides, slaves and hunting dogs' as listed by Strabo. From c. 10 BC until the conquest, the volume of trade appears to have increased. During this period the wheel-thrown pottery, thought to have been initially introduced by 'Belgic' settlers, continued to be produced until after the invasion. In its latest phase 'Belgic' ware is characterised by the addition of new forms to the repertoire, like the butt beaker (fig. 4.5) and shallow platter (fig. 20.5). The butt beaker is a particularly distinctive vessel form, with a barrel-shaped body which is normally divided by horizontal grooves and cordons into a series of panels often filled with vertical combing (fig. 4.5).

The introduction of the butt beaker, together with girth beakers (fig. 4.3) and other forms derived from Gallo-Belgic originals (plate 21), is generally attributed to the period after 15 BC, based on the premise that Rome signed a treaty with Tincommius, King of the Atrebates, which promoted trade between Britain and Roman Gaul.[18] Stevens concluded that by 15 BC the Atrebates were *clientes* and that the importation of Continental fine wares, such as Gallo-Belgic ware and Arretine ware, should be dated from this time. The traditional view of this treaty is that it was an alliance between Tincommius and Rome against the Catuvellauni. Had the treaty been negotiated solely with the Atrebates, it follows that the initial imports should be concentrated in Sussex and Hampshire, their tribal area, only later spreading north of the Thames. In fact the distribution of Arretine ware in Britain follows a converse pattern, with the principal area of imports situated north of the Thames, even into Gloucestershire and East Anglia, basically corresponding to the heartland of Catuvellaunian territory. The Catuvellaunian tribal centre at Wheathampstead was abandoned at about this time, with the move to Verulamium (St Albans). Wheeler's excavations at Wheathampstead revealed neither butt beakers nor platters, which presumably means the *oppidum* was occupied before the introduction of Gaulish wares following the treaty with Rome. At Verulamium, the new tribal capital, butt beakers, girth beakers and Arretine platters are all represented.[19]

Early in the first century AD, under King Cunobelinus, the capital of the joint kingdom was moved to the Trinovantian centre at Camulodunum (Colchester). By this time Arretine and samian were being imported in increasing quantities. The sources varied – from workshops at Arezzo, Puteoli and the environs of Rome in Italy, to Lyons, Lezoux and La Graufesenque in Gaul, indicating a broad trading network. Hawkes has even postulated that the move to Camulodunum may have been in response to the need for a major port on the east coast to handle the increasing volume of foreign trade. The presence and purchasing power of the Roman armies in the Rhineland were creating a large demand for merchandise in the north. At Colchester, which has produced the largest collection of early Arretine and samian from any British site, so much of the pottery can be paralleled at Haltern (one of the forts built on the river Lippe by Drusus during the campaign east of the Rhine and occupied from 11 BC to AD 16) that direct trade between Britian and the Rhineland must have already begun. Local copying of the imports also occurred, particularly the Gallo-Belgic platters and beakers, which were themselves derived from the imported Italian and Gallic tablewares and produced in Gallia Belgica and the Rhineland in response to the demands of the occupying army (plate 21). Perhaps even more surprising is the evidence from Skeleton Green, Herts, suggesting that a Roman trading post had been established there by c. AD 10.[20] Although it only had a brief existence, it is hard to imagine it existed in an atmosphere hostile to Rome.

It can be seen that imported goods, far from being restricted to the territory of the Atrebates, occur widely in south-eastern Britain and trade was not apparently controlled by a single tribe. It might be that 'free trade', organised by enterprising, freelance merchants was little affected by political treaties. On the other hand, the Catuvellauni may not have been considered to be the enemy of Rome and an alliance was made with both the Atrebates and the Catuvellauni.[21] A treaty with both British kingdoms would have been more advantageous to Rome, creating wide commercial possibilities north of the Thames.

Roman

FINE WARES

The Roman invasion of AD 43 increased the level of trade between Britain and the Continent, as an army of about 50,000 men had to be supplied and maintained. The years after the conquest saw a flood of imported fine wares, south Gaulish samian and colour-coated drinking vessels. The development of the Gallic samian industry has been seen in terms of a gradual move north of the production areas, from Italy to East Gaul, due to the insatiable demand of the cities and armies of the Rhineland. Therefore, the eventual areas of production mirrored the areas of maximum demand.[22] This view has been modified in recent years by the discovery of Augustan kilns at Lyons and at other sites such as Pisa, revising the idea of a straight move from Arezzo to La Graufesenque in southern Gaul.

The situation was far more complicated, with the development of branch industries in Gaul, perhaps initially in response to the demand of the military market in the Rhineland and the expected campaigns east of the Rhine. Samian of Italian type was produced at Lyonasse near Lyons as early as 30 BC. This was succeeded by an industry at La Mutte on the bank of the Saône, producing wares almost identical to Arretine, made in imported and local moulds by Italian potters, and supplying quantities of samian to Haltern. Fine ware beakers of ACO type, again almost identical to Italian vessels, with relief-moulded decoration, created by the potter ACO and usually signed with his name, were also made at La Mutte. Vegas has demonstrated, with a distribution map of ACO beakers made in North Italy and at Lyons, that the products of the latter workshop largely went to the military installations on the Lower German and Upper Danube frontier.[23] However, the industry seems to have declined in the Tiberian period, c. AD 25, probably due to the growth of factories at La Graufesenque and other south Gaulish sites.

The industry at Lyons did not recover until the late 30s and 40s, at a time of renewed military expansion which saw the construction of many new forts on the Rhine and the extension of the Upper Danube frontier to the line of the river. It is probably no coincidence that the expansion of the Lyons colour-coated industry occurred at the same time as Caligula's plans for further conquests in Germany and Britain. Yet samian production did not recommence at Lyons, due no doubt to the strength of the south Gaulish industry. If, as seems likely, the Lyons industry was connected with the northern military market, and was eminently well placed to do so, what was the purpose of the potteries at Montans, La Graufesenque and Lezoux which were started some 20–30 years later? Both Montans and La Graufesenque are further south, away from the northern markets. Hofmann[24] has argued that each was taking a certain market area, La Graufesenque to southern France and Spain, Montans to Aquitaine, and Lezoux to north-west France. If this was initially so, the situation did not last for long, for by the Claudian period La Graufesenque had totally outstripped Montans and Lezoux. Even more strange is the collapse of Lyons which was in a far better geographical position than La Graufesenque to supply northern France and the Rhineland.[25] The latter was situated in a totally unsuitable location for trade, hemmed in by the Cevennes to the north and apparently only partially interested in the markets of Aquitaine. Instead the main outlet route appears to have been south by 70 miles of road to the coast of Narbonne. If La Graufesenque had been originally intended to supply the Mediterranean market the situation soon changed, for by c. AD 16 its products were reaching Vindonissa, Switzerland. The industry eventually supplied a vast area, from North Africa to Britain, probably exploiting the old trade routes of Arezzo and Lyons. The next 80–90 years of production saw little change in the area supplied. Instead the real expansion was in quantity. At its peak in c. AD 60–80 the output was emormous, reaching hundreds of thousands of vessels a year.

The establishment of these potteries in Gaul was probably undertaken or encouraged by *negotiatores*. In the late Republican-early Imperial period the role of the *negotiator* gradually changed from a purely monetary backer of all manner of activities to one more closely engaged in actual commerce. In the mid-first century these men were not actively involved in the details of trade, which were handled by their agents, *mercatores* and guilds of *nautae*, sailors. The founding of branches of well-known Italian industries in Gaul was financially attractive to such men. Although it was expensive to move and re-equip the potters, this was soon offset by sales to the military market and, in the longer term, by sales to the increasingly Romanised households of Gaul. The military authorities could at the same time be assured of the availability of basic supplies for the newly founded garrisons, at lower prices than direct imports from Italy. This does not imply direct military contracts. The army and the State relied heavily on independent merchants and did everything to enable them to operate freely.[26] It is now thought that the army did not supply pottery directly to the troops, except in the case of military workshops, but nevertheless had to ensure that it was available. Good profits for *negotiatores* were probably the best incentive for the creation of plentiful supplies, whether Arretine to Augustan forts in Germany or black-burnished ware to Hadrian's Wall.

The fine wares that reached Britain came, ultimately, through the activities of *negotiatores*. However, the cargoes that travelled by the tributaries and large rivers of Gaul before being loaded into ocean-going vessels were probably never seen by the men who financed them. Many other loads may have been the joint efforts of *mercatores* sharing space in composite cargoes. The pottery will have been brought from local markets or direct from the kilns by agents of *negotiatores* or by *mercatores*. The potters themselves may have been unaware of the destination of their products and it was probably of little concern to them, as they were often slaves or freedmen running workshops on the land of rich aristocrats. The existence of 'contracts' between the army and the kiln sites would, therefore, be unlikely. Any connections would have been with the *negotiatores*, whose expertise and finance were undoubtedly used by the government.

SAMIAN

Samian with moulded decoration was made in a surprisingly restricted range of forms, only a few of which are at all common. Plain forms are more numerous, with about twenty main types. The carinated bowl, Drag 29, is associated with the early years of the occupation of Britain, from 43–70 (fig. 27.29). This form went out of use in c. 85 to be replaced by the hemispherical bowl, Drag 37 (fig. 27.37; plate 20) which continued into the third century. The only other common bowl, Drag 30, (fig. 27.30) was made throughout the first and second centuries, although always relatively less abundant than 29 and 37. The undecorated Drag 15/17, (fig. 28) a dish with internal quarter-round moulding at the junction of the base and wall, largely dates to the Claudio-Neronian period. Two main types stand out, the shallow

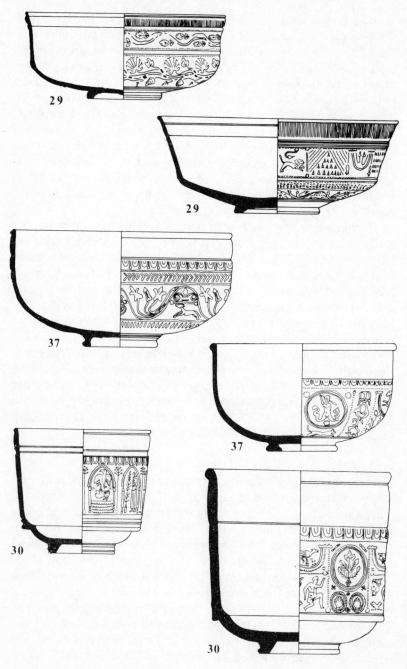

29

29

37

37

30

30

15/17 and the deeper 15/17R, with a rouletted circle on the floor. This was superseded in the Flavian period by Drag 18, a simple dish with a beaded rim, again subdivided according to the absence or presence of a rouletted circle on the floor. This form developed gradually into the 18/31 and 18/31R, which are characteristic of the first half of the second century, finally evolving into the 31 and 31R (fig. 28). By then the vessel had become so deep that it might be more correctly termed a bowl. This form is particularly common in late Antonine deposits. Cups are more prominent in the repertoire than beakers. Drag 24/25 dates to the first century, almost entirely to the pre-Flavian period (fig. 28). The commonest first-century cup, Drag 27, made until the middle of the second century, was gradually overtaken in popularity by Drag 33 (fig. 28). The latter also appeared in the first century, becoming the most common cup form during the second century. Two forms important in the late second century were Drag 38, a flanged bowl, which was frequently imitated in non-samian fabrics and Drag 45, the commonest samian mortaria, with its spout moulded separately in the form of a lion's or bat's head (fig. 28).

COLOUR-COATED WARE

As well as samian, many of the workshops produced colour-coated wares – mainly cups and beakers. The latter were not particularly well represented in samian. Often, as at La Graufesenque and Trier, they were made in the same fabric as, or a very similar fabric to, the samian but with a dark colour-coating. Moulded and non-moulded vessels were produced, the latter often elaborately decorated with appliqué and barbotine designs (plate 10). Fine-ware cups and beakers should not be viewed as a cheaper alternative to samian but rather as vessels with a specialized purpose. It is generally assumed that they were primarily used for drinking, as borne out by the use of vine leaves and bunches of grapes as decorative motifs.

Such drinking vessels continued to be made up to and beyond the end of the major samian industries in the third century AD. It was only when the industry started to decline and exports were reduced, that the range of colour-coated fine wares began to expand, to include flagons, bowls and dishes, in order to replace samian as an all-purpose

---

Fig. 27 **Common decorated samian forms**

Upper 29 Claudio-Neronian, south Gaulish

Lower 29 Flavian, S.G.

Upper 37 Flavian, S.G.

Lower 37 Antonine, central Gaulish

Upper 30 Flavian, S.G.

Lower 30 Antonine, C.G.

Scale 1:4 After Hartley

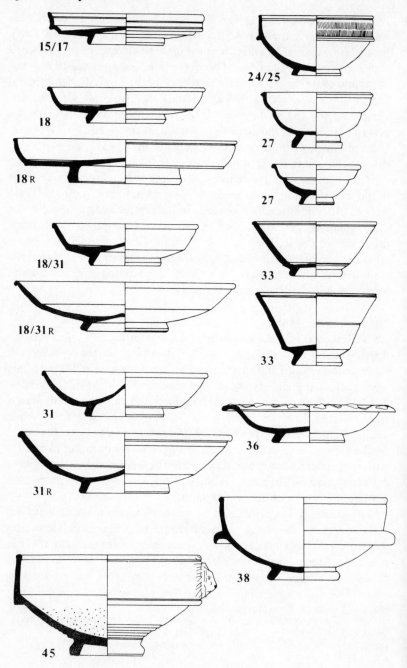

tableware. Prior to this the two types of tableware were largely interdependent. However, colour-coated fine wares were not exclusively produced by samian potters. At some centres, like Cologne, they were manufactured alongside coarse wares, such as flagons, mortaria and other kitchen wares.

LYONS FINE WARE

In the pre-Flavian period the main producer of colour-coated fine wares was Lyons. This is a very distinctive ware, made of clay as fine as samian but usually pale cream in colour with a dark-greenish brown lustrous colour-coating. The standard products were small hemispherical cups and beakers with a high rounded shoulder and everted rim (fig. 29).[27] All Lyons vessels were decorated in some way, if only with simple roughcast sand. A wide range of decorative schemes was used on the cups but all these designs were applied free-hand using plastic clay, as opposed to the barbotine method used on contemporary vessels from Gaul, Spain, Italy and the Lower Rhineland. Particularly distinctive are the vessels decorated with 'raspberry roundels' (fig. 5.5), imbricated scales, (figs 5.4, 29.4) and 'hair pins' or gadroons. The beakers rarely have any form of decoration other than roughcast, made with fine sand on small vessels and coarse sand on the larger ones (fig. 29.5).

The distribution of Lyons ware (fig. 30) reflects the general market area of the industry, with heavy concentrations in Britain and the Rhineland due no doubt to the large military garrisons stationed in both areas.[28] In France the lack of publications may make the map unrepresentative but contemporary Lezoux products may have monopolised the market in central Gaul. The absence of Lyons ware in Gallia Narbonensis and southern Aquitainia seems certain. So the map may be taken as a reliable indication of the principal markets of the Lyons industry, namely the Rhineland, Raetia and Britain.[29] Lyons ware was outstandingly successful. In Britain it cornered 83 per cent of

---

Fig. 28   Common plain samian forms

15/17 pre-Flavian, S.G.	Upper 27 Claudian, S.G.
18 pre or early Flavian, S.G.	Lower 27 Hadrianic-Antonine, C.G.
18 R pre or early Flavian, S.G.	Upper 33 Flavian-Trajanic, S.G. or C.G.
18/31 Hadrianic, C.G.	Lower 33 Antonine, C.G.
18/31 R Hadrianic, C.G.	36 First and second century, S.G. or
31 Antonine, C.G.	C.G.
31 R Antonine, C.G.	38 Antonine, C.G.
24/25 Claudio-Neronian, S.G.	45 Antonine, C.G.
	Scale 1:4 After Hartley

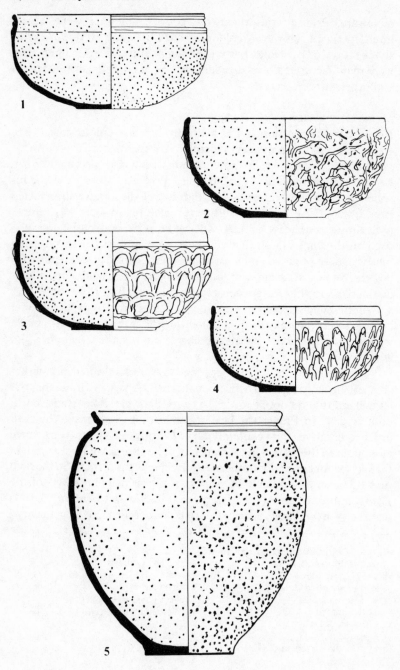

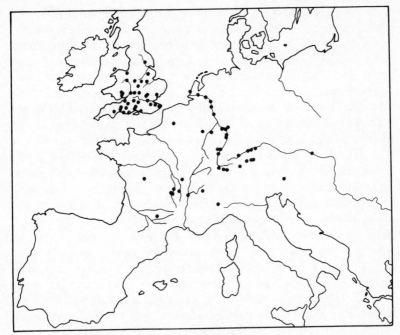

Fig. 30   Distribution of Lyons ware. *After Greene*

the market with the remaining 17 per cent shared between six other competitors, some made much closer to Britain. For example the fine wares imported from the Rhineland, the nearest Continental source, were certainly contemporary and equally good for their purpose. The German ware is exceedingly common in its own area, taking up to 60–80 per cent of the local market. It possessed the advantage of direct shipment from the Rhine to Eastern Britain, compared with the routes from Lyons which inevitably involved long land, river and sea journeys.

Some influential factor must lie behind the outstanding success of Lyons ware. It may be the highly organised way the ware was

Fig. 29   Lyons Ware
1 Cup decorated with sand roughcast from Aislingen, Germany (Greene type 1.5)
2 Cup with rustication from Vindonissa, Switzerland (Greene type 2.1)
3 Cup with three 'arcades' from Vindonissa (Greene type 8)
4 Cup with applied pointed scales from Nijmegen, Netherlands (Greene type 4.1)
5 High-shouldered beaker with sand roughcast from Cirencester, Gloucestershire (Greene type 20.4)
Scale 1:2 After Greene

marketed. The local pottery was probably transported to the garrisons of the Rhine and Upper Danube by *negotiatores*, who gradually became more closely involved in commerce. The existence of *vinarii* and a *diffusor olearius ex Baetica* at Lyons suggests that the volume of trade represented by the consignments of cups and beakers was small compared to the cargoes of wine, oil and other perishable goods, Many other items, including south Gaulish samian, were assembled at the port and sold to civilian merchants or military quarter-masters for redistribution. The *negotiatores ars cretariae*, who are attested at Lyons, probably did not deal with the locally made fine wares, as the titles of such men imply involvement in large-scale operations, like the organisation of the samian trade.[30] However, their subsidiary network of *mercatores* and other agents could easily have included more exotic wares in the cargoes they assembled such as beakers from central Gaul, glazed wares from the Allier and cups and beakers from Lyons itself. The port at Lyons must have seen many cargoes unloaded and reconstituted into mixed boatloads destined for a variety of places.

Merchants and traders were attracted to Lyons because of its position. The city was ideally located for trade, placed at the centre of a network of roads and waterways. Strabo tells us that 'Lugdunum (Lyons) itself is situated beneath a hill at the meeting place of the Saône and the Rhône and is occupied by the Romans. It is the most populous of all the cities of Gaul with the exception of Narbonne, for the people use it as a trading-centre and the Roman governors mint both silver and gold money there'.[31]

The river pattern of Gaul was crucial to the dispersal of goods, from Spain and Italy through Gaul to Britain and Germany. The Rhône was navigable to a great extent, even for large cargoes, covering a wide area of the country with its tributaries, which were also largely navigable. The Rhône joins the Saône at Lyons and above this junction the Doubs flows into the Saône. The Doubs was important as it provided a connection with the Rhine. Today a modern canal connects the Doubs with the Rhine near Kembs. From here cargoes could be shipped upstream to the mouth of the Aare, via Basel and Augst, reaching Vindonnisa in Switzerland. A little further up the Rhine another tributary, to the north, leads via a short overland journey to the Danube at Hüfingen, providing access to at least 14 Danube forts in Raetia. Downstream from Kembs all the important Rhine frontier garrisons could be reached, including Strasbourg, Mainz, Bonn, Köln, Neuss, Xanten and Nijmegen. A more direct route would also have been available by an overland journey from the upper Saône to the Mosel, giving access to Trier. Conveniently, the Mosel flows into the Rhine at Koblenz, leading to the most densely occupied section of the Rhine frontier. From the upper reaches of the Saône cargoes could also be moved overland as far as the Seine and 'from this point the merchandise moves down to the ocean and to the Lexobii and Caleti and from these to Britain in less than a day's sailing'.[32] As the Rhône was swift and therefore difficult to navigate against the current, some goods, like those for the Arverni, were taken overland to the Loire and then travelled west to the Atlantic.

The disappearance of Lyons colour-coated ware may reflect the commercial concentration at Lyons. The sixties were a bad time for the city. A severe fire in AD 65 was followed by further troubles in 68, when it was besieged by the rebel Vindex during his revolt against Nero. Both of these incidents must have damaged the local industries. Due to this resistance to Vindex, the revenues of the city were confiscated by Galba when he became Emperor. The revolt of Civilis, AD 69–70, disrupted the Rhineland, while in Raetia, Noricum and Pannonia the conflicting loyalties of the garrisons during the civil war of 68–69 led to the destruction of many Upper Danube forts. Once peace was restored, legionary garrisons on the Rhine-Danube frontier were changed and units from distant bases were brought in to replace them. It is hardly surprising that Lyons ware disappeared after the disruption first of its production and distribution centre and then of its main markets.[33] The new legions had different ceramic tastes, judging by the pottery made for *X Gemia* at Nijmegen and *XI Claudia* at Vindonissa after AD 70. The early Flavian period also saw a change in fashion, away from the cup towards the beaker, sealing the fate of the Lyons industry.

An indication of the extent of colour-coated wares exported to Britain in the pre-Flavian period is that a serious attempt was made at imitation at Colchester but the vessels only achieved a small, local distribution. The long chain from the potter through the agents of the *negotiator*, from shipper to distributor and finally from shopkeeper or quarter-master to customer worked so efficiently that a legionary at Vindonissa could have exactly the same type of drinking vessel as his fellow at Usk in Wales.[34]

The large quantities of Gallic fine wares (both samian and colour-coated ware) imported into Britain have led to the impression that Gaul, rather than Germany, was the 'natural trading partner' of Britain as far as pottery was concerned.[35] In the early conquest period this is to be expected, as Gaul was better equipped for widespread trade. Southern Gaul had been exposed to Greek and Roman influences for a considerably longer period. Long before any Roman merchants or troops arrived, the Greek cities had been trading with Gaul. In addition to wine, some tablewares were traded as early as the seventh century BC. This trading network was presumably inherited in 121 BC when Rome acquired the Province of Gallia Narbonensis. The campaigns of Caesar in the 50s would have required elaborate arrangements for supplying the army, stimulating the development of the economy of Gaul. This grew steadily up to the next major military campaign, the conquest of Germany. A great deal of industrial change must have resulted from the early stages of Romanisation. In the pottery industry the tastes of the Roman garrisons and *coloniae* shaped the output of the native Gallic potters. The siteing of foreign fine-ware industries in southern and central Gaul contributed to this development.

This was the situation when the armies of Augustus advanced to the Rhine and beyond it. As well as the importation of Italianate fine wares and samian, mostly from Lyons, the presence of the army in the area also stimulated the production of Gallo-Belgic wares which imitated Italian originals (plate 21). At this stage the Rhineland was an important trade-route to Britain, as it had been in the pre-conquest period, and most of the apparent links between Britain and the Rhine provinces are due to similar sources of supply.[36] Few Lower Rhineland products, like colour-coated cups, find their way to Britain, although they are extremely common in the Rhineland itself. Furthermore few were exported south of Mainz. The reason for this was the concentration of military installations and civilian settlements in the Lower Rhineland, which provided a massive 'home' market. There was little incentive for long-distance trade.

In the late first and second centuries this pattern was to change, when the Rhineland grew in importance not only as a trade route to Britain, with direct shipping to the Tyne and the Forth, but as an exporter, with local products travelling both north and south. During this period fine-ware and samian industries developed along the Rhine and the Mosel, their output being mainly counterparts of Gaulish items. Cologne (Köln), the capital of Germania Inferior and situated on a principal water course and trade route, possessed the necessary attributes of a major distribution centre. A large fine-ware industry grew up in and around the city, whose wares were exported as far afield as Britain and the Danubian Provinces.

COLOGNE FINE WARE

Cologne ware has a fine white fabric with a glossy colour-coat, ranging in colour from black to orange-brown. In the pre-Flavian period the potters imitated Lyons vessel forms and Spanish barbotine designs to produce their own types of cups and beakers with elaborate foliate barbotine decoration (fig. 31.1–3; plate 11). After *c.* AD 80 until the close of the second century, the bag-shaped beaker with cornice rim was manufactured (figs 31.5–7, 32.1; plate 13). Individual vessels can be more precisely dated by observed typological developments (fig. 31.7 cf. 32.1). A new form was adopted in the early second century, derived from a samian beaker form, with a bulbous body, short curved neck and simple rim (fig. 32.2). This form was probably introduced into the Rhineland with the start of samian production at Trier in *c.* 120–30. The Trier potters also made colour-coated fine ware vessels similar to those produced at Cologne, but in a red fabric. In the latter part of the second century these gave way to a new distinctive range of vessels referred to in Britain as 'Rhenish ware' (plates 17, 18). Also towards the end of the century the bulbous beaker with a short-curved neck was gradually evolving into the long-necked bulbous beaker so typical of the third century (fig. 5.3). This was produced at Trier in Rhenish ware (plate 17, left) but not apparently at Cologne, where by this time production may have been in decline.

In Germany, Cologne remained the most important producer of colour-coated fine wares until the late second century, when it was superseded by Trier. The potters at Cologne were certainly some of the most inventive, producing 'hunt cups' and 'gladiator beakers' in colour-coated ware and a wide range of other exotically decorated beakers in lead-glazed and coarse fabrics (plates 14, 16). It was the direct influence of Cologne that stimulated the production of similar vessels first at Colchester and then in the Lower Nene Valley. The industry at Colchester had further links with the Rhineland, through the samian produced there by potters from the Sinzig-Trier workshops. The production of colour-coated fine ware at Cologne had been known for some years[37] but its importance as a traded commodity was not fully appreciated since there was no evidence for exportation to Britain. Indeed it was considered to be unlikely, as the workshops established at Colchester and in the Lower Nene Valley would have supplied cheaper products to the British market. 'The white fabric of many of the vessels made in the Nene Valley makes them so similar to Cologne products that trade in either direction would be difficult to detect but at the same time unlikely'.[38] This implied that it was easier to

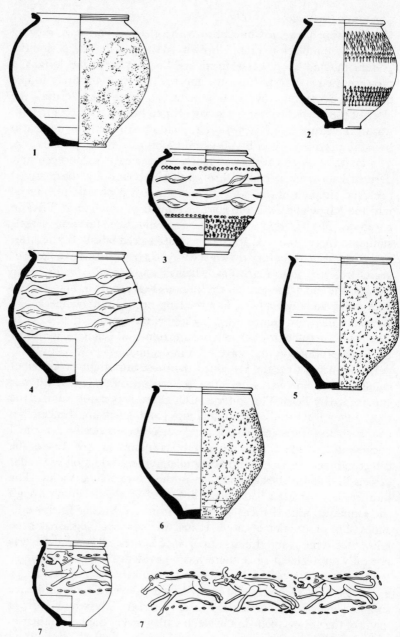

establish workshops in Britain than to trade directly with the Rhineland.

This outlook has been completely changed by the chemical analysis of Cologne and Lower Nene Valley products.[39] The object of the analysis was to determine how well a sample of 79 sherds, mostly of hunt cup or roughcast type, from central and southern British sites, generally considered to be from the Nene Valley, compared with a sample of 47 sherds from a number of different Nene Valley kilns. To compare with the Nene Valley control sherds, a small sample was obtained from kiln sites in Cologne. Of the 79 test cases included in the analysis, 50 were assigned to Cologne Group A, 16 to the sub-group of Cologne A and 12 to Nene Valley Group A. Fourteen samples of bag-shaped beakers with roughcast decoration were analysed and all fell within Cologne Group A. Of the 52 hunt cup sherds analysed the majority (29 sherds), belonged to Cologne A, while only 16 samples were associated with sub-group B. Nene Valley A accounted for only 7 sherds. Assuming these results indicate a general trend in central and southern Britain, it would seem that any hunt cup found there is unlikely to have originated from the Nene Valley. This study has established beyond doubt the importation of Cologne colour-coated ware to Britain.

From c. AD onwards there was a small but continuous trickle of such vessels to Britain, with an increase in the quantity from c. AD 120 when a shipping route was opened up from the mouth of the Rhine to the Tyne. Direct contact between the Rhineland and the northern frontier zone is suggested by an inscription dredged from the Tyne at Newcastle, which records the arrival of reinforcements for all three British legions from the armies of both German provinces under the governorship of Julius Verus. As might be expected, Cologne ware is present on both Hadrian's Wall and the Antonine Wall. Due to the geographical proximity of south-east England to the Rhineland it is hardly surprising that the greatest quantity of Cologne fine wares would appear to be concentrated in this part of the country. Consign-

---

Fig. 31 Cologne ware
1 High-shouldered beaker with sand roughcast, c. AD 40–80
2 High-shouldered beaker with rouletting, c. 40–80
3 High-shouldered beaker with barbotine foliate decoration, c. 40–80
4 Globular beaker with cornice rim and barbotine foliate decoration, c. 80
5 Bag-shaped beaker with cornice rim and clay roughcast, c 80–160
6 Bag-shaped beaker with cornice rim and clay roughcast, c. 160–190
7 Bag-shaped beaker with barbotine hunting scene, c. 120–160
Scale 1:4

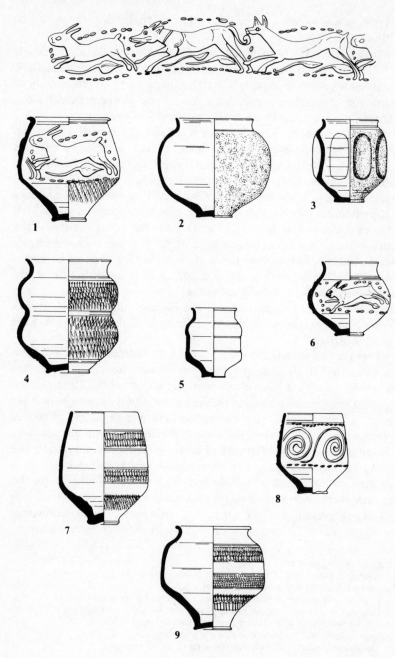

ments probably entered via eastern ports such as Dover, Richborough, and London. On the Upper German Limes, Cologne fine wares faced competition from vessels manufactured in the Middle-Upper Rhineland but despite this they are dispersed as far afield as Regensburg and Straubing (fig. 33).

Like Lyons, Cologne possessed the necessary mechanisms for trade, amply illustrated by the inscriptions referring to *negotiatores* either originating from, or operating there. Various *negotiatores* are listed by Hassall[40] but of particular importance here is one C. Aurelius C L Verus (Cologne: CIL XIII. 8164 [a]), who is referred to as a *negotiator Britannicianus*. This inscription illustrates the trading connections between Britain and Cologne, although the objects of such trade were more likely to be salt, oil and wine. Two further inscriptions from Colijnsplatt-Domburg mention *negotiator cretarius Britannicianus*, traders who were presumably engaged in the shipping of east Gaulish samian from Trier and Rheinzabern, and 'Rhenish ware' to Britain, who may have included Cologne products in their cargoes. These men operating in the late second and early third century probably bore little resemblance to those described by Caesar nearly two centuries earlier, for whom the financing of merchants selling goods to the natives was probably only a minor activity. These later *negotiatores* were far more involved in actual trading operations. Colijnsplatt and Domburg were both shrines to the goddess Nehalennia, near the important harbours at the mouth of the Waal and the Scheldt. These harbours served ships trading between the Rhineland (via the Waal) and Gallia Belgica (via the Scheldt), and the east-coast ports of Britain and coastal regions of Gaul. Cologne was a particularly well placed entrepôt for distributing its products as well as goods brought from the immediate hinterland and from further afield, such as the Mosel Valley and the Upper Rhineland. It would have been the ideal venue for assembling composite cargoes.

Fig. 32 **Cologne ware**
1 Bag-shaped beaker with cornice rim and barbotine hunting scene, *c.* AD 160–90
2 Bulbous beaker with short-curved neck and clay roughcast, *c.* 120–190
3 Indented bulbous beaker with short-curved neck and clay roughcast, *c.* 120–190
4 Constricted bulbous beaker with short-curved neck and rouletting, *c.* 120–190
5 Constricted bulbous beaker with short-curved neck, *c.* 120–190
6 Bulbous beaker with short curved neck and barbotine hunting scene, *c.* 120–160
7 Bag-shaped beaker with plain rim and rouletting, *c.* 150–250
8 Bag-shaped beaker with plain rim and barbotine abstract decoration, *c.* 150–250
9 Bulbous beaker with inclined neck and everted rim, with rouletting, *c.* 180–250
Scale 1:4

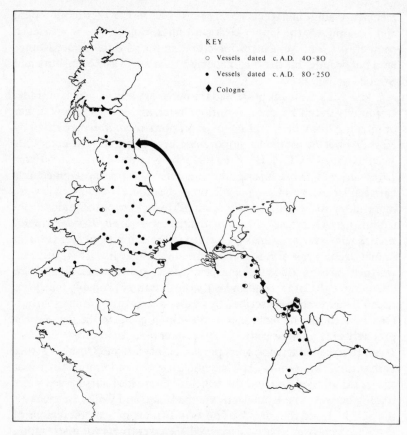

KEY

○   Vessels   dated   c. A.D.   40-80

●   Vessels   dated   c. A.D.   80-250

◆   Cologne

Fig. 33   Source and distribution of Cologne ware

It is no longer true to say that 'trade with the Rhine provinces may thus be stated to have been negligible as far as pottery was concerned'.[41] However, a large part of Cologne's industrial output would have been consumed by the extensive home market. The Lower Rhineland, with its large cities and fortresses, encouraged production geared to satisfy local demand. All the major urban centres attracted artisans who made the essential consumer goods, like pottery and metal utensils, for the home market. This resulted in the various workshops remaining on a small scale, probably representing individual family concerns. As well as fine wares the potters also manufactured coarse wares, figurines and lamps, and this lack of specialisation suggests that the artisans involved were anxious to provide a wide range of products for prospective purchasers. Such lack of specialisation also restricted the quantity of any one type that could be manufactured, reflecting a reliance on the large local market rather than on long-distance trade, which required massive production like that seen at La Graufesenque and the other samian workshops. Those fine wares that were exported were undoubtedly part of composite cargoes, consisting of samian, lamps and figurines and other commodities such as the locally produced glass. The density of urban markets in the Lower Rhineland encouraged self-sufficiency in consumer goods, and exportation outside the area was a by-product rather than a primary concern.

Production at the various kilns in and around Cologne appears to cease in the early third century. This may have been partly due to the disruption of the industry's export market, as the Upper German Limes was irrevocably dislocated by the Great Alemannic invasion of AD 233. It was not until 257 that the Lower German Limes was seriously damaged by invading Franks. Although a small amount of pottery was produced in the fourth century at Cologne this was purely for local consumption.

CENTRAL GAUL

In addition to the commercial connections with the Rhineland, Gaul was an important trading partner of Britain throughout the second century. Perhaps surprisingly Lezoux, the main workshop in central Gaul, did not assume the role of Lyons as the leading producer of fine wares. Instead that industry too went into decline, albeit temporarily, in c. 75. After that date Lezoux continued to produce, in colour-coated ware, distinctive barrel-shaped beakers first seen in the pre-Flavian period, up to Hadrianic times (fig. 9.6). South Gaul continued to produce masses of samian but no fine wares for export. After c. 120 Lezoux started to mass-produce samian for exportation, but the output never reached the scale of that at La Graufesenque and by this time the structure of the industry had completely changed. A new repertoire of colour-coated fine wares was introduced in the Antonine period. These vessels were manufactured in a samian fabric with a black colour-coating. In this respect they are similar to the 'Rhenish ware' produced at Trier but different decorative techniques were employed (fig. 34). Central Gaulish colour-coated ware belongs to the samian tradition and the bag-shaped beakers, so characteristic of the Rhineland industries, do not appear to have been included in the repertoire. Apart from distribution in Gaul, most central Gaulish samian was exported to Britain, though some reached the Rhineland and rather larger

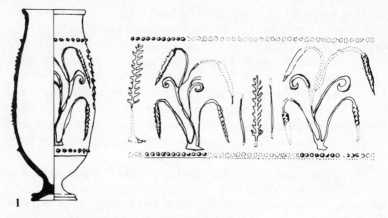

Fig. 34   Central Gaulish colour-coated ware
1 Beaker with barbotine decoration, Antonine. *After Webster*

quantities went to the Danubian provinces.[42] Much of the samian that reached Britain came by the Loire outlet. The Pudding Pan Rock wreck and finds from the New Fresh Wharf site in London give a clear indication of this trade.

NORTH GAUL

The late first and second centuries saw the creation of many new samian industries in addition to Trier and Rheinzabern in north-eastern Gaul, like the Argonne group which includes the workshops at Lavoye, Avocourt and Les Allieux. In contrast to the industry in the Lower Rhineland, production in this area was not concentrated in or around large urban centres, but was a rural industry, like that in central Gaul, situated close to the natural resources necessary for making pottery (i.e. clay, water and wood). The difference in location determined a reliance on long distance trade, rather than dependence on a large home market. The north Gaul industry was undoubtedly an offshoot of that in central Gaul, as both the samian and fine wares were inspired by vessels from Lezoux. Bag-shaped beakers, with a tulip-shaped profile and grooved cornice rim were produced (fig. 35.2). Some vessels have the barbotine tear-drop and hair-pin motifs so common on central Gaulish beakers. More commonly they were decorated with roughcast. Production of this form spread to western Britain but it was never adopted by the Rhineland industry or its off-shoots in south-east Britain. After c. 140 the form ceased to be made by the north Gaulish potters, when new forms were introduced, including

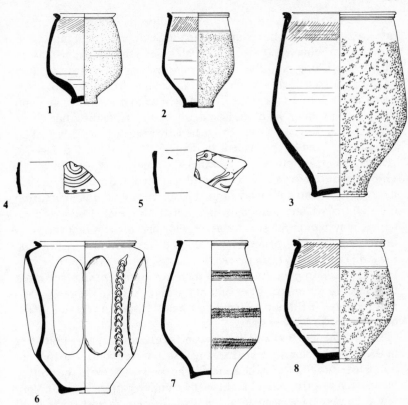

Fig. 35 North Gaulish vessels
Bag-shaped beaker with cornice rim and clay roughcast, c. AD 140–60+
2 Bag-shaped beaker with grooved cornice rim and clay roughcast, c. 80–140
3 Bag-shaped beaker with grooved cornice rim and clay roughcast, c. 80–140
4 Bag-shaped beaker with barbotine abstract decoration
5 Bag-shaped beaker with barbotine hunting scene, c. 120–140+
6 Indented bag-shaped beaker with grooved cornice rim and barbotine 'wishbones', c. 80–140
7 Bag-shaped beaker with grooved cornice rim and rouletting, c. 80–140
8 Bag-shaped beaker with grooved cornice rim and clay roughcast, c. 80–140
Scale 1:4

the short-curved neck bulbous beaker and its successor, which were invariably manufactured in a samian fabric with a black colour-coat. These changes may be correlated with the introduction of the new range of drinking vessels at Lezoux, also in c. 140, when the non-samian fine wares apparently ceased to be made in favour of the black colour-coated vessels.

Production was fragmented, with small potteries scattered across north-eastern Gaul, clustering around the Seine and its tributaries. In this area the Seine was the main arterial trade route. As Strabo tells us, 'this river (Rhine) and the Seine do enclose some territory in their windings but not so very much. Both of them flow from the south to the north and in front of them lies Britain, so near to the Rhine that Kent, the eastern promontory of the island, can be seen from there but a little further away from the Seine. It was here that the deified Caesar set up his shipyard when he sailed to Britain'.[43] Due to the lack of centralisation, output never reached the same level as that at La Graufesenque or even Lezoux. A combination of the following factors created small, comparatively limited industries: small manufacturing units, kilns which could only take relatively small loads, and no apparent system in the area for assembling and distributing goods, as illustrated by the paucity of recorded inscriptions mentioning *negotiatores*. Samian from the north-east Gaulish workshops is always much less common in this country than that from central Gaul and it may account for only 4–5 per cent of the finds, though the proportion may be higher in the northern military area.[44] Obviously the bulk of the output went to local markets.

During the late first and early second centuries, large quantities of north Gaulish colour-coated drinking vessels were exported to Britain. The apparent reliance on the Seine for the transportation of the pottery has created an east to west bias in its distribution pattern (fig. 36). Very few examples have been found east of Strasbourg and none at all recorded in the Lower Rhineland. This western bias may have been in part due to the presence of workshops in the Rhineland making similar wares. In Britain the distribution also appears to be largely confined to the west, especially Wales and the West Country. In contrast the pottery is rarely found on eastern sites but did reach the Stanegate and Hadrian's Wall. In broad terms, the distribution pattern relates to the line of the Fosse Way, with a higher proportion falling to the west than to the east and this may reflect the ports of entry used. The distribution of samian provides corroborative evidence. Argonne samian was also shipped to the south and west of Britain from the second to the fourth century, as indicated by the high percentage of Argonne stamps at Carlisle (20 per cent of all the east Gaulish samian) and Chester (25 per cent) as compared to York (where it accounted for only 5.9 per cent).[45] Ports of entry can be suggested. At Clausentum (Bitterne, Southampton) a collection of second-century central Gaulish vessels may represent a load of dumped breakages.[46] An inlet port has been

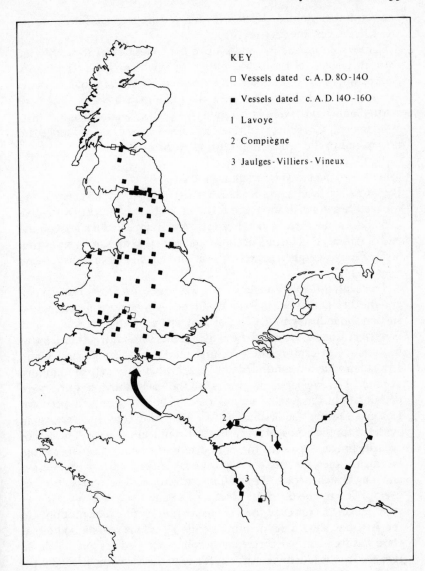

KEY

□ Vessels dated c. A. D. 80 - 140

■ Vessels dated c. A. D. 140 - 160

1 Lavoye

2 Compiègne

3 Jaulges - Villiers - Vineux

Fig. 36   Sources and distribution of north Gaulish vessels

conjectured at Bosham Harbour, near Chichester, handling cargoes from Lezoux in the first century.[47]

Cargoes of samian, fine wares and other commodities were shipped from the mouth of the Seine, either directly across the Channel to Southampton or Chichester or by first coasting east to Boulogne, across the Channel and then west along the British coast. Vessels of north Gaulish type were imitated in the west, at Wanborough, Wilts, Wilderspool, Cheshire, and Caerleon, Gwent, but this influence did not extend to the production centres of the east.

END OF THE GALLIC FINE-WARE INDUSTRIES

By c. 190–200 production of samian at Lezoux had virtually ceased and the factories in north and eastern Gaul could not even cope with local demand. In most areas when Lezoux ware disappeared it signalled the end of samian. Production declined and ceased in the same way as that at La Graufesenque, suggesting that similar factors may have been responsible.

The central Gaul-Rhineland area was crucial to Lezoux's survival and the distant markets in Britain and the Danube were not enough to sustain the industry in the face of a collapsing 'home market'.[48] The pattern at Rheinzabern and Trier also seems similar, where there was no attempt to capture the potential markets in Britain and Gaul. Instead production continued until c. 220 when they in turn went into decline. The barbarian invasions of the early third century were perhaps only the final straw, as the 196–7 civil war had been for Lezoux. During the second half of the third century there is no evidence for the export of fine wares to Britain on any scale. The lack of security prevailing during this period, after the eventual collapse of the German Limes, was not conducive to large-scale pottery production and long-distance trade. The trading patterns of the second century, as exemplified by the distribution of samian and fine wares, were never re-established. However, the late fourth-century fine ware produced in the Argonne should be mentioned (fig. 9.4). This red-slipped tableware was frequently decorated with roller-stamped designs. It can be regarded as the fourth-century successor to the early Imperial Gaulish samian tradition. In 1975 some 120 examples were known from 28 sites in England and Wales.[49]

ROMANO-BRITISH FINE WARES

After c. 200 Britain had to become self-sufficient as far as fine wares were concerned. The rapid growth of the Oxfordshire industry can be seen as an attempt to replace the tablewares no longer supplied from the Continent. The red colour-coated wares made there, like those produced in North Africa and the Argonne, followed the samian tradition but completely moulded vessels were not included. Instead, other decorative techniques, like painting, stamping and rouletting were used. The earliest vessels closely copy the latest imported samian forms, like Drag. 31, a dish, 38, a flanged bowl and 45, a mortarium. Imitations of 36, a shallow bowl with a broad rim (figs 28, 36), were also manufactured with white painted scrolls replacing the original barbotine leaf pattern on the rim. This ware was distributed over most of Britain, particularly south of the Trent.

At the same time the Lower Nene Valley industry increased the range and output of its colour-coated wares. During the last half of the second century this was restricted to beakers and 'castor boxes', a type of lidded bowl. Beakers continued to be made throughout the third century, keeping pace with the latest Continental fashions by copying the white painted decoration found on Rhenish 'motto pots'. The repertoire now expanded to include flagons, jars and bowls and samian type vessels. Copies of Drag. 31, 36, 37, 38 and 45 were made until the late fourth century, but not on the same scale as at Oxford.

The New Forest potters also produced red colour-coated vessels of samian type. Some forms and decorative techniques were shared with the Oxford potters, like copies of Drag. 31, 38 and 45, but these vessels were mainly used locally. It should be remembered that these large industries produced many other types of pottery besides colour-coated vessels, including parchment ware, mortaria and grey kitchen wares for local consumers.

Not only did Britain become self-sufficient in the production of fine wares but actually exported pottery to the Continent, notably Oxford-shire red colour-coated and Dorset black-burnished wares. The former was Britain's largest source of tablewares and the main competitor of Argonne pottery. It has been identified on eight or nine European sites, represented by about 20 examples. Dorset black-burnished ware has been found on eight sites, with some 30 sherds recorded. Two pieces of New Forest pottery have been recognised at the site of Alet in Brittany.[50]

THE MORTARIA INDUSTRY

The Roman army made a considerable impact on coarse-ware production in Britain, importing vessels not previously used here, like flagons and mortaria, from the Rhineland, Gallia Belgica, Gaul and

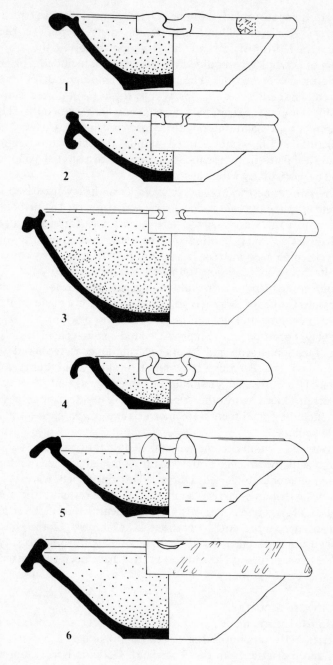

even Italy. The mortaria maker Q. Valerius Veranius may have moved his workshop from Bavai in Gallia Belgica to Kent in order to exploit the new market. By AD 60–70 there were several potteries specialising in mortaria in south-east England, supplying the army further north and the southern settlements, like Verulamium, Canterbury, Silchester and Colchester, which had experienced Roman influences long before the conquest. Britian became self-sufficient by the end of the century and the import of mortaria virtually ceased. During this period the principal potteries were those south of Verulamium, at Brockley Hill and Radlett and those at Colchester but by the early second century they had declined and were superseded by new centres. The very large pottery established in the Hartshill-Mancetter area, near Nuneaton, Warwickshire, operated for almost three centuries. At least one potter, G. Attius Marinus, previously at Colchester and Radlett moved there in c. AD 100. This vast industrial area, covering about 25 square miles soon became one of the main suppliers of mortaria to the northern military zone and it also dominated the Midland market, taking over the markets previously served by the potteries south of Verulamium. Its products are, however, rare in the south. Characteristic are vessels in a fine, white 'pipe clay' fabric with red-brown grits on the inside. By the mid-second century the fashion was for smaller flanges, which were less hooked and more flaring and had more prominent rounded rims (fig. 37.5). Towards the end of the second century the potters began to make hammer-head rims which were sometimes decorated with reeding or, after c. 230, with groups of painted vertical strips (fig. 37.6). Large-scale production continued until the last quarter of the fourth century.

The main rival of this industry was the large pottery which developed around Oxford at the beginning of the second century. Although this started on a smaller scale than at Mancetter, it grew and flourished until the end of the Roman era, with its main market in the southern Midlands and the south but also capturing the west Midlands, Wales, Essex and the Verulamium region from local

Fig. 37   Development of Oxford and Hartshill/Mancetter mortaria
1 Oxford mortarium with illegible potter's stamp on the flange, c. 100–160
2 Oxford mortarium, late second to early third century
3 Oxford mortarium typical of c. 240–400+
4 Hartshill/Mancetter mortaruim, mid-second century
5 Hartshill/Mancetter mortarium, late second century
6 Hartshill/Mancetter mortarium with hammer-head rim, late third-fourth century
Scale 1:4 After Swan

potteries. North of Mancetter, Oxford could make little impact as the former saturated the area (fig. 38), but its mortaria are found in small numbers both in the north Midlands and the North. The vessels manufactured at Oxford were cream in colour with distinctive multi-coloured translucent quartz internal grits, instead of the ironstone used at Mancetter. Typical mid-third- to fourth-century examples have prominent rims with rolled over or square flanges (fig. 37.3).

Although Mancetter and Oxford were inland, this did not prevent the use of water-borne transportation. No doubt the many rivers in southern England, which flow to coastal harbours, were used. The Anker flows through the Mancetter area, joining the Tame at Tamworth which in turn flows into the Trent. The Oxfordshire potters were never far away from the Thames and its tributaries. By these means all the major industrial centres were within reach of the sea.

ROMANO-BRITISH COARSE WARES

The production of kitchen wares was also stimulated by the arrival of the Roman army. In those areas where a thriving industry already existed it was fully exploited. The army relied on local potters, who often adhered to their traditional techniques and forms but added the new types – flagons and mortaria – to meet military needs. Colchester already possessed a large industry, producing 'Gallo-Belgic' forms, like butt beakers and girth beakers, which were quickly taken up by the army. It is not surprising that mortaria production soon began in this area, undoubtedly due to the expertise of the local potters and that, through pre-conquest trade, this had become the most Romanised part of the country. In the south-west large quantities of Durotrigian black-burnished ware occurs on Roman forts, like Waddon Hill in Dorset. A pottery was established at Corfe Mullen, Dorset, which supplied a large military base at Lake farm with native wares and flagons, and mortaria in white or buff fabrics. As the army moved north and west into areas which were either aceramic or where the quality of the local wares was inadequate, the army sometimes brought in potters. This was cheaper and more efficient than trading over long distances for cheap kitchen wares which were constantly in demand. At the Neronian supply fortress at Usk in Wales pottery was produced locally, in a highly distinctive range of forms, quite unlike those found on south-eastern sites.[51] The Usk forms have more in common with contemporary pottery from the Rhineland. As Usk lay in frontier territory with virtually no pre-Roman Iron Age pottery tradition, the

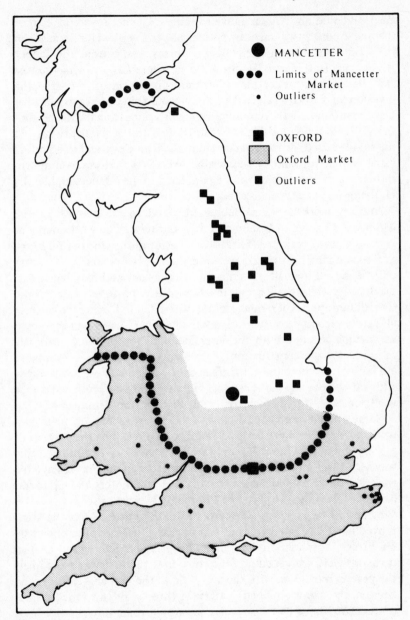

**Fig. 38 The markets covered by the Hartshill/Mancetter and the
Oxfordshire kilns.** *After Hartley*

garrison could not rely on native suppliers. Hence, 80–90 per cent of the coarse pottery was made by potters who had worked for the army on the Continent and, judging by the forms, came from the Upper Rhineland. In this area lies Strasbourg, where *Legio II Augusta* was stationed prior to the conquest of Britain. The legion formed part of the invasion force in AD 43 and a detachment could have been garrisoned at Usk. As three out of the four invasion legions came from the Rhineland, the *XX* from Neuss and the *XIV* from Mainz, it is hardly surprising that the soldiers used forms then current in the Rhineland and that potters came from there to supply their needs. So many of the forms common in the early conquest period can be paralleled in the Rhineland, like the Hofheim flagon and the reeded-rim bowl.

Military workshops, producing tiles and coarse pottery for the legions, are known in Britain and the Continent. The works depot at Holt served the legionary fortress at Chester during the period *c.* 75–120, manufacturing tiles, coarse pottery and even fine wares. The latter only represent a small percentage of the output and may have been produced to offset the shortage in tablewares at this time, caused by the dwindling supplies of samian from southern Gaul. During the late first and early second century nearly all the legionary bases had their own workshops to cope with the large demand for building materials required for the construction of permanent fortresses. The smaller auxiliary forts sometimes had their own workshops, especially those situated in isolated positions. The kilns at Grimscar produced coarse wares and tiles for the nearby fort at Slack in the Pennines.

Some civilian craftsmen followed the army, setting up their own workshops, to exploit the local military market. The production of pottery known as Trent Valley ware may have been stimulated this way. At Margidunum, Nottinghamshire, a fort on the Fosse Way, this ware accounts for about 80 per cent of the coarse pottery and it is found on other forts in the region, like Thorpe by Newark, also on the Fosse Way and as far afield as Chesterfield in Derbyshire. After the army moved north in *c.* AD 80 output almost ceased. Its presence obviously encouraged production but after the garrison left either civilian demands were not yet sufficient to sustain the industry or more likely the potters moved on with the army. So in the first and early second century the army obtained pottery in three main ways: from local potters stimulated by the arrival of the army, from military workshops connected to the local garrison, or from civilian potters who established workshops in the vicinity of forts.

The construction of Hadrian's Wall marked a dramatic and major change in the supply of pottery to the army. The Wall replaced the earlier, Flavian-Trajanic, Stanegate frontier which was supplied from military works depots along its line. With the building of the Wall a different system was introduced. From then on the army rarely produced its own coarse pottery. Instead goods were supplied to the troops, in considerable quantities, from all parts of the Province, particularly black-burnished ware from Dorset (BB1) and mortaria from Mancetter. All the primary construction levels of Hadrian's Wall have produced large quantities of BB1. Petrological analysis has shown that this pottery was made in the Wareham-Poole Harbour area and represents a continuation of the local Iron Age potting traditions[52] (figs 10,11). It is found along the entire length of the Wall, with a specific range of forms constantly recurring.

The appearance of the ware in the north and its domination of both the military and civilian markets for over 200 years has led to much speculation. Originally the sudden expansion of the market area of the Dorset industry, with a distribution along the western seaboard to the northern frontier (fig. 39), was explained in terms of a contract to supply the garrisons with pottery. The evidence for the official organisation of such mundane supplies has recently been reviewed and other explanations advanced. The pottery may have accompanied much more important official supplies, like grain. The western bias in the distribution may be the result of sea transportation. On the Wall itself there is a rough division between east and west supply patterns, which became more apparent with the study of the distribution of Severn Valley ware.[53] Although this ware is only found in small quantities, it has a definite western bias which suggests that the pottery came by sea to the mouth of the Solway and then along the wall, travelling from west to east. BB1 was probably distributed along the Wall in a similar way. It continued to be supplied to the north until *c.* 367, when the Barbarian Conspiracy may have disrupted such long-distance supply patterns.

In *c.* 140 the building of the Antonine Wall resulted in a similar development in long-distance trade along the eastern seaboard. The appearance of BB2 in the north marks this new trading pattern (fig. 39). This ware copies BB1 but has a finer fabric and was wheel-thrown. Petrological analysis suggests that a major production centre for much of the BB2 found on northern military sites lay in the Colchester area. Its manufacture probably began soon after the mid-first century. Colchester mortaria and fine wares also travelled north with supplies of BB2. No doubt these goods were shipped directly from the Thames

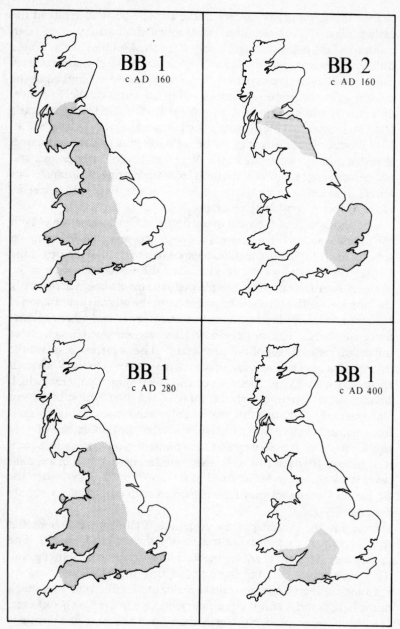

Fig. 39 Distribution of black-burnished ware 1 and 2. *After Gillam*

estuary to the Forth. This is demonstrated by the mortaria distribution which indicates two concentrations of material, one in the south-east and the other, quite removed, on the northern frontier. This arrangement existed until *c.* 250, after which BB2 reached the north infrequently. Using the pottery as an indication of trade, it would seem to imply that the most intense movement of goods along the eastern seaboard was during the mid-second to early third century, presumably reflecting the new arrangements required to meet first the Antonine advance into Scotland, *c.* 140–163 and then subsequent Severan campaigns, *c.* 208–211. As the campaigning and new military positions were both concentrated in the east, on the coastal plain of eastern Scotland, it is logical that the troops were supplied from the south-east and it is tempting to see the distribution of BB2 and Colchester mortaria as corroborative evidence. However, BB1 is also found on the Antonine Wall and on other Scottish forts, once again concentrated in the west, indicating that the western route was still operating. After the troops were withdrawn from Scotland the eastern seaboard route appears to have gone out of use, but goods continue to travel north by the western seaboard until the middle of the fourth century.

If supplying the army was the main generator of this traffic it is reasonable to have expected similar evidence for the west and east throughout the Roman period.[54] Perhaps trade in the north-west was organised on a different basis, as there was less civilian authority in this region due to the presence of permanent military garrisons. The area was also less developed than the south-eastern civil zone. The economy of the highland areas was biased towards pastoral farming, producing a surplus of meat, hides, wool and dairy produce, perhaps more than was needed for local purposes, which could have been sold to the southern markets. Shipping travelling back and forth to the area could have supplied deficiencies in cereal products and manufactured goods from the developed civil zone. If it is accepted that pottery accompanied perishable cargoes, the ceramic evidence has considerable implications for the economy of western Britain. If it is due to army supply it points to the inadequacy of local farming to meet all needs, but if it is due to commercial activitiy it implies a great deal about the productivity of western Britain.[55]

In the third and fourth centuries production became increasingly concentrated at fewer but larger potteries. The large manufacturing centres around Oxford, in the New Forest and the Lower Nene Valley were dependent upon the sophisticated monetary system and safe communications to sell their wares. Even grey kitchen-ware, like the pottery made at Alice Holt, Surrey, was mass-produced and traded over long distances. After *c*. 400, when the army was withdrawn and Britain ceased to be an official Roman Province, the long-distance trading networks quickly collapsed. They could not be maintained during a period of political and social upheaval. The Oxfordshire potteries which were apparently still flourishing at the close of the Roman period had ceased to function well before the Saxon settlement of the area in the middle of the fifth century.

Conclusion

The study of Roman pottery enables the archaeologist to examine a part of the economy that would otherwise be totally unknown. Through the examination of pottery the existence of a widespread network of trade, penetrating to the humblest and remotest parts of the Empire, is revealed. This network also carried other goods and acted as a means of communication, for spreading news. Trade was essential as a way of converting agricultural surplus into useable goods, without which Roman society could not have existed. Politically and socially trade furthered the process of Romanisation far more than any other individual factor. Rome saw the activities of traders as a legitimate way of infiltrating native society, with the men themselves acting as useful go-betweens who could spread official propaganda. Success meant tax-income and more importantly political influence. The movement of pottery enables the archaeologist to see such trade in action.

6 Pottery and Industry

Location

Throughout much of prehistory pottery-making appears to have been a domestic craft, made in the home for immediate use. It was usually hand-made, without the use of a wheel or turntable, and production may have been seasonal, undertaken by both men and women. For these reasons it has been assumed that prehistoric pottery must express local traditions. Yet even at this early stage, some pottery was produced by specialist craftsmen, demonstrated by the high and uniform standards of certain types. These potters could have worked from home, travelled from place to place supplying the local needs before moving on to the next settlement or in established workshops, dispersing their products by trade or exchange.

INDIVIDUAL WORKSHOPS

An individual workshop serving the local community could still have been run on a part-time or seasonal basis, in conjunction with farming or some other activity, but making pottery would have been a major source of income. Before the results of petrological studies were known most Iron Age pottery was regarded as a household product, seldom, if ever, travelling far, but now Glastonbury ware and saucepan pots are considered to be the work of specialist potters, perhaps operating from permanent workshops. The pottery could have been marketed commercially or redistributed through reciprocal exchange. Most Roman coarse wares were made in this way and distributed locally or, at best, regionally.

Individual workshops may be found in rural or urban contexts but they are more common in the countryside, as a lucrative urban market is likely to have to encourage a nucleated industry (i.e. one based on a multiplicity of units). A limited range of kitchen vessels, in wheel-made grey coloured fabrics, was the typical product. Many Roman pottery assemblages are dominated by such vessels, which are often difficult to assign to a specific source. At Portchester heavy mineral analysis suggests that about 75 per cent of the grey wares came from within a 5–10-mile radius or less, while only 25 per cent came from further afield (some 20–30 miles) and most of that was obtained from either the New Forest or Alice Holt.[1] In the area around Portchester there were many small, scattered workshops producing grey wares, and this pattern was generally repeated throughout the civilian zone of Roman Britain. Nearly every large population centre had kilns close by, located close to the natural resources necessary for making pottery, i.e. clay, water and wood, and to the local market.

The selling price of pottery has to cover manufacturing, transport and marketing cost, and must leave a profit. For the Mediaeval period there is evidence that transport costs were as much as 25 per cent of the purchase price. So the cost of pottery will rise as the distance from its source increases. It has been calculated that, during the late Roman period, carriage by inland waterways cost 4.9 times as much as by sea, while overland haulage was 28 to 56 times as much.[2] The workshop, which had only a small to medium output, could not rely on mass-production as the nucleated industries did, to keep down its costs, but maintained a low purchasing price with cheap transport and market-ing. This was achieved in two ways. Products could be channelled through permanent shops and the daily market in a nearby town, with perhaps additional sales in the surrounding minor settlements by traders or by pedlars, moving according to the cycle of market days in what is called a 'periodic ring'. In the countryside a temple or shrine may have been the focus for regular fairs and markets. In this way 'the more humdrum products of trade and industry penetrated through the periodic markets to the poorest peasants of the deepest countryside'.[3] Pottery could also be distributed by using the main roads. As the distance from the kilns increased, transport costs claimed a greater percentage of the purchase price, so that beyond a certain point it became uneconomic for the potters to trade any further. The quicker and easier movement provided by main roads, as in the Roman period, extended their market area. It was only by using the roads providing access to and from the workshop, that a reasonable price could be maintained. Bulk movements by cart or pack animal without the main roads, especially in the winter, resulted in slower movement, possibly more breakages and higher costs. Marketing models often assume a circular trading area around the distribution centre but roads and other important lines of communication, like waterways, exist only in certain directions, so that transport costs will increase irregularly.

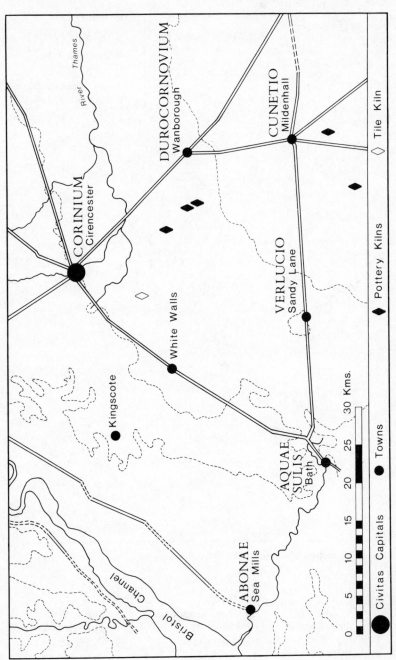

Fig. 40 The Roman kilns sited near Wanborough, Wiltshire. *After Anderson*

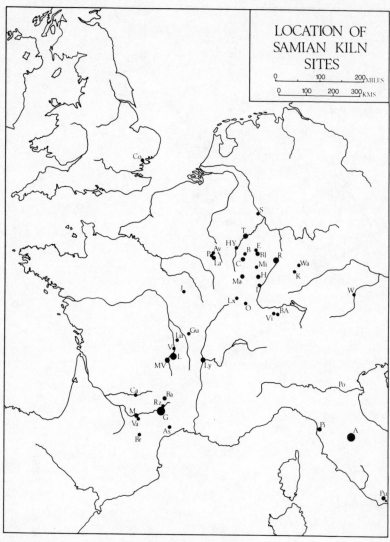

Fig. 41   Location of samian kiln sites. *After Marsh*

Italy
   Arrezo (A)
   Po Valley (Po)
   Pisa (Pi)
   Puteoli (Pu)

South Gaul
   La Graufesenque (G)
   Le Rozier (Rz)
   Banassac (Ba)
   Aspiran (As)

   Bram (Br)
   Montans (M)
   Valery (Va)
   Carrade (Ca)

In Roman Britain workshops clustered around the towns and other large settlements. The Province was divided into semi-autonomous self-governing areas, called *civitates*, each with a dominant town providing a centre for justice and administration. In many cases the *civitates* were created from existing Iron Age tribes. The tribal area of the Atrebates became a *civitas* with Silchester, Calleva Atrebatum, the original tribal capital, acting as its administrative and economic centre. One of its neighbours was the *Civitas Dobunnorum* with its centre at Cirencester, Corinium Dobunnorum. These administrative divisions may even have affected regional trade.

Towns of lower status also stimulated production for the local market. The potters at Whitehill Farm in the vicinity of Wanborough, Durocornovium, a small town on the main road from Cirencester to Silchester, made kitchen wares for its inhabitants (fig. 40). Another kiln-site in the area produced both grey wares and colour-coated fine wares, which generally travelled no further than Wanborough, where over 200 vessels of north Wiltshire colour-coated ware have been found.[4] Although much smaller in number, the second largest group is from Cirencester, with other examples found at White Walls, Cricklade and other sites close to Wanborough. This ware did not reach Gloucester, perhaps due to the presence of the steep Cotswold scarp. The drift of the distribution pattern is undoubtedly north and west

---

Central Gaul
Lyons (Ly)
Lezoux (L)
Les Martres de Veyre (MV)
Vichy and Terre France (V)
Lubié (Lu)
Gueugnon (Gu)
Jaulges-Villiers-Vineux (J)

East Gaul
Rheinzabern (R)
Trier (T)
Sinzig (S)
Haute-Yutz (HY)
Boucheporn (B)
Chémery-Fauquelmont (C)
La Madeleine (Ma)
Eschweilerhof (E)
Blickweiler (Bl)
Mittlebronn (Mi)

Heiligenberg (H)
Ittenweiler (I)
Luxeuil (Lx)
Offemont (O)

Swiss and Trans-Rhine
Waiblingen (Wa)
Kräherwald (K)
Vindonissa (Vi)
Baden-in-Aargau (BA)
Westerndorf-Pfaffenhofen (W)

Argonne
Lavoye (La)
Avocourt and Les Allieux (Av)
Pont-des-Rèmes (P)

Britain
Colchester (Co)
Aldgate-Pulborough (unlocated)

rather than south, with no examples at Silchester. The lopsided pattern of finds may be related to Wanborough's sphere of influence.

This can be predicted by Reilly's 'Law of retail gravitation'. Using this formula, a market area can be constructed around a centre according to the size and location of neighbouring places. In this case the distribution centre was Wanborough, with the pattern demonstrating not only dependence on a town for a major part of the marketing, but also the importance of main roads in the movement of goods from the town. Cirencester was near enough to receive the pottery in reduced quantities but Silchester was too far away and so an uneconomical proposition. It also demonstrates that fine wares tend to travel further afield than grey kitchen wares produced at the same workshops. This pattern is repeated at the larger nucleated industries, like the New Forest and Oxford potteries. The potters themselves could have supplied the local market with cooking pots, peddling their wares and selling through markets, while the more distant customers who required the fine wares were supplied by traders.

Difficulties can arise when studying the marketing of products from isolated workshops, as the distribution of the wares can be so local that there are insufficient find-spots to observe any pattern. The products of a late first-century kiln at Shedfield, Hampshire are virtually unknown away from the kiln's site, which lies deep in the countryside, between Winchester, Chichester and Bitterne (Clausentum). The virtual absence of Shedfield pottery at these sites presumably reflects its very local market. Some workshops were much better organised. The individual workshops around the Thames estuary which produced BB2, and those in the Severn Valley which manufactured a number of characteristic forms in a distinctive orange to buff fabric, appear to behave as if they had been a single industry. In both these areas small scattered rural potteries were linked by a common repertoire and fabric as well as the same home and long-distance markets.

NUCLEATED WORKSHOPS

Fine wares were normally produced by individual workshops concentrated in a small area, where costs could be minimised by the mass-production of pottery. Samian was made in this way, with the potteries usually in rural locations which were sometimes situated in the most unlikely places (fig. 41). The workshops at La Graufesenque were near the small town of Condatomagus, in the heart of the Cevennes massif. Export to the Mediterranean involved an expensive haul over the Causses, while the northern markets were blocked by the Massif

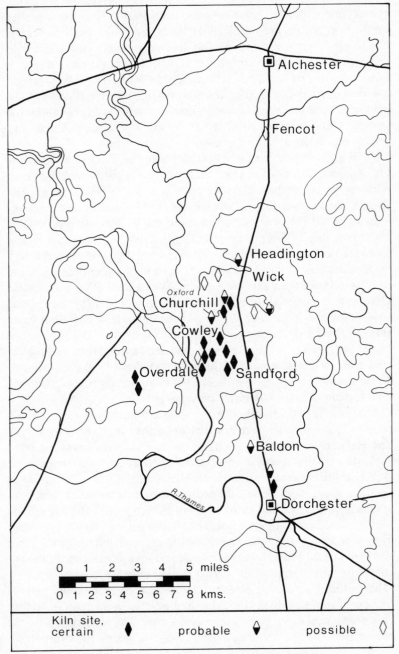

Fig. 42 Roman kiln sites in the Oxford region. *After Young*

Central. This reflects the nature of an industry in which the making and selling of pottery were separate activities. It may explain why production centres are found in such isolated positions. The central Gaulish industry was more sensibly located on the northern fringe of the Massif Central and connected via the Allier and the Loire to a coastal outlet (fig. 41), but it is hardly in a commercially strategic position like Lyons. Production in north and eastern Gaul was also primarily rural in character, with workshops scattered throughout the region. Only in rare cases, as at Trier, was a samian industry established in an urban environment.

In Britain the production of both fine wares and coarse wares at the Oxford potteries, sited in the country between the Roman towns of Alchester and Dorchester-on-Thames, was also on a very large scale (fig. 42). As a result, the industry was able to produce cheaper products which flooded the local market. Sites in the vicinity often produce a high percentage of fine pottery, even though many of them are not near a road. In conclusion, many of the industries that made pottery on a large scale were in rural areas, not related to or dependent upon the nearest town for their existence. Some, like Lezoux, Rheinzabern and Oxford, were close to the main waterways providing cheap transportation which was necessary for long-distance trade. These industries relied on a well-developed communication system for the dispersal of their wares, based on the provincial road network and river and coastal traffic. Rural developments of this kind would not have been possible without *negotiatores* or other traders, who were willing to travel into the countryside to make wholesale purchases.

More rarely, workshops clustered in or around large urban centres. The Arretine potteries were in an urban setting, like those in the Greek and Hellenistic world. If a town had the necessary resources, i.e. clay, fuel and available space, it would attract potters and other artisans, as did the more important military establishments. The concentration of wealth would also be an incentive, attracting a wider range of specialists. Cologne had its own urban industry, with the workshops and kilns situated either immediately outside the city on the main arterial roads or within the confines of the city walls (although the latter may predate the founding of the *colonia* and are generally considered to mark the outer limits of the earlier pre-Roman settlement) (fig. 43). This industry served the extensive home market, producing a greater variety of products than the individual isolated workshop, including fine wares, coarse wares, figurines and lamps. This variety shows that the artisans were providing a wide range of goods for prospective

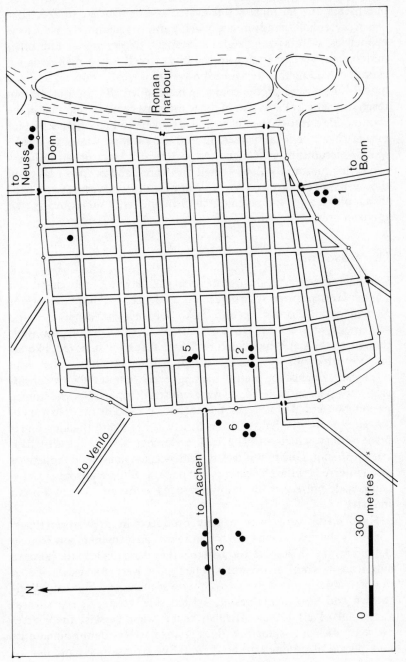

Fig. 43   Location of Roman pottery kilns at Cologne. *After Lung*

purchasers in a far more sophisticated and demanding market. The urban potter had the advantage of being able to sell directly in the local market as well as wholesale to traders. *Negotiatores* and other middlemen were operating in the city, which was a major market centre, providing facilities for exportation of local products, so that a higher output and profits could be maintained. But output did not reach the same levels as that of the workshops grouped together in the countryside due to the lack of specialisation in production, and reliance primarily on the local market. Indeed, exportation was often due to special circumstances. Colchester possessed a large urban industry producing mortaria, colour-coated fine wares, and probably BB2 but they were not exported on any scale until *c*. 140 when there was a need to supply troops campaigning in Scotland and subsequently the garrison on the Antonine Wall.

Organisation

Demonstrating the production of pottery in the home, implying that it was made on the premises where it was used, in either the prehistoric or Roman periods is not an easy task. Surprisingly few houses and settlement sites are known from the prehistoric period, due it is thought to their ephemeral nature. Those that have survived, like the late Neolithic villages at Skara Brae and Rinyo on Orkney, have not produced evidence for pottery making, even though they are considered to be part of the Grooved ware cultural complex. For the Roman period, household production has not been proved by the discovery of any equipment in a house, but as little was needed for making hand-made pottery, which could be fired in a kitchen hearth, this is perhaps not surprising. Due to this lack of evidence, a home-based industry is often inferred by the character of the pottery. Simple unsophisticated hand-made pottery is invariably regarded as the product of a home industry.

Hand-made wares were widely produced in prehistoric times. Similarly they have long been recognised as an element of any Roman pottery group. It has been thought that they were made in the home to supplement wheel-made wares when they were too expensive or unobtainable. Some writers have found it inconceivable that wheel-thrown and hand-made vessels existed side by side. Yet the most successful of all Romano-British coarse-ware vessels, the Dorset black-burnished cooking pot (fig. 11) was hand-made throughout its long period of production. So it would be wrong to assume that all hand-made wares were only of local significance or that they were produced solely in the home by women and did not form an important means of livelihood.

Up to *c*. 120 most Dorset black-burnished ware was used by the local inhabitants and the army units stationed in Dorset and Devon. The limited typology, simple techniques of manufacture, and restricted distribution have been taken to indicate a household industry – part-time domestic production possibly in the hands of women.[5] The industry was located on barren heathland in the Wareham-Poole harbour area. Little is known about how the pottery was made, except that as few kilns have been found it is assumed that the bonfire method was used. The known production sites are in isolated positions, not apparently linked to any specific community. Indeed the industry was established in an agriculturally impoverished area with few settlements.

After *c*. 120 the increased output precludes the idea of a part-time domestic industry linked to agriculture. It seems more likely that by now the work was a specialised job, a livelihood which could have involved both men and women for much of the year. Despite the continuation of simple technology, production undoubtedly took place in workshops. The wide distribution of the pottery could only have been achieved through traders, who arranged bulk shipments to the northern frontier. Pottery may not have been their prime interest; they may have been dealing in more valuable commodities like Dorset salt, Purbeck marble and Kimmeridge shale. Indeed the pot-making may initially have been linked in some way with the extraction of salt. Clearly some hand-made pottery was produced in workshops and it should be appreciated that hand-made wares functioned as well as those made on a wheel, that some types display high standards of craftsmanship in design and decoration, and that many were widely distributed. It would be wrong to assume that all such pottery was produced domestically.

THE OWNERS OF WORKSHOPS

Although household pottery production was undoubtedly important, the more specialised types were made by craftsmen, probably with their own workshops, implying that pot-making was a trade. It could still be a part-time seasonal activity but it was a livelihood. Aids like the wheel and the kiln became necessary to increase output and efficiency and the owner of the workshop could employ assistants, perhaps at first members of his own family, as the work load increased. Most Roman pottery was manufactured in individual workshops. Typical products were grey kitchen wares which were seldom transported very far. Although small and isolated, these workshops are ubiquitous and have cumulative importance. Some were run by indigenous potters who adopted the full range of equipment associated with the workshop. In other cases potters came from the Continent to establish workshops, exploiting the new military and civilian markets. The men who ran these concerns were either part-time potters, who were also farmers, or full-time professionals. Some military workshops are known, like that at Holt near Chester where pot-making was secondary to tile making, run by soldiers with possible civilian assistance.

In the case of civilian potters the question of land ownership still remains a problem. At the moment there is little evidence to indicate that these workshops operated as part of the villa economy, even though it has been suggested that the development of large potteries in the countryside was due to the entrepreneurial activities of landowners.[6] The upper classes were not overtly involved in trade, as their wealth was largely generated by land ownership, but the large estates, or *latifundia*, normally included a number of manufacturing industries. The production of *dolia* is specifically mentioned by Varro, providing rare literary evidence that ceramic products were made on estates. It can be reasonably inferred that the manufacture of amphorae and other ceramic containers was for the storing and transporting of estate produce. In those cases where there is actual evidence for estate production it largely relates to the manufacture of bricks and tiles, rather than vessels, which was common practice in Italy. Even in those proven instances it is still difficult to establish the relationship between the landowner and the pottery producer. The potter could have been employed by the landowner but equally might have been an independent tenant paying rent.[7] It is unlikely that the potters who ran individual workshops also owned the land and the concept of a tenant potter-farmer seems the most attractive at the moment.[8] However, in late Imperial times, rural potters were apparently so poor that they were excused the *collatis lustratis*, a tax on trade which was levied every five years. This could mean that the profits of the industry were not going to the potters but the landowner.[9]

THE ARRETINE INDUSTRY
Much of our knowledge of the organisation of the Arretine and samian industry comes from the study of potters' stamps. The Arretine stamps in their earliest and most informative phase bear the name of the works

owner followed by that of one of his slaves. Occasionally the servile status is directly referred to, as on the stamp of Surus Sari L (uci) S (ervus). These stamps show that the industry of the late first century BC was based on slavery but, as the slave's name appears besides that of his master, it must surely indicate that he was a valued and respected craftsman. Rasinus had no fewer than 60 slaves working for him, while C. and L. Avillius had only one. Perennius with about 13 slaves probably represents the norm. Relatively few firms had more than twenty slaves, many between ten and twenty and even more had less than ten, although it is not known how many slaves were working at one time.

Five hundred slaves have been identified but, as only the key craftsmen would have been recorded, there must have been a large number of labourers for the more menial tasks, like the extraction and preparation of the clay. Only some 40 slaves are associated with the manufacture of decorated vessels. The workshop owner may not have been actively engaged in the manufacture of the pottery, for had he been it is unlikely that he would have given his slave's name such prominence on the stamps. Instead he may have dealt with administration and marketing. So the industry was based on the individual workshop run by its proprietor with the aid of skilled slave potters and other workers.

It is apparent that numerous separate firms existed at Arezzo. About 90 have been recorded but not all were working at the same time. There may have been a great deal of co-operation and co-ordination between workshops, as illustrated by standardised forms and fabric. Some form of central controlling office has even been postulated.[10] Installations, such as tanks for preparing the clay or the kilns, may have been used communally but the stamps show that the workshops operated independently, so that when the establishments of Rasinus and C. Memmius were joined together for a time the vessels produced carry the stamp Rasini Memmi. Later when the association ended one of the names was deliberately erased from the stamp. There are other examples of stamps bearing the names of two or more owners but in most cases the names appear to belong to the same family, implying family businesses.

Excavations have uncovered a number of structures at Arezzo which also suggest a collection of individual units. The workshop of Ateius appears to have been completely self-contained. The great levigation tank (see below) of M. Perennius and his kiln are probably typical of the equipment possessed by most of the workshops. There is no reason to accept that the standardisation of fabric and forms necessarily implies co-operation. The nature of the fabric was largely conditioned by the raw materials obtainable in the area and the specifications of the ware. Typological standardisation occurs throughout the Roman world, from the fine-ware industries of Gaul and the Rhineland to the production of coarse wares in Dorset.

The industry at Cologne was in an urban setting. The production sites scattered around the city represent small working units, with their own kilns and other equipment. Each unit appears to have operated independently and yet each produced a range of items that were virtually identical. All the major urban centres attracted artisans who manufactured goods for the local market. The output of the workshops remained on a comparatively small scale, although larger than isolated examples and they were undoubtedly run as individual family concerns.

THE SAMIAN INDUSTRY

The stamps on Gaulish samian have also been used to ascertain how the industry was organised and how it functioned. They generally take the form of a name followed by F, FE or FEC (*fecit*-made by) and M or MA (*manu*-by the hand of), presumably denoting the name of the potter, or by OF (*officina* – workshop), indicating the owner of the establishment. It has been suggested that they were used to differentiate the work of various potters who made the same forms. Slaves are not mentioned on samian stamps, so it may be assumed that the workers are free. However, there is a graffito from La Graufesenque which records a monthly tally of tasks carried out by various slaves.[11] At least five people are listed as being engaged in activities ranging from visiting other places to the preparation of the clay for throwing and woodcutting. The latter was presumably used for firing the kilns. The dates on the graffito indicate that pottery production went on in the summer, when conditions were good enough to avoid the use of drying kilns. This suggests that slaves may have been employed as labourers rather than potters and thus they were not included on the stamps. They certainly appear to have played a lesser role than at Arezzo. So the names on the stamps represent either the owner of the workshop or the potter, although in some small firms they are likely to be the same man. In the case of Cinnamus, the largest of the Lezoux firms, he was probably the owner, as seven potters' names are associated with his bowls, suggesting that they were his mould makers or finishers. However, they may have been independent craftsmen who purchased moulds from Cinnamus to use in their own workshops. Failing to differentiate the sale of moulds from the founding of branch factories can cause confusion, so that the bowls stamped CINNAMIOF from Vichy could indicate the sale of moulds from Lezoux or the setting up of a branch of the Cinnamus firm.

As at Arezzo the workshops may have been run as family concerns. At La Graufesenque the *officina* of Mommo was active from pre-Claudian times down to the reign of Vespasian – some 45 years. As this period of activity represents more than the life span of one man it suggests that the business was handed down from father to son.

There was a high level of specialisation in production. The prominent name-stamps in the decoration, like those of Cinnamus, are thought to be advertisements deliberately included by the work's proprietor. The mould maker's name usually occurs in cursive script below the decoration (plate 22). The bowl finisher, who trimmed the rim and formed the foot-ring after removal from the mould, added his mark on the rim of Drag 30 and 37 (fig. 27.37). Even the making of the poinçons (stamps) was a specialist job and these were sometimes signed. One bowl could have been worked on by several potters, as on a production line. It is clear that samian firms could range in size from very large establishments, employing independent craftsmen who performed different tasks, to much smaller concerns where the potter-owner coped with all the stages of production. The south Gaulish potter Masclus stamped his bowls on the base and also signed his name amongst the decoration, indicating a small firm which was responsible for all operations.

The organisation of the industry at La Graufesenque was quite different to that in central and eastern Gaul. Tally lists indicate that kiln loads were communal at La Graufesenque, fired by specialist kiln operatives. The kilns may have been attached to the larger works or operated independently, serving numerous small concerns. These kilns were extremely large and in them thousands of vessels could be fired at a time. In contrast Lezoux has not produced a single tally list, although they have been found at Blickweiler and Rheinzabern. The dearth of comparative material from these sites suggests that commu-nal firings were the exception rather than the rule. Instead the central and east Gaulish industries seem to have been composed of many individual contained units. The workshop of Comitalis at Rheinzabern had several kilns, buildings and other structures, such as levigation tanks and wells. The size and number of these installations indicates a small workshop. The same picture emerges at Lezoux, where over 200 kilns have been recorded, implying a scatter of small workshops.

The different methods used in southern Gaul are also apparent in the forming and decorating of the vessels. South Gaulish samian is characterised by a confusing combination of decorative motifs, so that it is difficult to distinguish the work of individual potters by their style. In contrast in central and eastern Gaul the styles of different firms stand out quite distinctly. Also the south Gaulish output was on a far greater scale than that of central and eastern Gaul. This suggests radically different methods of production. In south Gaul potters appear to have been grouped into large communal manufactories, in which specialist craftsmen dealt with different aspects of production, from mould-making to bowl-finishing. In central and eastern Gaul small contained workshops were the rule, with the potter-owner increasingly performing all the tasks of manufacture. Even Cinnamus had few 'associates' compared with the large number of slaves connected with many of the Arretine firms. The samian industry appears to have fragmented into smaller working units resulting in a lower output capacity. The individual potters who moved to join an already established indigenous industry would have used the existing local marketing system. Their wares would have only achieved local distribution. Many of the small east Gaulish workshops operated in this fashion. Only with the mass migration of potters to a single area would the industry be large enough to attract traders and maintain a wide distribution, as was the case at Lezoux and Rheinzabern.

LARGE INDUSTRIES IN BRITAIN

Some of the large industries could still have operated on a part-time seasonal basis, perhaps still run by 'potter-farmers'. In Britain the kilns in the New Forest were clearly repaired on a number of separate occasions by plastering the walls with clay before use. Also the lack of substantial workshops may imply part-time activity. The differential distribution of wares, fine types travelling further afield than coarse, may suggest that the potters sold their coarse wares locally, through county fairs and the markets in the *civitas* capitals of Winchester and Dorchester, with merchants trading the finer wares further afield. The Oxford potteries operated on a much larger scale, with kilns spread over some 50 square km. Workshops, clay mixing tanks and various pits have been recognised. Particularly significant are the T-shaped driers thought to have been used for drying pottery, which suggest an attempt to prolong the working season. Although the kilns are small, the seasonal patching, so noticeable on New Forest examples, has not, so far, been found. The Oxford industry appears to have been more sophisticated, operating for a longer season each year. Grey coarse wares were marketed locally, while the colour-coated fine wares spread throughout southern England. Without traders the Oxford potteries could not have achieved their prominent position.

Not all the major industries in the countryside relied on fine wares for their existence. The potteries which made Derbyshire ware consisted of a series of workshops in the Holbrook-Hazelwood area to the north of Derby. The most extraordinary feature of this industry is that its products were exclusively jars, either with or without a prominent lid-seating, made in an extremely granular, rough fabric. A number of rural kilns were, therefore, producing a ware that would normally be associated with the individual workshop. The distribution is surprisingly broad for a ware of this type, covering all Derbyshire, parts of Lincolnshire, north Yorkshire and even beyond. Up to the end of the second and the beginning of the third century the ware was distributed fairly locally but from the mid-third to the fourth century it reached a much wider area. It is clear that the marketing pattern changed, with perhaps the intervention of traders who carried the ware further afield, but why should they take an interest in such a coarse ware which would have been sold very cheaply and generated little profit? The answer may be that the pots were containers for local produce and, after the contents had been consumed, they became kitchen vessels. This would explain the very limited and specialised repertoire. The jars with a lid-seating were designed to be sealed, so it has been suggested that they contained Celtic beans or possibly honey.[12] A similar reason, in this case the transportation of a liquid commodity, has been postulated for the wide distribution of Alice Holt grey wares, the product of another large rural industry in Surrey, in the late third and fourth centuries.[13]

THE STATUS OF THE POTTER

It can be seen that the status of the Roman potter changed during the course of time. The men who made Arretine wares were mostly slaves and their masters, who owned the workshops, were Italian citizens, like Cn. Ateius. By the time an industry was established at La Graufesenque slaves were mainly given more menial tasks. The potters themselves, from their name-stamps, were probably free independent craftsmen. The east Gaulish bowl finisher, Lutaeus, stamped the products of at least three different proprietors, Reginus, Satto and Ianus at Heiligenburg and Rheinzabern, suggesting that he was either an independent craftsman not attached to any specific workshop or he obtained moulds from the larger firms for use in his own workshop. In the latter case, owner and potter had become one and the same man. It is, therefore, surprising that few samian potters in Gaul used the *tria nomina*, the three names used to indicate Roman citizenship, a practice which had become virtually universal by the reign of the Emperor Claudius. At Montans the initials of the *tria nomina* were used quite frequently, as for example S (extus) Iv(lius) Prim(us) who worked during the Flavian period. In general it seems that even when a Gallic potter was a citizen he tended to stamp only his last name, or *cognomen*. Increasingly the industry was predominantly run by the local inhabitants, *peregrini* or non-citizens. This impression is reinforced by the graffiti, which indicate that the Celtic language was in common use in the south Gaulish workshops. It is further demonstrated by the names of the potters, which were either overtly Gallic, such as Viducus, Bitrix and Litugenus or, due to the ever-increasing effects of Romanisation, Latinised Gallic names, like Regulus and Divixtus. Latin when it is used in the tallies and stamps is often of a low standard. Meaningless stamps, vaguely suggesting letters, were commonly used by illiterate potters. All these features point to a strong Gallic element in the samian industry.

A similar pattern has emerged in the organisation of the Romano-British mortaria industry. Of the stamps recorded, only a few have the *tria nomina*, and these men were probably expatriates from Gaul or further afield who moved to Britain to take advantage of the new markets. Q. Valerius Veranius, with two of his associates, both Quinitii, and perhaps his freedmen, Suriacus and Esuneratus, probably moved from Gallia Belgica to Kent for this reason. C. Attius Marinus migrated at least twice in his working career which began in Colchester in the late Flavian period, moving first to Radlett, Herts, before finally settling at Hartshill-Mancetter, Warks. Q. Rutilius Ripanus was active at Brockley Hill from the mid-60s to mid-90s of the first century. The remainder of the names recorded on the stamps can be divided into two groups, those with Latin names, such as Saturninus and Vitalis, numbering over 60, and those with Celtic or definitely barbarous names such as Aesico and Amminus, of which there are twice as many.[14] Some are clearly Romanised Celtic names, like Bellicus, Messor and Senilis. There are also some fine examples of compound names, such as Setibogius and Tamesubugus. The latter is a rare example of a late potter, known from a graffito scratched before firing on a mortarium found near Oxford. The first element in his name is certainly appropriate for a potter working in the Thames valley. However, it could be a place name, with the ending standing for *burgus*. It is clear that most of the coarse pottery used in Britain during the Roman period was made by Britons.

Equipment

The Roman potter's workshop normally consisted of a building, containing a tank for preparing the clay and working areas, with kilns, wells and clay pits outside. Unfortunately few such establishments have been found in Britain. One of the best examples, found at Stibbington in the Nene Valley, was a rectangular building with a square stone-lined tank and paved working areas with an external kiln, well and clay-pit. Semi-circular or round houses have been found on pottery-making sites, as at Whitehill Farm, Wiltshire[15] (fig. 44) and Oxford.[16] The kilns were usually placed outside the building, perhaps to reduce the risk of fire. Most of the buildings seem to have been used exclusively for working and it has rarely been demonstrated that potters lived on site, but this may be because excavations have been too limited.

Pottery is made in stages, with associated specialised equipment. Once the clay has been dug it has to be prepared, as no clay can be immediately worked. The clay was purified in tanks by the process of levigation, which involves mixing the clay with water and allowing the coarser and heavier inclusions to settle out. These tanks could also have been used to store or to moisten the clay rather than to levigate it. A number of clay or stone-lined tanks are known from sites in Britain, including the Nene Valley, Brockley Hill and Oxford. Similar pits are also known from Rheinzabern but the most spectacular tanks have been found at Arezzo, where the one belonging to Perennius could hold at least 10,000 gallons. The large amounts of water used when cleaning the clay and shaping the pots required a good supply. Not surprisingly wells are common. Sometimes they may have been replaced by drainage gullies and ditches, like those found at Whitehill Farm (fig. 44). Clay is normally worked with the feet, to mix in additives like sand filler and to remove any air bubbles, usually on a dry flat area. This may have been done on the paved areas found in and around workshop buildings, like those at Stibbington.

TURNTABLES AND WHEELS

Pots were formed using a variety of methods. Many of the vessels

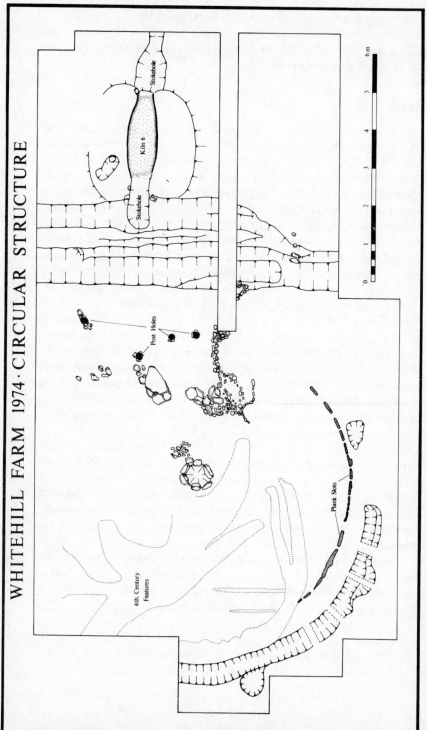

WHITEHILL FARM 1974 · CIRCULAR STRUCTURE

Stokehole

Kiln 6

Stokehole

Post Holes

4th. Century Features

Plank Slots

6 m

Fig. 44   Whitehill Farm 1974: the circular structure, *After Anderson*

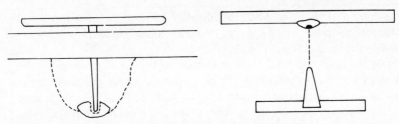

Fig. 45 **Pivoted and socketed potter's wheels.** *After Peacock*

classed as 'hand-made' are smooth enough and regular enough to have been made on a turntable. Often the finish of the rim, especially of Dorset black-burnished cooking pots, shows that it was turned, although the body was undoubtedly hand-formed. Most Roman pottery was produced on a fast wheel. It is thought that these took the form of fly-wheels rather than double or kick wheels. Such simple wheels were probably designed to rotate either on a fixed spindle or on an axis that was fixed to the wheel and pivoted on the ground[17] (fig. 45). A low fly-wheel of this kind could have been turned by an apprentice or slave while the master-potter formed the vessel. Most Roman fly-wheels must have been made of wood as so few have survived, although a remarkable exception is a wheel from Speicher, Germany, made from Mayen lava. It looks like the upper stone of a quern, or flour mill, but has holes on the upper edge which may have held the tip of a pole used to turn the apparatus (plate 23). Fragments of querns or mills have been found on other pottery production sites but these could have been used to grind materials. Double wheels cannot be entirely dismissed as one is illustrated on a Hellenistic relief from Egypt.

Very little is known of the potter's ancillary equipment for throwing and shaping pots. It must be assumed that most of these tools were of wood or bone and that is why they rarely survive, but the Musée National, St Germain, near Paris, has a collection of tools from pottery sites including iron spatulas which could have been used for shaping and turning. Production of the more elaborate types of pottery, like samian, required a wide range of equipment. Numerous bowl moulds, individual moulds for appliqué and poinçons, (the stamps used to make the designs) as well as two-piece moulds for making terracotta figurines and lamps have been found at Trier (plate 6). The potter's name-stamps were specially made in bronze or pottery or simply cut into the end of an old piece of samian (plate 4). In the Museums für Vor-und Frühgeschichte, Frankfurt, there is a bronze wheel with a design cut into it, presumably originally mounted on a wooden haft, resembling a modern pastry-cutter, and undoubtedly used to produce rouletted decoration (plate 24). This was found at Niola (Hedderheim), along with other potters' tools made of iron.

Before firing the pottery has to be thoroughly dried, to minimise the risk of warping or bubbling. As many potteries only operated in the summer, no special provisions for drying were necessary but the season could be extended by using drying sheds or ovens. A rectangular building with a system of flues was found at Mancetter, Warwickshire, dating to the mid-second century.[18] Drying ovens have been found at the Churchill potteries, Oxford, taking the form of small 'T'-shaped structures.[19]

FIRING TECHNIQUES

Although kilns were used in the late Iron Age on the Continent they are rare, and in England the only examples are prefabricated surface structures. P. Woods[20] discovered some slight surface structures in the Upper Nene Valley in which Belgic wares were fired, dating to the period immediately after the Roman conquest. Ephemeral structures such as these have little chance of survival. However, pottery can be effectively fired in surface bonfires or clamps, although again these are difficult to detect. Much prehistoric pottery must have been fired in this way or in domestic hearths. Pottery can be fired in almost any open hearth. A clay that is well weathered and full of organic or mineral fillers can be treated in this fashion without fear of breakage. Vessels may be rotated in the fire by degrees until all the parts of it are baked. Though this method is primitive it is effective and much of the pottery made in the home during prehistoric and Roman times was probably fired in this manner.

BONFIRE METHOD

The stacking together of a number of pots and their firing under a bonfire is only one stage removed from using a domestic hearth. This method of firing may indicate the communal production of pottery. A bonfire, once lit, will normally rise fairly quickly to its maximum temperature and thereafter the temperature will gradually fall. This simple, effective and cheap way of firing pottery was still used extensively after the Roman conquest as with Dorset black-burnished ware. Unfortunately these sites are very difficult to find, because the waste was left lying on the ground and hence easily destroyed and dispersed. At best all that remains are layers of ash and sherds of black-burnished ware, many of which are uncharacteristically red in colour having been reheated in an oxidising atmosphere. As black-burnished

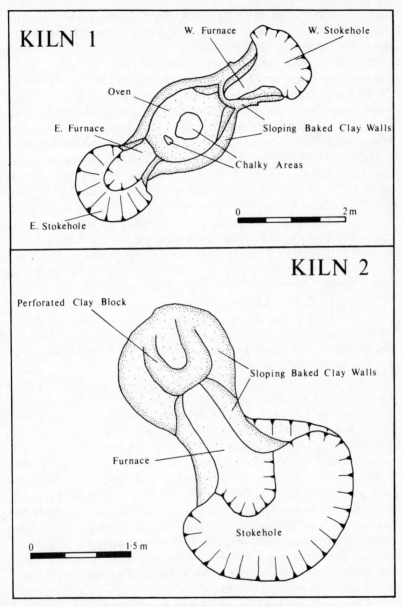

Fig. 46 Savernake Forest 1957–58: Kilns 1 and 2. *After Anderson*

ware is heavily tempered, the failure rate must have been low. Rejected pots tend to be discoloured or cracked rather than warped and so it is not easy to recognise them as wasters.

Some of the kilns in the Savernake Forest, Wiltshire,[21] are no more than elaborate versions of the bonfire technique. This type of kiln is sometimes referred to as the horizontal draught kiln. Kiln 1 consisted of a central oval-shaped oven dug into the natural clay sub-soil (fig. 46). At both ends of the oven the walls narrowed into flue channels leading into the stokeholes. The floor of the oven was flat with the walls sloping sharply up to a height of 356mm, although this was presumably less than the original height. The kiln had been refloored and clay cheeks added to the west end of the oven where it joined the flue. This type of kiln was rapidly and easily constructed, making good use of the local geology. The original hollow dug for the oven, once fired, provided adequate kiln walls without additional material being required. Some alterations to the structure were necessary, presumably to increase efficiency, particularly at the west end of the oven, and the floor was relaid, possibly because of damage incurred during an earlier firing, perhaps during the raking out of ashes.

At Whitehill Farm, Wiltshire[22] eight kilns were of the two-flued variety. These kilns can be dated to the second century AD. The basic design of these two-flue kilns is similar to that of Savernake Forest Kiln 1, but whereas the latter possessed an oven constricted at either end to form flue tunnels, the Whitehill Farm examples are less sophisticated and lack such well defined flues. Instead they look more like an elongated barrel (fig. 47). The distinguishing features of these kilns are the trench construction (formed by digging a long, shallow basin-shaped trench into the natural clay to produce, after firing, a kiln with a somewhat uneven floor and sloping walls), a long barrel-shaped oven lacking distinctive narrow flues, and a flue opening at either end of the oven into an adjacent stokehole (plates 25, 26). In some cases it appears that the kilns were set into moulds of clay that had been deliberately built up higher than the surrounding areas, presumably to improve firing conditions and assist drainage on a very wet site (fig. 47; plate 26). Another feature of the kilns was the total replacement of kiln floors and sometimes walls, rather than minor localised repairs, indicating continuity of use over a considerable period.

The interior of Whitehill Farm Kiln 2 revealed the existence of five different floor-levels (plate 27). Some of these total refloorings involved the rewalling of the kiln as well. All the floors were well laid and even, having been fired to produce a hard grey surface. Each

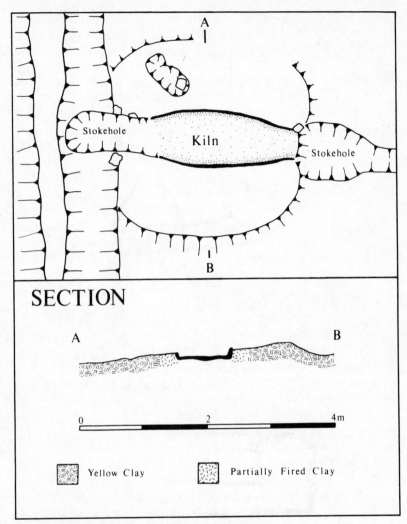

SECTION

0   2   4 m

Yellow Clay   Partially Fired Clay

Fig. 47 Whitehill Farm 1974: Kiln 6. *After Anderson*

operation consisted of laying a quantity of clay 80–100mm thick on top of the preceding floor, the top 20–30mm forming the hard-baked floor surface. In the case of Kiln 1 the damaged walls and floor were repaired by the insertion of pot sherds and clay plates. These plates, made from lumps of unfired clay and flattened on grass, were pushed into gaps in the kiln floor and smoothed in with the already fired areas. Eventually large parts of the kiln floor were repaired in this way. During firing,

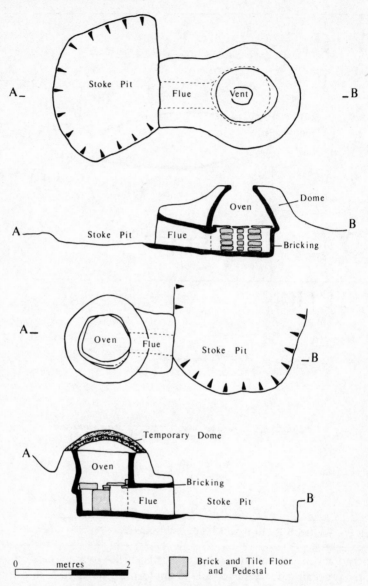

Fig. 48 Experimental Romano-British type up-draught kilns constructed at Barton-on-Humber
Kiln A: pottery placed on a permanent, supported, fired clay floor with vent holes
Kiln B: pottery placed on a temporary floor of fire-bars radiating from a central support.
After Bryant

pottery was stacked on the oven floor in an inverted position. The pottery was probably covered over with bracken, straw and wood and perhaps sealed with turf. The whole structure was then fired and the fire fed with fuel through the two stokeholes until the required temperature was reached. After firing the kiln would have been left to cool, perhaps for several days, so that when opened the pottery would not crack from being exposed too suddenly to cold air.

UP-DRAUGHT KILNS

The up-draught kilns introduced after the Roman conquest and subsequently adopted by native potters are quite different structures. This change in firing practices can be accounted for in a number of ways but the most likely is that native potters who worked for a while in the vicinity of military installations learnt the new methods from potters who had come to Britain with the army. Basically an up-draught kiln is any structure in which the fire is set in a pit below the pottery, which is itself enclosed in a dome, or similar structure, with a vent or blow-hole to allow the smoke and gases to escape (plate 28). Such kilns are generally round, oval or square and may have one or more stokeholes. The pottery may be placed on a permanent fired clay floor (fig. 48A) with vent holes (either supported or free-standing), or on fire-bars, radiating from a central support or traversing the width of the oven, which forms a temporary floor (fig. 48B). The central pedestal may be permanent or removeable. The top covering was probably not permanent, indeed few survive, since it had to be broken away after each firing to gain access to the pottery (fig. 48). Up-draught kilns vary considerably in design and sophistication.

The up-draught kilns found in the Savernake Forest, alongside and contemporary with the trench type discussed above, are rather primitive structures. Kiln 2 (fig. 46) was circular in shape with a single flue leading to a large stokehole. This kiln had been constructed in the same way as Kiln 1 on the same site, using the natural clay sub-soil as walling but in places patches of clay had been applied to repair the walls. In the centre of the furnace was an unusual pedestal which had undergone a variety of alterations. In its original form the pedestal was a 'V'-shaped structure with two arms of fired clay rising from the lower part of the kiln. This pedestal presumably formed a support for fire bars used to create a temporary floor. Subsequently two further clay 'skins' were added to the pedestal, probably to repair damage, and finally the two clay arms were extended back, attaching the structure to the rear furnace wall. At Whitehill Farm up-draught kilns, with one

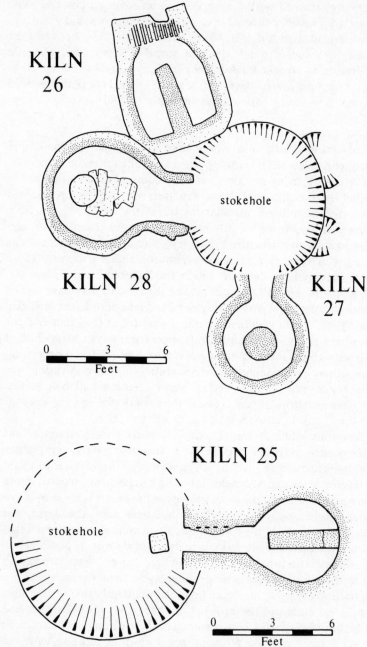

Fig. 49   Roman kilns at Colchester: Endsleigh School 1955, Kilns 25–28.
After Hull

flue and stokehole, also occurred alongside the two-flued trench variety. Four kilns of this type were uncovered.

The kilns at Colchester (Hull, 1963) were much more sophisticated affairs.[23] Colchester Kiln 26 (fig. 49) was squarish in plan, typical of many first-century examples. It was built of broken tiles laid in clay and the walls were about 28cm thick. The walls stood from 41–61cm high. The central support was of the same construction, with tiles laid in clay, and was attached to the back wall of the furnace. The arch leading into the flue, which faced north, still stood. The south wall of this kiln backed onto Kiln 28. This kiln was pear-shaped with a wide flue facing east and opening onto the same shallow stokehole as Kiln 27. The central support was not connected to the back wall of the furnace and it was constructed of a round column of clay with a jumble of fragments of tiles in front. Unfortunately little remained of the floor of the oven. Kiln 27 was circular with a short flue. The central support was also circular, free-standing, made of clay and 55cm in diameter. Kiln 25 (fig. 49) was pear-shaped with a central support fixed to the back wall which was built of rectangular clay blocks. The walls were built of tiles laid in courses, and little survived of the floor or the dome. These kilns presumably had temporary floors constructed of fire-bars radiating from the central supports.

The samian kilns found at Colchester were even more elaborate with hollow pipes embedded in the walls, used to circulate the heat and at the same time to prevent the pottery coming into direct contact with the furnace gases and smoke.[24] The oven also contained a series of hollow pipes, extending from below the permanent floor to the top of the structure again to circulate the heat more evenly. These were capped with chimneys to allow the gases and smoke to escape. These special precautions were taken so that the pottery was fired consistently at a high temperature thus ensuring even baking (plate 29).

There is still a great deal to be learnt about Roman potting techniques and production sites. Surprisingly little is known of the layout of individual workshops and the relationship between kiln sites clustered together in a small area. Many excavations have only dealt with the kilns and not even attempted to find ancillary buildings and equipment. The latter are often difficult to locate, as even a minor pottery may be spread over several acres. Large-area excavations have only recently been carried out and it is hoped that future work will investigate the entire industrial unit rather than just concentrate on kiln structures.

Conclusion

Archaeology incorporates many disciplines ranging from art history to advanced scientific methods of analysis. It is the aim of the archaeologist to blend together these diverse elements, which include history, social anthropology, mathematics and medicine, and so to attempt to recreate man's past. Archaeology is concerned with studying all aspects of past cultures and societies, not just political events and the lives of important people. The study of pottery mirrors the discipline as a whole. The form and decoration of vessels are the province of crafts and art historians, graffiti and name-stamps are of interest to the epigraphist, the fabric can be analysed by the geologist, chemist and physicist, while production techniques and distribution will be the concern of the social-anthropologist and economist.

The real object of studying pottery is to combine all this information together to form a coherent picture of the life of man in the past. The study of pottery, or any other artefact, in isolation or for its own sake would be far too limiting. There is always the danger with a subject so inherently complicated as pottery that it will become over-specialised. Due to its vast complexities pottery is usually studied period by period. Each specialist tends to stay in the compartment of his or her choice, either Neolithic, Bronze Age, Iron Age, Roman or Mediaeval and there is little overlapping or even exchanging of information. Common traits binding all the periods together are invariably overlooked. The problems that arise at the point where two periods merge, such as the interface between the Iron Age and the Roman periods, often remain unanswered as each specialist denies responsibility. Not only do people concentrate on their respective periods but they specialise further in one particular aspect.

This is especially true of the Roman period with the division of the ceramic material into so many different sections culminating in specialists for individual industries. With so many divisions there is a danger that the wider implications of pottery studies will be completely lost in a mass of indigestible information. New scientific techniques are applied to pottery without any real regard to the archaeological significance, largely because it is fashionable to do so. The outcome of such experiments is often no more than a contribution to methodology which adds little to our real knowledge of the pottery and has little relevance to the past. Indeed with the proliferation of pottery types and styles, due to increasing statistical and compositional analysis, we are in danger of learning more and more about less and less. Pottery studies are becoming increasingly parochial with some specialists losing sight of their ultimate goal. The real value of such studies lies in the resulting implications whether chronological, economic or social. Ultimately, as Wheeler said, archaeology is about people not things.

Pottery is a subject worthy of detailed study, not for its own sake but because of the wider implications which may contribute to our understanding of man's past. It is hoped that the preceding chapters have illustrated the many and varied ways in which pottery can be used by the archaeologist. Above all, because of its interest and potential, pottery will always remain an important source of information, retaining its pre-eminent position in archaeology.

Select Bibliography

A.C. Anderson *A Guide to Roman Fine Wares* Vorda I 1980

B. Cunliffe *Iron Age Communities in Britain* 1978

A. Detsicas *Current Research in Romano-British Coarse Pottery* CBA 10, 1973

J.P. Gillam *Types of Roman Coarse Pottery Vessels in Northern Britain* 1970

D.W. Harding *The Iron Age in Lowland Britain* 1974

C. Johns *Arretine and Samian pottery* British Museum 1978

N. Langmaid *Prehistoric Pottery* Shire Archaeology 1980

J.V.S. Megaw & D.D.A. Simpson *Introduction to British Prehistory* 1980

M. Millet *Pottery and the Archaeologist* Institute of Archaeology, London 1979

F. Oswald & T.D. Pryce *An introduction to the study of Terra Sigillata* Revised 1945

D. Peacock *Pottery and Early Commerce: characterisation and trade in Roman and later ceramics* Academic Press 1977

D. Peacock *Pottery in the Roman World: an ethnoarchaeological approach* 1982

S. Piggott *Neolithic Cultures of the British Isles* 1954

A.C. Renfrew *British Prehistory: a new outline* 1974

J.A. Stanfield & G. Simpson *Central Gaulish Potters* 1958

V. Swan *Pottery in Roman Britain* Shire Archaeology 1975

G. Webster *Romano-British Coarse pottery: a student's guide* CBA 6, 1976

Notes and References

Abbreviations used in the Notes
Antiq. J. Antiquaries Journal
Arch. J. Archaeological Journal
BAR *British Archaeological Reports*
CBA *Council for British Archaeology*
PPS *Proceedings of the Prehistoric Society*
Rep. Res. Comm. Soc. Antiq. London – Reports of the Research Committee of the Society of Antiquaries of London
Rom. Stud. *Journal of Roman Studies*
TCWAAS *Transactions of the Cumberland and Westmorland Antiquarian and Archaeological Society*

1 Why Study Pottery?

1 A.H.L. Pitt-Rivers, *Excavations at Cranborne Chase, near Rushmore,* Vol IV 1898
2 See Verulamium. S.S. Frere, *Verulamium Excavations Vol I,* Rep. Res. Comm. Soc. Antiq. London, No. 27 1972
3 R.F.J. Jones, 'Why pottery', in M. Millet (Ed) *Pottery and the Archaeologist,* Institute of Archaeology, London 1979
4 Strabo, *Geography,* iv, 199
5 D. Peacock, 'Neolithic pottery production in Cornwall,' in *Antiquity,* 43 1969, 147

2 Pottery and Research

1 G. Daniel, *A short history of Archaeology,* Thames and Hudson 1982
2 S. Piggott, 'Abercromby and after: the beaker cultures of Britain re-examined,' in L. Alcock and L. Foster (Eds), *Culture and Environment,* 1963
3 S. Piggott, *Neolithic cultures of the British Isles,* Cambridge 1954

4 S. Piggott, *The West Kennet Long Barrow: Excavations 1955–56,* Ministry of Works Archaeological Reports No. 4, London 1962
5 I.H. Longworth, 'The origins and development of the primary series of collared urns in England and Wales', *PPS* 27 1961, 263–306
6 Charles Roach Smith, *Illustrations of Roman London,* London 1859
7 H. Dragendorff, 'Terra Sigillata' in *Bonner Jahrbucher,* 96, 1895, 18–155
8 J. Dechelette, *Les vases céramiques ornés de la Gaule Romaine,* 2 vols, Paris 1904
9 R. Knorr, *Topfer und Fabriken verzierter Terra-Sigillata des ersten Jahrhunderts,* 1919
Terra Sigillata-Gefasse des ersten Jahrhunderts mit Topfer-namen, 1952
10 W. Ludowici, *Katalog V: Stempel, namen und Bilder romischer Topfer aus mein en Ausgrabungen in Rheinzabern,* 1901–14, 1927
11 E. Folzer, *Die Bilderschusseln der ostgallischen Sigillata-Manufacturen,* Bonn 1913

12 F. Oswald, *Index of potters' stamps on terra-sigillata, 'Samian Ware'*, 1931

13 J.A. Stanfield and G. Simpson, *Central Gaulish Potters*, Oxford 1958

14 J. Curle, *A Roman frontier post and its people: the fort of Newstead in the parish of Melrose*, Glasgow 1911

15 T. May, 'The Roman pottery in the York Museum' in *York Phil. Soc. Reps*, 1908–11

16 T. May, 'Catalogue of the Roman pottery in the Museum, Tullie House, Carlisle', TCWAAS, N.S.17, 1917

17 T. May, *The pottery found at Silchester*, Reading, 1916

18 T. May, *Catalogue of the Roman pottery in the Colchester and Essex Museum*, Cambridge 1930

19 J.P. Bushe-Fox, *Excavations at Hengistbury Head, Hampshire in 1911–12*, Rep. Res. Comm. Soc. Antiq. London No. 3, 1915

20 W. Whiting, W. Hawley and T. May, *Report on the excavations of the Roman cemetery at Ospringe, Kent*, Rep. Res. Comm. Soc. Antiq. London No. 8, 1931

21 J.P. Bushe-Fox, *Excavations of the late Celtic urnfield at Swarling, Kent*, Rep. Res. Comm. Soc. Antiq. London No. 5, 1925

22 J.P. Bushe-Fox, *First report on the excavations of the Roman Fort at Richborough, Kent*, Rep. Res. Comm. Soc. Antiq. London No. 6, 1926 Second Report 1928 Third Report 1932

23 T. May, *Warrington's Roman Remains*, Warrington 1904

24 T. May, *The Roman forts at Templeborough, Near Rotherham*, 1922

25 G. Webster, 'Reflections on Romano-British pottery studies – past, present and future', in J. Dore and K. Greene (Eds), *Roman pottery studies in Britain and Beyond*, BAR Supp Series 30, 1977

26 J.P. Bushe-Fox, *Excavations on the site of the Roman town at Wroxeter, Shropshire in 1912*, Oxford 1913

27 R.E.M. Wheeler, *Prehistoric and Roman Wales*, Oxford 1925

28 R.E.M. Wheeler and T.V. Wheeler, *Verulamium: A Belgic and two Roman cities*, Rep. Res. Comm. Soc. Antiq. London No. 8, 1936

29 see chapter 1 note 2

30 K. Kenyon, *Excavations at the Jewry Wall Site, Leicester*, Oxford 1948

31 J.P. Gillam, *Types of Roman coarse pottery vessels in Northern Britain*, Newcastle 1971

32 *Ibid* Page 11

33 E. Gose, *Gefasstypen der Romischen keramik in Rheinland*, Köln 1950

34 H.H. Thomas, 'The pottery' in D.M. Liddle 'Excavations at Hembury Fort, Devon,' *Proc. Devon Arch. Expl. Soc.*, 11 135

35 H.H. Thomas in D.M. Liddle 'Excavations at Hembury Fort, Devon,' *Proc. Devon Arch. Expl. Soc.*, 1929–32. Three annual reports

36 I.W. Cornwall and H.W. Hodges, 'Thin sections of British Neolithic pottery – Windmill Hill, a test site,' *Bull. Inst. Arch. London Univ.* IV 29, 1964

37 See chapter 1 note 5

38 D. Peacock, 'The black-burnished pottery industry in Dorset' in A. Detsicas (Ed), *Current Research in Romano-British coarse pottery*, CBA 10 London 1973

39 P. Corder, 'A pair of fourth-century Romano-British kilns near Crambeck,' *Antiq. J.*, XVII, 1937, 392–412
'A Roman pottery of the Hadrianic-Antonine period at Verulamium,' *Antiq. J.*, XXI, 1941, 271–298
A Romano-British kiln on the Lincoln Racecourse, University of Nottingham 1949

40 M.R. Hull, *The Roman Potters' Kilns at Colchester*, Rep. Res. Comm. Soc. Antiq. London No. 32, 1963

41 V. Swan, 'Aspects of the New Forest late Roman pottery industry in A. Detsicas,' (see Note 38)

42 M. Fulford, *New Forest Roman pottery*, BAR Brit Series 17, 1975

43 C. Young, 'Oxfordshire Roman Pottery', BAR Brit Series 43, 1977

44 A. Anderson, *A Guide to Roman*

Fine Wares, Vorda I 1980.
M.D. Howe, J.R. Perrin and
D. Mackreth, *Roman Pottery from
the Nene Valley: a guide*,
Peterborough City Occasional Paper
No. 2, 1981
45 K. Greene, *Report on the
Excavations at Usk 1965–76. The
Pre-Flavian Fine Wares*, Cardiff
1979
46 A. Anderson, M. Fulford, H.
Hatcher and A.M. Pollard,
'Chemical Analysis of Hunt Cups
and Allied Wares from Britain',
Britannia 1982, Vol XIII

3 Pottery and the Archaeologist

1 A. King, 'A Graffito from La
Graufesenque,' *Britannia* XI, 1980
2 A.K.B. Evans, 'Pottery and History'
in A.C. Anderson and A.S.
Anderson (Eds), *Roman Pottery
Research in Britain and North-West
Europe*, BAR Int. Series 123,
Oxford 1981, 521
3 See note 1, page 141
4 See note 2, page 522
5 F.O. Waage, 'Vasa Samia', *Antiquity*
II 1937, 46–55
6 F.O. Waage, *Excavations in the
Agora at Athens*, 1933
7 J.W. Hayes, *Late Roman Pottery*,
London 1972
8 See note 2, page 524
9 See note 1, page 142
10 See note 2, page 522
11 Governor Pownall, 'Memoire on the
Roman Earthen ware fished up
within the mouth of the River
Thames', *Archaeologia* 5 (1779),
282–290
12 S. Lysons, 'Some account of Roman
Antiquities discovered at Carhun',
Archaeologia 16 (1812), 127–134
13 Galen, *de Simplic. Medic. Temp. ac
Facult*, 9, Chapter 2
14 G. Webster, *Romano-British Coarse
Pottery: A student's Guide*, CBA Res.
Rep. No. 6 1976, 17
15 *Ibid*, 18
16 *Ibid*, 20
17 K. Greene, *Report on the excavations
at Usk 1965–76: The Pre-Flavian*

Fine Wares, Cardiff 1979, 20
18 P. Bidwell, 'Early black-burnished
ware at Exeter' in J. Dore and
K. Greene, *Roman Pottery Studies in
Britain and Beyond*, BAR Supp.
Series 30 1977, 189–98
19 *Ibid*, 192
20 J.P. Gillam, 'Coarse fumed ware in
North Britain and Beyond', in
Glasgow Arch. Journal 4, 1976, 57
21 *Ibid*, 63
22 E. Birley in I.A. Richmond and
E. Birley, 'Excavations on Hadrian's
Wall in the Birdoswald-Pike Hill
sector', *TCWAAS* NS. XXX
169–205
23 See note 20, page 70
24 See note 20, page 63
25 J.A. Ford, 'A quantitative method
for deriving cultural chronology,'
Washington: Pan American Union
1962
J. Deetz, *Invitation to Archaeology*,
New York 1967, 27–30
26 S. Champion, *A Dictionary of Terms
and Techniques in Archaeology*,
Oxford 1980, 130
27 P. Corder, *The Roman Town and
Villa at Great Casterton, Rutland*,
University of Nottingham 1951
28 G. Webster, 'Reflections on
Romano-British pottery studies;
past, present and future', in J. Dore
and K. Greene (see note 18) page
321
29 R.E.M. Wheeler and T.V. Wheeler,
*Verulamium: A Belgic and Two
Roman cities*, Rep. Res. Comm. Soc.
Antiq. London No. 11, 1936, 58
30 D. Breeze, *The Northern Frontiers of
Roman Britain*, London 1982, 76
31 *Ibid*, page 118
32 B. Hartley, 'The Roman occupation
of Scotland: the evidence of the
samian ware.' *Britannia* 3, 1972, 1–65
E. Birley, 'Excavations at
Corstopitum, 1906–58', in *Arch.
Aeliana* 4S XXXVII 1959, 1–32
33 See note 30, page 129
34 J.Y. Akerman, 'An account of
excavations on the site of some
ancient Potteries in the western
district of the New Forest',
Archaeologia 35 (1853) 91–9

35 H. Sumner, *Excavations in New Forest Roman Pottery Sites*, London 1927

36 K. Hartley, 'The marketing and distribution of mortaria', in A. Detsicas (Ed), *Current Research in Romano-British Coarse Pottery*, CBA 10, London 1973, 42

37 H.W.M. Hodges, 'The examination of ceramic materials in thin section', in E. Pyddoke (Ed), *The Scientist and Archaeology*, London 1963, 10

38 D. Peacock, 'Neolithic pottery production in Cornwall', *Antiquity* 43, 1969, 145–9

39 D. Peacock and A. Thomas, 'Class 'E' imported post-Roman pottery: a suggested origin,' *Cornish Arch* 6, 1967, 35–46

40 D.F. Williams, 'The Romano-British black-burnished industry: an essay on characterisation by heavy mineral analysis,' in D. Peacock (Ed), *Pottery and Early Commerce*, 1977

41 D. Peacock, 'Roman Amphorae in pre-Roman Britain', in D. Hill and M. Jesson (Eds), *The Iron Age and its Hill forts*, University of Southampton Monograph Series 1971

42 A.C. Anderson, M. Fulford, H. Hatcher and A.M. Pollard, 'Chemical analysis of Hunt Cups and Allied wares from Britain,' *Britannia* XIII 1982

43 *Ibid*

44 See note 26, page 38

45 See note 38, page 147

46 See note 36, Fig 7

47 I. Hodder and C. Orton, *Spatial Analysis in Archaeology*, Cambridge 1976

48 See note 26, page 132

4 Pottery and History

1 H.H. Thomas, 'The Pottery' in D.M. Liddle, 'Excavations at Hembury Fort, Devon,' *Proc. Devon. Arch. Expl. Soc.* II, 1935

2 I.F. Smith, *Windmill Hill and Avebury: Excavations by A. Keiller*, Oxford 1965, 43

3 D. Peacock, 'Neolithic pottery production in Cornwall', *Antiquity* 43, 1969

4 See note 2, page 46

5 I.F. Smith 'The Neolithic' in A.C. Renfrew (Ed), *British Prehistory; A new outline*, 1974, 110

6 *Ibid* page 111

7 J.V.S. Megaw and D.D.A. Simpson, *Introduction to British Prehistory*, Leicester 1979, 171

8 G.J. Wainwright and I.H. Longworth, *Durrington Walls: Excavations 1966–68*

9 See note 7, page 177

10 A.S. Henshall, *The Chambered Tombs of Scotland II*, 1972

11 See note 5, 111

12 D.L. Clarke, *Beaker Pottery of Great Britain and Ireland*, 2 vols 1970

13 J.N. Lanting and J.D. Van der Waals, 'British Beakers as seen from the Continent', *Helenium* 12, 1972, 20–46

14 H. Case, 'The Beaker culture in Britain and Ireland', in R.J. Mercer (Ed), *Beakers in Britain and Europe*, BAR Suppl Ser 26, 1977, 71–101

15 J. Abercromby, *A study of the Bronze Age Pottery of Great Britain and Ireland*, 2 vols 1912

16 See note 7, page 186

17 See note 7, page 188

18 C.B. Burgess and S. Shennan, 'The Beaker phenomenon: some suggestions,' in C.B. Burgess and R. Miket (Eds) *Settlement and Economy in the third and second millennia B.C.*, BAR Brit. Ser. 33, 1976, 309–26

19 F.R. Hodson, 'Some pottery from Eastbourne – the 'Marnians' and the pre-Roman Iron Age in Southern England,' *P.P.S.* 28, 1962, 154

20 *Ibid*, page 154

21 D.W. Harding, *The Iron Age in Lowland Britain*, London 1974, 13

22 B. Cunliffe, *Iron Age Communities in Britain*, London 1974, 31–57

23 D. Allen, 'The origin of coinage in Britain: a reappraisal,' in S.S. Frere (Ed), *Problems of the Iron Age in Southern Britain*, 1958, 97–308 'Celtic coins', in Ordnance Survey,

Map of South Britain in the Iron Age, 1962, 19–32

24 A.J. Evans, 'On a late-Celtic urn-field at Aylesford, Kent,' *Archaeologia* 52, 1890, 315–88

25 J.P. Bushe-Fox, *Excavations of the Late Celtic Urnfield at Swarling, Kent*, Rep. Res. Comm. Soc. Antiq. London 5, 1925, 1–55

26 A. Birchall, 'The Aylesford-Swarling culture: the problem of the Belgae reconsidered,' *P.P.S.* 31, 1965, 241–367

27 See note 21, page 210

28 J.B. Ward-Perkins, 'An early Iron Age site at Crayford, Kent,' *P.P.S.* 4, 1938, 151–168

29 See note 21, page 199

30 K. Kenyon, 'The Roman theatre at Verulamium, St Albans', *Archaeologia* 84, 1934, 213–261

31 F. Oswald, 'A third-century well at Margidunum', *J. Rom. Stud.* 16, 1926, 36–44

32 P. Corder, *Excavations at the Roman town of Brough, East Yorkshire*, East Riding Antiq. Soc. 1936

33 G. Webster, 'Reflections on Romano-British pottery studies; past, present and future', in J. Dore and K. Greene, *Roman Pottery Studies in Britain and Beyond*, BAR Supp Ser. 30, 1977, 320

34 M.R. Hull, *Roman Colchester*, Rep. Res. Comm. Soc. Antiq. London 20, 1958

35 G.C. Dunning, 'Two fires of Roman London', *Antiq. J.* 25, 1945, 48–77

36 H. Chapman, 'Excavations at Aldgate and Bush Lane House in the City of London', *Trans London and Middx Arch. Soc.* 24, 1973, 4–7

37 R. Merrifield, *The Roman City of London*, London 1965

38 S.S. Frere, *Verulamium Excavations I*, Rep. Res. Comm. Soc. Antiq. London 27, 1972

39 P. Corder, *The Roman Town and Villa at Great Casterton, Rutland*, University of Nottingham 1951

40 D. Atkinson, *Report on the Excavations at Wroxeter 1923–27*, Birmingham Arch. Soc. 1942

41 G. Simpson, *Britons and the Roman Army*, London 1964

42 S.S. Frere, 'Verulamium-Three Roman Cities,' *Antiquity* 38, 1964, 103–112
J.S. Wacher, *The Towns of Roman Britain*, London 1974

43 G. Marsh, 'London's samian supply and its relationship to the development of the Gallic samian industry', in A. C. Anderson and A. S. Anderson (Eds), *Roman pottery research in Britain and North-West Europe*, BAR Int. Ser. 123 1981, 173–238

44 See note 33, page 323

45 J. Ward, *The Roman Fort at Gellygaer*, London 1903, 97–8

46 V.E. Nash-Williams, *The Roman frontier in Wales*, Cardiff 1954

47 F. Oswald and T.P. Pryce, *An Introduction to the study of Terra Sigillata*, (Revised Edition) 1945

48 See note 43

49 C. Goudineau, 'La céramique dans l'économie de la Gaule', *Les dossiers de l'archéologie* 6, 1974, 101–9

50 See note 43, page 208

51 See note 43, page 210

52 B. Hartley, 'Some wandering potters', in J. Dore and K. Greene. See note 33, 251–61

53 T.W. Potter, *Romans in North-West England – Excavations at the Roman forts of Ravenglass, Watercrook and Bowness on Solway*, TCWAAS Res. Ser. I, 1979, 237–269

54 B. Hartley, 'Samian pottery', in G. Webster, 'An excavation of the Roman site at Littlechester', Derby 1960, *Derbyshire Arch. J.*, 81, 1961, 85–110

55 See note 43, page 214

56 B. Hartley, 'The Roman occupation of Scotland: the evidence of the samian ware', *Britannia* III, 1972, 1–65

57 See note 56, page 39

58 D. Breeze, *The Northern Frontiers of Roman Britain*, London 1982, 129

59 J.C. Mann and J.P. Gillam, 'The North British frontier from Antoninus Pius to Caracalla,' *Arch Aeliana* 4th. Series 48, 1970, 1–44

60 See note 56
61 See note 56, page 48

5 Pottery and Trade

1 C.J. Young, 'The value of the study of pottery in the late Roman period', in H. Howard and E. Morris (Eds), *Production and Distribution: a ceramic viewpoint*, BAR 120 1981
2 D. Peacock, 'Neolithic pottery production in Cornwall', *Antiquity* 43, 1969, 46
3 J.V.S. Megaw and D.D.A. Simpson, *An Introdution to British Prehistory*, Leicester 1980, 167
4 I. Smith, 'The Neolithic', in A.C. Renfrew (Ed), *British Prehistory: A new outline*, 1974, 113
5 *Ibid*, page 114
6 B. Cunliffe, *Iron Age communities in Britain*, London 1978, 300
7 D. Peacock, 'A contribution to the study of Glastonbury ware from South-Western Britain' *Ant. J.* 49, 1969, 41–61
8 See note 6, page 53
9 See note 6, page 111
10 C. Blackmore, M. Braithwaite and I. Hodder, 'Social and cultural patterning in the late Iron Age of Southern Britain', in B. Burnham and J. Kinsbury (Eds), *Space, Hierarchy and Society*, BAR Sup. Ser. 59, 1979
11 D. Peacock, 'Glastonbury Ware: An alternative view', (see note 10 above)
12 *Ibid*, page 114
13 *Ibid*, page 113
14 D. Peacock, 'A petrological study of certain Iron Age pottery from Western England', *P.P.S.* 34, 1968, 414–27
15 Note 6, page 299
16 Note 6, page 157
17 D. Peacock, 'Roman Amphorae in pre-Roman Britain', in D. Hill and M. Jesson (Eds) *The Iron Age and its Hill Forts*, University of Southampton Monograph Series 1971
18 C.E. Stevens, 'Britain between the Invasions (54 BC–AD 43): a study of ancient diplomacy', in W.F. Grimes

(Ed), *Aspects of Archaeology in Britain and Beyond*, 1951, 332–44
19 R.E.M. Wheeler and T.V. Wheeler, *Verulamium: A Belgic and Two Roman cities*, Res. Rep. Comm. Soc. Antiq. London, No. 8, 1936
20 C. Partridge, *Skeleton Green – a Late Iron Age and Romano-British site*, Britannia Monograph Series 2, 1981
21 G. Webster, *The Roman Invasion of Britain*, London 1980, 53
22 G. Marsh, 'London samian supply, and its relationship to the development of the Gallic samian industry', in A.C. Anderson and A.S. Anderson (Eds), *Roman Pottery Research in Britain and North-West Europe*, BAR Sup. Ser. 123, 1981, 173–238
23 M. Vegas, ACO-Becher, *Acta Rei Cretariae Rom. Fautorum*, 11–12, 1969–70, 107–24
24 B. Hofmann, 'Les secteurs de vente de la céramique sigillée de la I er siècle de notre ère', *Forum* 4, 1974, 9–11
25 See note 22, 207
26 K. Greene, *Report on the excavations at Usk 1965–76 – The Pre-Flavian Fine Wares*, Cardiff 1979, 140
27 *Ibid*, page 13
28 *Ibid*, fig 15
29 *Ibid*, page 17
30 *Ibid*, page 141
31 Strabo, *Geography* IV, 11, 2
32 *Ibid*, IV, 1, 14
33 See note 26, page 141
34 See note 26, page 143
35 K. Greene, 'Roman trade between Britain and the Rhine Provinces: the evidence of the pottery to *c*. AD 250', in J. du Plat Taylor and H. Cleere (Eds), *Roman shipping and trade: Britain and the Rhine Provinces*, CBA Res. Rep. 24 London 1978
36 *Ibid*, page 52
37 W. Lung, 'Zur vorr-und frühgeschichteichen ceramik im Kölner Raum', *Kölner Jahrb*, 4, 1959, 45–65
38 See note 35, page 53
39 A.C. Anderson, M. Fulford, H. Hatcher and A.M. Pollard, 'Chemical analysis of Hunt cups and

allied wares from Britain', *Britannia* XIII 1982

40 M. Hassall, 'Britain and the Rhine Provinces: epigraphic evidence for Roman trade', in J. du Plat Taylor and H. Cleere (Eds), *Roman shipping and trade: Britain and the Rhine Provinces*, CBA Res. Rep. 24, London 1978

41 See note 35, page 57

42 B. Hartley, 'Samian or terra sigillata', in R.G. Collingwood and I. Richmond, *The Archaeology of Roman Britain*, London 1969

43 Strabo, *Geography* IV, 111, 3

44 See note 42, page 238

45 B.M. Dickenson and K.F. Hartley, 'The evidence of potters' stamps on samian and on mortaria for the trading connections of Roman York', in R.M. Butler (Ed), *Soldier and Civilian in Roman Yorkshire: Essays to commemorate the nineteenth centenary of the foundation of York*, 1971

46 M. Bulmer, *An introduction to Roman samian ware*, Chester Arch. Soc. 1980

47 G. Dannell, 'The samian from Bagendon,' in J. Dore and K. Greene, *Roman Pottery Studies in Britain and Beyond*, BAR Sup. Ser. 30, 1977, 229–34

48 See note 22, page 212

49 M. Fulford, 'The interpretation of Britain's late Roman trade: the scope of mediaeval history and archaeological analogy', in J. du Plat Taylor and H. Cleere (Eds), *Roman Shipping and trade: Britain and the Rhine Provinces*, CBA Res. Rep. 24, 1978, 59–69

50 *Ibid*, page 60

51 K. Greene, 'The pottery from Usk', in A. Detsicas (Ed), *Current Research in Romano-British coarse pottery*, CBA 10, 1973

52 D. Peacock, 'The black-burnished pottery industry in Dorset', (see note 51 above)

53 P.V. Webster, 'Severn Valley ware on Hadrian's Wall', *Arch Aeliana* 50, 1972, 191–203

54 M. Fulford, 'Roman pottery:

towards the investigation of economic and social change', in H. Howard and E. Morris, *Production and Distribution: a ceramic viewpoint*, BAR 120, 1981, 203

55 *Ibid*, page 203

6 Pottery and Industry

1 M. Fulford, 'The pottery in B.W. Cunliffe, *Excavations at Portchester Castle*', Rep. Res. Comm. Soc. Antiq. London, 32, 1975

2 A.H.M. Jones, *The Roman Economy*, 1974

3 S.S. Frere, *Britannia*, 1967, 263

4 A.S. Anderson, *The Roman pottery industry in North Wiltshire*, Swindon Arch. Soc. Report no. 2 1979 Wiltshire fine wares in P. Arthur and G. Marsh (Eds), *Early Fine Wares in Roman Britain*, BAR Brit. Ser. 57, 1978

5 D. Peacock, *Pottery in the Roman World: an ethnoarchaeological approach*, London 1982, 86

6 C.J. Young, *Oxfordshire Roman Pottery*, BAR Brit. Ser. 43, 1977

7 See note 5, page 129

8 *Ibid*, page 94

9 C.J. Young, 'The value of the study of pottery in the late Roman period' in H. Howard and E. Morris (Eds), *Production and Distribution: a ceramic viewpoint*, BAR 120 1981

10 C. Goudineau, *La Céramique arétine lissé*, Paris 1968

11 A. King, 'A graffito from La Graufesenque', *Britannia* XI, 1980

12 S.O. Kay, 'The Romano-British Pottery Kilns at Hazelwood and Holbrook, Derbyshire,' *Derbyshire Archaeological Journal*, 82, 1962

13 M.A.B. Lyne and D.S. Jefferies, *The Alice Holt/Farnham Roman Pottery industry*, CBA Res. Rep. 30, 1979, 57

14 A. Birley, *The people of Roman Britain*, 1979, 133

15 A.S. Anderson, *The Roman pottery industry in North Wiltshire*, Swindon Arch. Soc. Report No. 2, 1979

16 See note 6, fig 11–12

17 See note 5, page 55 and fig 24
18 K. Hartley, 'Mancetter', *West Midlands Archaeological News Sheet*, 8, 1965, 12–13
19 See note 6, page 20
20 P.J. Woods, 'Types of late Belgic or early Romano-British pottery kilns in the Nene Valley', *Britannia* V, 1974, 262–81

21 F.K. Annable, 'A Romano-British pottery in Savernake Forest, Kilns 1 and 2,' *Wilts Arch. Mag.* 58, 1962, 142–55
22 See note 15
23 M.R. Hull, *The Roman Potters' kilns at Colchester*, Rep. Res. Comm. Soc. Antiq. London no. 32, 1963, 157
24 *Ibid*, fig 12 and 13

Index